The River Palace

The River Palace

Walter Lewis & Rick Neilson

DUNDURN PRESS
TORONTO

Copyright © Walter Lewis & Rick Neilson, 2008

All rights reserved. No part of this publication may be reproduced, stored in a retrieval system, or transmitted in any form or by any means, electronic, mechanical, photocopying, recording, or otherwise (except for brief passages for purposes of review) without the prior permission of Dundurn Press. Permission to photocopy should be requested from Access Copyright.

Copy-editor: Nigel Heseltine
Designer: Jennifer Scott
Printer: Marquis

Library and Archives Canada Cataloguing in Publication

Lewis, Walter
    River palace : the many lives of the Kingston / Walter Lewis, Rick Neilson.

Includes bibliographical references and index.
ISBN 978-1-55002-793-8

    1. Kingston (Steamboat) 2. Steamboats--Saint Lawrence River-- History. 3. Steamboats--Great Lakes (North America)--History. I. Neilson, Rick II. Title.

VM383.K46L48 2008   386'.2243609713   C2008-900716-6

1   2   3   4   5   12   11   10   09   08

  Conseil des Arts   Canada Council      ONTARIO ARTS COUNCIL
      du Canada   for the Arts   CONSEIL DES ARTS DE L'ONTARIO

We acknowledge the support of the Canada Council for the Arts and the Ontario Arts Council for our publishing program. We also acknowledge the financial support of the Government of Canada through the Book Publishing Industry Development Program and The Association for the Export of Canadian Books, and the Government of Ontario through the Ontario Book Publishers Tax Credit program and the Ontario Media Development Corporation.

Care has been taken to trace the ownership of copyright material used in this book. The author and the publisher welcome any information enabling them to rectify any references or credits in subsequent editions.

J. Kirk Howard, President

Printed and bound in Canada

www.dundurn.com

Dundurn Press	Gazelle Book Services Limited	Dundurn Press
3 Church Street, Suite 500	White Cross Mills	2250 Military Road
Toronto, Ontario, Canada	High Town, Lancaster, England	Tonawanda, NY U.S.A.
M5E 1M2	LA1 4XS	14150

Table of Contents

Acknowledgements		7
Foreword		9
Introduction: The Wreck of the *Cornwall*		11
1	The Iron Steamboat	22
2	John Hamilton's *Kingston*	41
3	The Floating Palace	46
4	The *Kingston* and the Canadian Navigation Company	59
5	The *Bavarian*	81
6	The *Algerian*	91
7	The *Cornwall*	119
8	The *Cornwall* and the Calvin Company	124

| 9 | The *Cornwall* and the Donnelly Salvage and Wrecking Company | 133 |
| 10 | The *Cornwall* and Sin-Mac Lines Limited | 140 |

Epilogue ... 145

Appendix A: Captains ... 146

Appendix B: Contracts and Descriptions ... 159

Appendix C: Accidents ... 173

Appendix D: Salvage Operations ... 183

Notes ... 202

Bibliography ... 233

Index ... 241

Acknowledgements

We would like to thank a variety of people for their assistance beginning with Ken McLeod and Bill McNeil. Others who have made a special contribution include Steve Salmon, who checked a few special sources in Ottawa; Maurice Smith, who stopped in at the archives at Glasgow University while in Europe on a conference tour; and Larry McNally who chipped in with some key references from his research. Others who contributed included Elizabeth Collard, Katherine Ferguson, and H. Ashley Hornell.

In the course of an extended project like this we have had the opportunity to work with a variety of archivists, librarians, and curators including Steve Salmon, Larry McNally, and Pat Kennedy from Library and Archives Canada; and Anne McDermaid, George Henderson, and Shirley Spragge of the Queen's University Archives. Earl Moorehead and Maurice Smith of the Marine Museum of the Great Lakes at Kingston; John Summers, with the former Marine Museum of Upper Canada; and the Toronto Harbour Commission's Michael Moir also provided assistance. Kingston Frontenac Public Library; the Halton Hills Public Library (Betsy Cornwell, Geoff Cannon, Mary Hughes, and Lorene Morwick); the ILLO staff of the Southern Ontario Library Service (Anne Church and her staff); the Archives nationales du Québec à Montréal; the University of Glasgow Archives; the staff of the Baldwin Room of the Metropolitan Toronto Reference Library, the Institute for Great Lakes Research (Jay Martin); the York University Libraries; Robarts Library at the University of Toronto; University of Guelph; the Archives of Ontario; and the City of Toronto Archives (Karen Teeple) deserve appreciation as well.

For pictures, thanks are due to Peter Blood and Toni Towle (underwater stills); Jonathan Moore (video footage); Adam Henley for the superb sketch of the wreck after less than an hour and a half diving on it; Gerry Girvin, Rochester (an illustration and information); Lorne Joyce; the Steamship Historical Society of America; Stanley Triggs, Notman Archives of the McCord Museum, Montréal; Alain Côté, Beloeil; Pierre Lambert; Daniel C. McCormick, Massena; National Gallery of Canada; Royal Ontario Museum (Canadiana Collection); Gordon Shaw; and the Bowmanville Museum

Among those who reviewed the text were Steve Salmon, Maurice Smith, Ken Macpherson (master of the semicolon), Gordon Shaw, Helen Lewis, Jan Hassard, Joan Murray, Gail Richardson, and Jim Pritchard. None of them saw the version you're holding so they cannot be held responsible for it. We also appreciate the work of the team at the Dundurn Group including Barry Jowett, Jane Gibson, Nigel Heseltine, Barry Penhale, Beth Bruder, and Kirk Howard.

For technical support we thank John Grozelle. We are also grateful to John and Sue Cornwell, whose loaned laptop went many miles over more years than any of us thought this would take. Thanks also to the Ontario Arts Council (OAC) for a grant.

A special thanks is due to Debbi Lewis for her patience and understanding.

Foreword

This is a biography of a ship — a steamboat — and a very special one at that. We have tried not to write a "life and times." Nevertheless, to understand the story of this ship we have had to touch lightly on a range of other stories, equally worthy of whole volumes on their own: the development of iron shipbuilding, the passenger trades on the lower Great Lakes, royal tours, turn-of-the-century salvaging.

It was never our intention to write business history, but in nineteenth-century Canada merchant ships existed to make money for their owners. How the *Kingston* was deployed in her various incarnations was dependent on the business decisions of a number of key individuals and boards of directors.

Nor has it been our intention to write a report on marine archaeology. This is not to say that a study of the site would not tell us a variety of things about nineteenth-century shipbuilding. The *Kingston* remains one of the oldest riveted hulls in North America.

But our approach to this vessel was one of historians and divers. And as a dive site she is one of the most fascinating, in an area of the Great Lakes known for its rich variety of dive opportunities. In no other place on the lakes can you explore the wreck of a mid-nineteenth century iron-hulled paddle-wheeled steamboat.

Kingston is perhaps unique among the vessels of her generation because a large amount of information about her has survived. Launched in the pre-dawn of the era of outdoor photography the number of pictures is simply overwhelming. Apart from the usual government records of the vessel (registrations and the like), we are fortunate to have access to the archives of the two companies that owned her for most of her working life. Combine this with a local press anxiously tracking major advertisers over her working career and we found ourselves confronting, for once, a historical jigsaw puzzle that still had most of the pieces. Part of this was simply the result of two major inquiries and the paperwork in the courts.

But for most people the *Kingston* remains the pre-eminent example of the nineteenth-century excursion steamer, not because she was the first, the biggest, or the most expensive. In an era when the claim "floating palace" was made of a long succession of vessels, *Kingston* had actually played the role. For forty years after the first and most extensive royal tour ever undertaken in North America, passengers were told that they were in the same vessel, and perhaps even in the same stateroom as the Prince of Wales. Nor was this fact ever forgotten by those who found different uses for the aging vessel.

Today, in the height of the summer diving season, the wreck again sees as many visitors as it did in the late days of the reign of Queen Victoria, visitors who can admire her fine lines, hold her taffrail in their gloved hands and think of days when this floating palace ran the rapids of the St. Lawrence River.

Introduction

The Wreck of the *Cornwall*

Divers, like archaeologists and palaeontologists, have a morbid fascination with the dead, though they tend to prefer the word "shipwreck." Ever since the proliferation of scuba gear in the 1950s, Kingston has been a mecca for divers drawn to the variety of shipwrecks in the area. For years, wrecks like the side-wheeler *Comet* and the schooner *George Marsh* have been popular dive sites.

As well, for years, researchers have been trying to locate and identify the other wrecks known to be in the area. Not the least of these was the *Cornwall*, also known during her long career as the *Kingston*, the *Bavarian*, and the *Algerian*. In 1989, fresh clues from one of the Donnelly family, Mrs. Cole, along with information supplied some years before by Vic Ruttle, combined to narrow the search to a small area near the ship graveyard off Amherst Island some ten to twelve miles (sixteen to twenty kilometres) out of Kingston. Using nothing more sophisticated than a chart recorder, a device working on the same basic principle as a Second World War sonar, and a Loran C Navigation system, Rick Neilson spent the summer turning the twenty-four-foot, aluminum-hulled *Restless* through section after section of the chart. Finally, on the Labour Day weekend, the recorder showed a jump of nearly twenty-five feet off the bottom. Repeated passes confirmed the location of something substantial in seventy feet of water.

The River Palace

A diver's view of Cornwall: *The ship lies on a soft bottom in some seventy feet of water, layers of decking spill off the after deck, the forward hold is bare to the angle iron joining her iron plates. Both feathering paddlewheels remain, one twisted out of its pillow blocks from the force of striking bottom. Also remaining are the great boilers, although the "A" frame, her walking beam and the cylinders were completely removed, probably for the scrap value of the metal.*

Three weeks later Rick returned with Paul Conley, an experienced and discreet dive buddy. They plunged into the relatively warm September water. Slowly descending the anchor line, Rick was having trouble clearing his ears. Paul dropped down ahead. A few seconds later he returned swinging his arm around in a great circle. A paddle-wheeler!

Closer inspection confirmed more details: a riveted-metal hull, smashed at the bow; two feathering paddlewheels. The dimensions checked out — the wreck of the *Cornwall* had been found!

Careful searches confirmed that the salvagers who sank the ship had left few archaeological treasures that would be at risk in an open dive site. Consequently, in 1990, a special mooring was placed off her starboard bow with the assistance of Steve Alford and the crew of the *Wreck Hunter*. Since then thousands of divers have had the opportunity to explore the wreck of the *Cornwall*.

Introduction

The windlass.

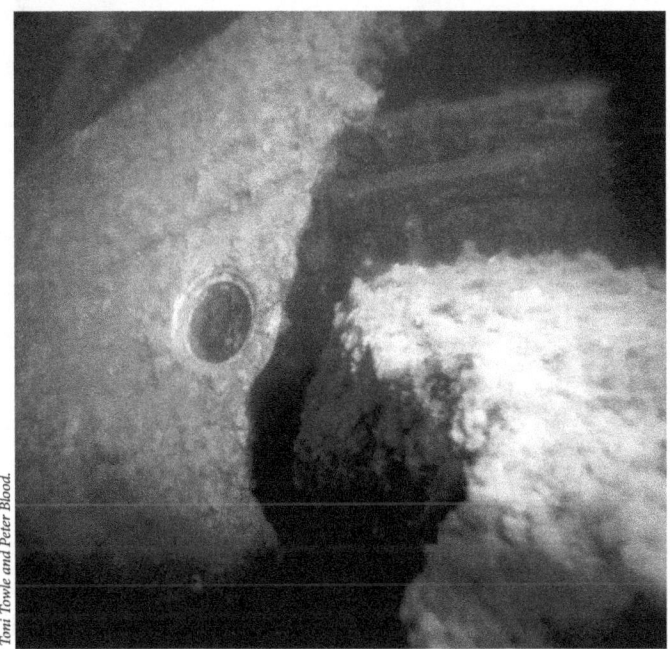

One of the port portholes, just ahead of the tear in the fabric of the hull.

The River Palace

Any tour of the wreck begins at the mooring line off the bow. Before the zebra mussels began clearing up the Lakes, visibility varied from as much as twenty feet to as little as five or six. For this reason, a short line leads the diver from the mooring line to the bow. The bow leans to starboard. The fine sharp lines created in a drafting room on the Clyde in the winter of 1854 are still evident as they sweep back from the stem. The forward part of the main deck has tumbled sideways off the hull, with a long strip of iron strapping still vainly reaching towards the surface.

On the forward deck are the remains of the dominant feature of the bow area, a large windlass. Still lying on the bottom, in the vicinity, are the hawse pipes, which admitted the anchor chain to the windlass on this deck. As one swims back on the port side of the hull, a rip in the fabric of the hull is evident, the result of wreckers' explosives or the final contact with the lake's bottom. The shattered remains of the main deck still cover a small part of the empty forecastle.

Another porthole, looking upwards along the inside of the hull. Two two-inch angle irons show the structure of the Cornwall's *internal framing. They support an overhang, which in turn carried the main deck.*

An experienced diver has little trouble manoeuvring through the wreckage into the confined space. You can still catch glimpses of the world outside the portholes. A small forward "crash" bulkhead is still in place, although opened so as not to interfere with her sinking. Silt quickly stirs from the movement of the diver.

Introduction

Behind the twisted decking the skeleton of the craft is laid bare. The iron plates forged on the Clyde, the angle-iron framing spaced precisely every two feet, the rivets hammered by the workmen in Bartley and Dunbar's St. Lawrence Engine Works in Montreal offer testimony to the durability of the workmanship in the hull. As you trace the course of the starboard side of the hull aft, a strange appendage appears along the hull. Just over two feet tall, a foot wide, and six inches thick, it looks for all the world like a wooden box. It isn't. It's a cement patch — perhaps one of those patches applied by the Donnelly's when, as the *Algerian,* she struck a rock in the rapids. The grain of the wood can still be traced in the patch. Unfortunately the outside of the patch lies nearly buried in the silt. Those who would search for it on the outside risk entanglement with the guards that still line both sides of the hull, supported by the iron struts or sponsons braced firmly against the hull. On the port side just forward of the engine room a small box contains some electrical equipment from the latter stages of the vessel's career.

Above: *The "Scotch tube" boiler, a favourite haven for eels.*

Left: *The valves on the top of the boiler.*

The River Palace

Behind it, out of the gloom, can be discerned the boilers, towering above the lower deck. With the valve attachments on top they reach over fifteen feet, well above the level of the main deck of the *Cornwall*. The fire tubes are exposed to the forward end and on the port boiler a small hole in the side reveals the tubes running to the back plate. In the after end of the starboard boiler, eels have been sighted. Nestled between the two boilers and set on the massive keelsons are the supports for the two paddlewheel shafts. They are all that remain of the over thirty-foot tall "A" frame that dominated the profile of the vessel. Little trace can be found in this neighbourhood of the midships bulkheads. Again, this is not surprising. Sin-Mac Line's wreckers may have found some value in the scrap iron plates, but at the end they were simply trying to ensure she would sink. The purpose of the bulkheads, by contrast, had been to keep her afloat. Their structural value may also be seen in the way that, in their absence, the sagging guards have pulled the sides of the hull outwards. Close to the lower deck, those not afraid of getting a little silt on their dive suit will see how the boilers are raised above the deck. The "double hull" in the engine room is nowhere more apparent than between the boiler and the hull. But by the time this detail has become apparent, the diver has been distracted by the most dramatic artifacts in the whole wreck.

Left: *A detail of the feathering blades, which pivoted to present the best angle at their entry into the water.*

Right: *The paddlewheel shaft: Normally the crank would have grasped this end of the shaft. The cranks were probably removed with the cylinder and the rest of the machinery and used as scrap.*

Introduction

Nineteen feet in diameter, her two feathering paddlewheels look almost capable of challenging the surface waters of the lake some seventy feet above. The wooden blades are embraced by the metal gearing designed to pivot them and keep them perpendicular to the water. Probably this gearing dates from the 1901 refit at Sorel, the *Algerian*'s last major overhaul as an R & O passenger vessel. Behind the starboard wheel those with a taste for detail can see where the elm sheathing reaches out from underneath the hull, where it protected the iron plating from rocks of the St. Lawrence rapids. This detail is also visible along the bottom by the bow.

Aft of the port wheel can be seen the davits — long rods curved at the end — that were installed on Garden Island to carry the lifeboats of the salvagers. Aft of them again lie pieces of decking and cabin work, slumping to the starboard side. Deck lies pancaked on top of deck. To the port side can be seen the guards and the rails and stanchions that kept the salvagers on board. Part of the counter stern has sprung away from the port side of

Landing of Prince of Wales at Quebec City: The royal tour of 1860 began in St. John's, Newfoundland, and had wound its way through Nova Scotia, New Brunswick, and Prince Edward Island. In late August it finally arrived in the Canadas (after Confederation the provinces of Quebec and Ontario). Feverishly preparing for her role in the next stage of the tour, Kingston *was among the steamboats welcoming the Prince.*

the hull carrying the rail with it. Finally, some 175 feet from the mooring line, the stern is reached. The rudder is there, swung hard to port against the hull. Above it, in the *Kingston*'s glory days, lovers and princes might have leaned on the taffrail watching the waters of Lake Ontario recede into the distance, the ship's wake spreading out across the water.

In the summer of 1860, the wreck we know as the *Cornwall* was a beautifully-appointed iron steamboat called the *Kingston*. With decks and cabins and brasswork scrubbed, painted, and polished, it was about to embark on the trip that would prove the high point of its long career. The Prince of Wales (later Edward VII) had come to North America. His itinerary included two especially important ceremonies — he was to officially open the great Victoria Bridge across the St. Lawrence River at Montreal and he was to lay the cornerstone of the new Parliament Buildings in Ottawa. It was feasible to undertake most of the journey through the Canadas by rail, but instead the Canadian provincial government had chartered the *Kingston* to serve as his "floating palace." From 23 August to 7 September, 1860, the *Kingston* and her passengers were the centre of attention of the continent, and indeed the British Empire.

The *Kingston*'s part in the tour began inauspiciously on 23 August. The prince had just endured four days of utterly miserable weather in Quebec City that had earned him the nickname "Raining Prince." Luncheons, levees, balls, tours, and fireworks had left the prince, and the rest of Quebec City society, exhausted. As the hour for his departure approached, one commentator described the city as "an exhausted beauty after a ball — the starch out of her dress — her hair somewhat dishevelled, her gloves and satin shoes considerably the worse for wear, and her whole motions exhibiting decided symptoms of fatigue."[1]

Meanwhile the *Kingston* lay at the Champlain market wharf. The owner's son, Captain Clarke Hamilton was back in command for the occasion.

Introduction

The steamer had been specially fitted for his [the Prince of Wales's] accommodation. The berths had been taken out of the state-rooms, and a comfortable bed placed in each. She had been thoroughly overhauled, and in addition to other ornaments a beautiful Prince of Wales [or more precisely his personal symbol] had been painted on each paddlebox, fresh carpets and furniture of all kinds had been supplied, and the sailors were all dressed in uniforms similar to that of the royal navy.

As soon as the Prince went on board his standard was hoisted at the fore, and was saluted by all the men-of-war in port, as well as by the citadel. The yards of the ships were manned, and their crews, as also the soldiers and the crowd assembled, cheered lustily.

The royal party, who were the only passengers, after going to see their rooms, went on the hurricane deck to enjoy the beautiful scene around. They remained close by the walking beam while the steamer moved away, which it did a few minutes before eleven o'clock.[2]

Attached to the royal party for this phase of the journey were Governor General Sir Edmund Head, with his civil and military secretaries; Lord Lyons and his two attachés; General Sir F. Williams, Colonel Rollo, and their two aides-de-camp; Commodore Lord Mulgrave; as well as Georges Ètienne Cartier, John Rose, Sir Allan MacNab, and Ètienne Taché of the Canadian government. In the bustle of ushering these worthies aboard, some time passed before thoughts of lunch led someone to wonder as to the whereabouts of the "clever New York caterer," Mr. Sanderson, and his assistants. Half an hour later the *Kingston* slunk back into port to pick up the cook.[3]

Fortunately for the prince and the *Kingston,* only one major setback would occur over the course of the tour, the details of which are in Chapter 3. *Kingston* would continue her work in various forms and under a succession of names for another sixty-five years. During that time, her owners would often boast about the summer of 1860 when she had served as the floating palace for the Prince of Wales.

The *Kingston* was to be the epitome of everything that people on the lower Great Lakes would come to expect in a late-nineteenth century steamer. For a steamboat she was reasonably fast. She was elegantly decorated by the best in the trade. But perhaps most important, her hull was made of iron, the material that would come to symbolize the age.

Iron was still a novelty in shipbuilding in 1853.[4] Commercial men had yet to build a iron-hulled vessel on the American side of the Great Lakes.[5] There were a limited number of iron-hulled government vessels, most notably the *Michigan* and the *Mohawk,* added to the American and British government fleets respectively during the sabre-rattling of the early 1840s.[6] The British government had even subsidized a consortium from Hamilton to build the *Magnet,* although she did not get into service until 1847 as the fuss was dying down.[7] But shortly before the *Magnet* came out, the Honourable John Hamilton had had the *Passport* built.[8] Less than ten years later, *Kingston* joined *Magnet* and *Passport* in the Royal Mail Line running between Montreal and Hamilton.

Both *Magnet* and *Passport* had been assembled in Upper Canada, using iron shipped out at great expense from Britain. The one attempt to steam a completed vessel across the North Atlantic resulted in her disappearance with all hands in the summer of 1854. In building *Kingston,*

Sir Henry Acland, The Royal Party Running the Lachine Rapids: *On August 29th after a picnic and a visit to Caughnawaga (Kahnawake) the Prince boarded the* Kingston *and was taken down the Lachine Rapids.*

Introduction

Hamilton would follow the earlier pattern and dispatched his order for the parts of an iron hull to Scotland.

Although this new generation of iron-hulled vessels operated in a world that was dominated by wooden schooners, wooden canal barges, and wooden steamboats, in the 1850s their biggest challenge was coming from the iron horse. The railways were threatening to take over the freight and passenger trades that were the life-blood of shipping. Although rail lines had encircled the lower Great Lakes by the end of the 1860s, the nemesis of the Royal Mail Line was the Grand Trunk Railway.

Grand Trunk Railway Route: The world as the railways re-defined it. Detail from A New and Complete Rail Road Map of the United States Compiled from Reliable Sources, *by William Perris, [1858].*

When completed the Grand Trunk ran from Portland, Maine, through the Eastern Townships, and across the St. Lawrence over the great Victoria Bridge to Montreal (a branch line ran to Levis, on the south shore of the St. Lawrence opposite Quebec City). From Montreal the main line ran parallel to the north shores of the St. Lawrence and Lake Ontario to Toronto, serving all the same river and lakefront communities as Hamilton's Royal Mail Line of steamboats. From Toronto the Grand Trunk swung away from the Great Lakes to Guelph, Stratford, and Sarnia. There the trains crossed the St. Clair River by ferry before being run on a subsidiary line that ran on to Detroit and ultimately Chicago. Today much of this line is still the busiest trackage in the Canadian National system east of Thunder Bay. In the 1850s it threatened to put the shipowners completely out of business.

1

The Iron Steamboat

The ashes and charred timbers were still warm along Kingston's waterfront the morning of 12 November, 1853. The ships and steamers that had been hauled away from their berths in the middle of the night drew slowly back to the shore. Smoke drifted up from the crates and barrels and bundles of freight stacked along the wharves waiting for shipment or delivery. Several storehouses lay in ruins.[1] It would not be Kingston's worst fire, or even the worst along the waterfront, but for those whose property and lives lay in its path, it had the potential to be devastating.

Amid the water-logged, fire-blackened wreckage that was the Commercial Wharf lay the remains of the storehouse and offices of its proprietor, John Hamilton. All his books and financial papers had been destroyed. Nearby, also in ashes, were the Kingston facilities of Hamilton's brothers-in-law, the Macphersons. The Honourable John Hamilton was at this stage a twenty-eight-year veteran of the shipping business, a man whose ships almost never lost a passenger, and who had never lost a ship to a major accident. The youngest of the seven sons of Robert Hamilton (founder of Queenston at the foot of the Niagara gorge), brother of George Hamilton (founder of the city that carries the family name), John was heir to a share of one of Upper Canada's greatest fortunes. Sent to Scotland to be educated after his father's death, trained in a Montreal counting house, John succeeded in business in a way that his elder brothers had not. Using a share of his father's estate, he had acquired the pioneer steamboat *Frontenac* in a mid-winter auction on that same Kingston waterfront in 1825. With his eldest brother he built a second steamboat, the *Queenston*. Even his marriage enhanced his business connections; his wife Frances Pasia was the sister of John and David L. (later Sir David) Macpherson. Their first son would be named John Macpherson Hamilton. From the 1820s his new brothers-in-law were the senior partners in what became the largest outfit transporting freight between Montreal and the Great Lakes. In the era before the railroad, all goods arriving by way of Quebec City and Montreal and destined for Upper Canada, whether transported up the St. Lawrence River, or up the Ottawa River and Rideau Canal passed into the care of Macpherson and Crane and their counterparts. If they were destined for ports above Kingston many of these imports moved on up Lake Ontario in the holds of a succession of steamboats built for John Hamilton. Part of John's success grew from the fact that he never tried to control the steamboat trade (many others also invested in it), he simply ordered some of the best, and most innovative, steamboats on the Lakes: the powerful *Great Britain* in 1830, the winter boat *Traveller* in 1835, and the *Ontario*, which in 1838 had been designed to challenge the rapids of the Long Sault.²

John Hamilton (1802–1882), from Topley Studios, Ottawa, April 1881.

Apart from his shipping interests John Hamilton had been a legislative councillor since 1831. He had described the appointment as "unexpected" and "undesired" but served there and in the Senate after

The River Palace

Passport *in Lachine Rapids: The* Passport *was launched at the Kingston Marine Railway in November 1846, the first commercial iron steamer west of Montreal. The cabin and staterooms on an upper deck were a major new innovation on Lake Ontario, and were a direct imitation of the new fashion on the Hudson River. She was the first of the Royal Mail Line to provide regular service down the Lachine Rapids and up the St. Lawrence canals.*

Confederation for fifty-one years until his death. Throughout that time, beyond the fact that he was frequently referred to as "the Honourable John Hamilton," he had perhaps the lowest "political" profile in the province. On the other hand he served for a significant number of years as the chairman of the board of trustees of Queen's College (later Queen's University) and also as the president of the Commercial Bank of Upper Canada, whose headquarters were also in Kingston. For all these activities John Hamilton was a fairly private individual who let others speak to the great controversies of the day. He appears to have attracted considerable loyalty, at least among his senior employees. Several agents, captains, and engineers were associated with Hamilton for decades in the activities of what would become known as the Royal Mail Line of steamboats.

Magnet *at Murray Bay: The iron for the hull of the* Magnet *followed that for the* Passport *across the Atlantic.* Magnet *was launched at Niagara in July 1847. She is seen here at the popular lower St. Lawrence resort town of Murray Bay.* Magnet *worked this route during the height of the summer season in the 1860s.*

Hamilton was one of the principal players in that part of a shipping industry that moved people and goods between Montreal and ports on Lake Ontario. He and his in-laws were threatened by the Grand Trunk Railway. With the line of the Grand Trunk being surveyed, with promises of millions in government subsidies, and millions more from British investors, why would Hamilton want to stay in the steamboat business? Why especially after the fire in November 1853? His brothers-in-law were selling out; David L. Macpherson was even taking up railway contracting.³ While we can be reasonably sure Hamilton thought about selling out, we cannot be sure why he did not.⁴

We do know he responded with the *Kingston*.

Hamilton's order was received early in 1854 in Govan, a small suburb of Glasgow on the south bank of the River Clyde. It was directed to James and George Thomson whose Clyde Bank Foundry would in time (after a shift downriver) grow into the famous Clydebank Shipyard. In the twentieth century the shipyard launched Cunard's *Queens*: the *Queen Mary*, the *Queen Elizabeth*, and the *Queen Elizabeth 2*. The Thomson brothers were experienced marine engine builders; a third brother, Robert, would become the superintending engineer for the Cunard Line, an invaluable connection for his brothers' firm. With more experience in working iron than traditional wooden shipbuilders possessed, the Thomson's moved into iron shipbuilding.[5] Hamilton's order was designated "Hull 15."

Unfortunately, in the vast archives of the Clydebank Shipyard there are few records from the earliest years of the firm. There are no plans for the hull, nor is there a record of her eventual name. However, the ledgers do show the firm received the first instalment of £500 sterling for Hamilton's hull on 23 February 1854 and equivalent payments on 27 March, 19 April, and 16 May. In contemporary terms a pound sterling (the official currency of Great Britain) traded about five U.S. dollars. The equivalent in British North America was expressed in "Pounds Halifax Currency" (or "Cy"), which was usually worth about four U.S. dollars. Canada would move to the dollar only four years later. An additional sum for "extras" was added on 16 May, bringing the bill to a total of £2,072 19s of which a profit of £429 13s 5d was posted by the Thomsons to their private ledger and the balance to the "boat yard" accounts.[6] Hamilton's account was small compared with Clyde Bank's other business because the shipyard did little more than prepare the iron for the hull. Thomsons charged Cunard £18,066 sterling for the *Jura* (2,240 tons), on the stocks from February 1853 to June 1854. Similar in size to Hamilton's vessel was the Australasian Steam Navigation Company's *Wonga Wonga* (662 tons) launched in May 1854 at a cost

George Thomson(1815–1866) of J. & G. Thomson, Clyde Bank Shipyard, Govan.

From Memoirs and Portraits of One Hundred Glasgow Men, Vol. 2, 320.

of £8,995 sterling. However, these orders were finished at the yard, and each included a pair of engines. By contrast, most of the work on Hamilton's hull was to be done in Montreal.

The pieces of the hull left port on May 15, immediately before the last payment was made.[7] By late August the next stage of the work was underway at the St. Lawrence Engine Works on the south bank of the Lachine Canal in Montreal. Much like James and George Thomson, the owners of the St. Lawrence Engine Works, Bartley and Dunbar, were

BARTLEY & DUNBAR,
ST. LAWRENCE ENGINE WORKS,
MONTREAL,
ARE NOW PREPARED TO EXECUTE ORDERS FOR
IRON STEAMBOATS,
LOCOMOTIVES,
Steam Engines and Boilers,
For Steamboats, Propellers, Saw and Grist Mills.
DREDGING MACHINERY,
WITH EVERY DESCRIPTION OF
WATER WHEELS & MILL WORKS,
Heavy Forgings,
From ten inches down to the smallest sizes.
ARCHITECTURAL CASTINGS FOR BUILDINGS,
PLAIN AND ORNAMENTED.
Pot Ash Kettles of the best quality, Cast Lip up.
With every other description of Iron and Brass Castings, all of the best material and workmanship, and on the
Most Reasonable Terms.

HAVING lately added to our already large stock, the whole of the TOOLS, MACHINERY and PATTERNS of the late Firm of MILNE & MILNE, and being situated on the CANAL BASIN, in possession of AMPLE WATER POWER, and SHIPPING ACCOMMODATION, for shipping and receiving everything our business requires, with DOCK ACCOMMODATION, for a number of Steamers, either under repairs or for the erection of new engines, within a few feet of our Shops, from these unequaled advantages we can do MORE WORK, QUICKER, BETTER and CHEAPER than any other Establishment in these Provinces.
We subjoin the names of a few Steamers as specimens of our work :—On the River St. Lawrence, Steamer TRENTON, Whitehall, Montreal Harbour Commissioners, Kingston Mail Line, Propeller OSHAWA, Detroit River, Steamer UNION, G. W. R. R. Co., Steam Engine and Grist Mill, DISTILLERY Messrs. T. & W. MOLSON, Montreal.

Montreal, October, 1857.

The Canada Directory for 1857–58, *1209.*

mechanical engineers, and not shipwrights. A "sketch" of the premises gives a sense of the true "birthplace" of Hamilton's new steamboat. The works consisted of:

> 1st A Smith's Shop, 65 by 50 feet, with 9 fires, with finishing and shearing machines, and a trip hammer, with which shafting 4 [feet] by 10 inches can be forged. 2nd, A Boiler Shop, 80 feet by 60, with 5 fires and a large quantity of machinery. Among the machinery is a punching machine, worked with a rack, whose work is mathematically correct, saving the tedious and expensive process of rimming holes to admit the rivet; and large rollers which will bend boiler plate lengthwise 9 1/2 feet long, with hammering; and a hydraulic pump for testing boilers. The machinery here is driven by a 30 horse-power water-wheel. 3rd, foundry, 70 by 60 feet, with facilities for making the heaviest castings required in this country. 4th, The Pattern Shop, 50 feet by 40, with accommodation for 10 or 12 pattern-makers. 5th, The Finishing Shop, 105 feet long by 50 feet wide, and three stories high, containing a large quantity of machinery of various sorts, of the best description, with the latest improvements, driven by a 25 horse-power water-wheel, and a 20 horse-power steam engine, when the water is drawn off the canal for repairs. The number of men and apprentices employed here is 160, receiving wages amounting to £190 or £200 per week, — they have gone as high as £325 per week. The work produced per annum is valued at £40,000, with capacity for extension to £70,000 or £80,000.... They possess peculiar facilities, with a boat shed, &c., on the bank of the canal for the construction of iron boats, and fitting the boilers and engines into steamers.[8]

A later description of the St. Lawrence Engine Works added:

As the name implies, engine and boat building are the principal business of the firm, but they also do a large business in the manufacture of all varieties of machinery for mills, boilers, hydrants, patent steam and other pumps, cranes, windlasses &c., besides railway work and all descriptions of iron castings and forgings.... They have also a very extensive stock of patterns for mill machinery; steam engines of various descriptions, viz.: beam, horizontal, oscillating with conic slide and Corliss' valves, several of each description having been made at these works and are now in successful operation.[9]

The shops stood on a pair of lots leased from the provincial Department of Public Works that lay between a basin of the Lachine Canal and the St. Lawrence River. Senior partner William P. Bartley had acquired control of the property in the spring of 1853 and brought James Dunbar into a partnership by the end of September. Shortly afterwards, a credit agency reported that the firm was financially dependent on Frothingham and Workman, "the largest hardware and iron wholesale firm in British North America."[10] A few weeks after forming their partnership, Bartley and Dunbar secured their first major client, the Honourable John Hamilton.

In November 1853, within days of the Kingston fire, Hamilton met with Bartley and Dunbar in Montreal to settle the terms of their agreement. The iron hull would be built at the St. Lawrence Engine Works for a 20 percent premium on their costs. In other words, Bartley and Dunbar would pay all the expenses and wages and supply all the tools, and Hamilton would reimburse that amount plus 20 percent. This part of the deal was a "no lose" situation for the Montreal engineers, who had no experience in shipbuilding. At the same time and on firmer ground, they undertook to build an engine for the steamer for £4,500 Cy. It was to be a "beam condensing steam engine [with] everything in proportion for an engine forty-two inches cylinder and ten feet stroke ... with Allen and Wells' patent cut off [valve]." They decided to build the boilers on the pattern of those in the American Great Lakes steamer, *Ontario*. Hamilton, however, retained the option of substituting a different design. Terms of payment and other details were settled in an exchange of letters in April 1854, shortly before the parts of the hull were shipped from Scotland. The final decision on the boiler design was not communicated until 23 August when the first instalments were paid.[11]

The only newspaper account of the construction of the *Kingston* appeared in the *Montreal Transcript* in September of 1854.[12] Hamilton's agent at the works, William McAuslan, escorted the *Transcript*'s reporter around the site. McAuslan was reprising the role he had had in the building of the *Passport*, remaining on site to supervise the construction in the owner's interest. In conducting the tour he emphasized the limiting dimensions of the *Kingston*'s design: "well calculated for the size of the canals," with particular emphasis on the light draught required for using the canals and running the rapids. For any given size of ship, iron construction produced a lighter vessel. Consequently, the *Kingston*, like the *Passport*, would have more internal space in comparison with the other vessels accommodated by the St. Lawrence canals. Moreover, many shipping men were confident that an iron hull was stronger than a wooden one — strength that was important in the rapids of the St. Lawrence.[13]

By mid-November 1854 the tedious task of hand-working the thousands of rivets in the hull was completed. On 15 November the steamboat was launched, sideways, into the waters of the lower Lachine canal basin.[14] We are not told who was present. John Hamilton was absent from his duties in the Legislative Council on 14–15 November and undoubtedly had come down from Quebec City.[15] The new steamer was christened *Kingston* after the community that would become her home port. The name had been used only once before in a Great Lakes' steamboat — a small vessel launched in 1833, which had been converted to sail in the 1840s.[16] Bartley & Dunbar submitted a bill for £150 for the launching, which would have covered the extra men on hand for the job and a keg or two with which to celebrate the occasion.[17]

As late as February Hamilton still hoped to have *Kingston* out early in the new season. His arrangements with Bartley & Dunbar were predicated on the delivery of the ship by 1 May 1855. At a mid-winter meeting with his associates, Hamilton tentatively assigned the ship to the "River Line," which carried the Royal Mail between Montreal and Kingston.[18] But all that winter her hull lay trapped in the lower basin of the Lachine Canal.

> ## JAMES SHEARER'S
> ## HOUSE JOINER-WORK MANUFACTORY,
> ### ST. GABRIEL LOCKS, LACHINE CANAL,
> ### MONTREAL.
>
> DOORS, Windows, Blinds, Architraves, Mouldings, Skirtings, Stairs, Handrails, Scroll Sawing, Turning, and every description of House Finishings
>
> **CONSTANTLY ON HAND AND MADE TO ORDER.**
>
> ## STEAMBOAT CABIN WORK
>
> PREPARED AND FITTED UP IN THE MOST MODERN STYLE,
>
> **Steering Wheels, &c., &c., &c.**
>
> BUILDERS, CONTRACTORS, and others ordering the above WORK may depend upon having it MADE IN THE BEST MANNER, and **WARRANTED NOT TO SHRINK.**
>
> ORDERS from Town or Country, promptly ATTENDED TO, and at ONE PRICE ONLY.
>
> BOXES, PACKING CASES and TRUNKS made to order. All kinds of SAWN LUMBER constantly on hand and for sale.
>
> real, October, 1857.

The Canada Directory for 1857–58, *1209*.

Complications arose. All the carpentry work had been contracted to James Shearer, a superb young Montreal carpenter who was becoming a specialist in steamboat interiors. Shearer's agreement with Hamilton also required delivery by 1 May 1855, but assumed that his men would be aboard in the fall of 1854. On 21 February 1855 he protested that he still did not have possession of the hull to get started![19] Bartley & Dunbar had to put the major pieces of the engine into the hull, the boilers, cylinder, and the like, because the decks and staterooms would enclose the mechanical works. They blamed their long delay on a late decision about the design of the boiler, and billed Hamilton another £200 for extra work.

All plans for having her on the line early in the season were frustrated. Her trials were delayed until the beginning of August. The engine promptly broke. Bartley & Dunbar immediately pointed the finger at Hamilton's men, exclaiming that the operators, not the engine builders, were at fault. Hamilton naturally disagreed, but was anxious to get the *Kingston* into service.

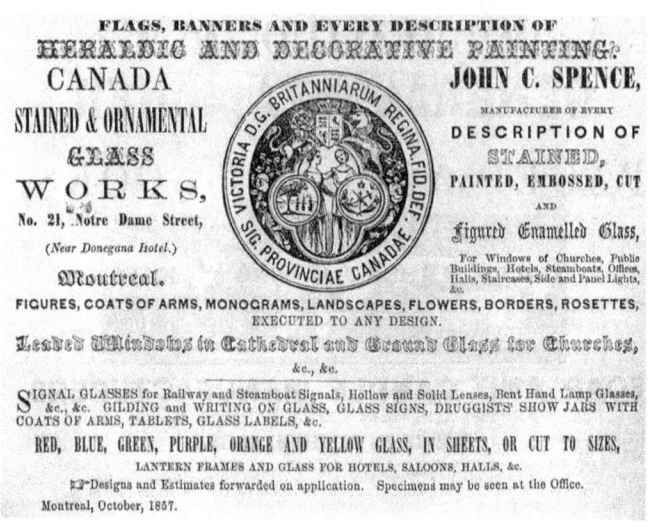

The Canada Directory for 1857–58.

The bill for construction continued to grow. Hamilton had already sent £2,072 19s sterling to Scotland for the fabrication of the hull. This was roughly equivalent to £2,300 Cy. The bill for shipping the iron to Montreal is lost. Bartley & Dunbar had then charged £1,987 10 1/2d Cy. for erecting and launching the hull, including their commission. The bill included a further £4,550 for the erection of the engine and two boilers. This more than doubled the cost to over £8,837 Cy. If the *Kingston* was at all comparable to other iron-hulled vessels built in the next few years, then these expenses would account for just under half of the actual cost of deploying the vessel. Much of the balance would have been the carpenters and joiners work contracted by James Shearer. After all a hull, engine, and boilers make a very plain vessel. Above the main deck rose a promenade deck, and above that the hurricane deck. These enclosed the public spaces on board as well as the private staterooms. Other smaller amounts would have been owed the Montreal tradesmen who supplied the stained glass and did the painting and gilding. The final major bill would have been for furniture that largely came from Hersee & Timmerman, the leading Buffalo suppliers to the railway steamers of Lake Erie.[20] If the *Kingston*'s bills were in proportion to those of other steamers of the era, we can crudely estimate that she would have cost over £19,000 Cy. or $76,000

U.S. Compared with the millions being poured into the construction of the Grand Trunk Railway this might seem like a trivial sum of money. To the deckhands aboard the *Kingston* earning perhaps £25 in a good season, the amount would have seemed enormous.[21]

The *Kingston* did not appear on the Great Lakes until the middle of August 1855, and then only to run up to Lewiston to receive her furniture. The enthusiastic write-ups of the *Montreal Daily Advertiser* were dutifully circulated by some newspapers along her route — each no doubt aware of the Hamilton advertising account.[22] Perhaps because ill feeling stemmed from the extended delays and the failed engine trials, this article generously awarded credit to the sub-contractors, and largely ignored Bartley & Dunbar. The contract for the *Kingston*'s carpentry work was one of the early highlights of a long career in steamboat work for James Shearer. Painting was undertaken by Walker & Little, gilding by Huell & Laird, and stained glass by Spence.[23] The *Daily Advertiser* concluded that neither "expense nor skill has been spared to make the *Kingston* the crack-boat on the route."[24]

What would the first visitors aboard the *Kingston* have seen as they crossed the gangplank onto her main deck? Beneath their feet was the lower deck. This was inside the hull and divided in the middle by an engine room occupying fifty-six feet of the 174-foot overall length of the hull. Because the engine room was placed in the widest part of the hull, it occupied over 40 percent of that space. A mere 26.2 feet wide, the engine room contained the great bulk of two boilers (each perhaps eight or nine feet in diameter), the base of the massive "A"-shaped frame that supported the walking beam some thirty feet overhead, and the base of the ten-foot tall casting that was her single cylinder. This cylinder, forty-two inches in its interior diameter, was probably enwrapped by wooden slats held tight by polished brass bands. At regular intervals in the *Kingston*'s passage up and down the Lakes she would stop for wood. From piles of cordwood stacked on a wharf, the crew would heave cord after cord of firewood down a hatch into a space next to the boilers. The firemen then had to hand feed it, piece by piece, into the furnaces of the two boilers to keep up steam. Cooled only by the water on the other side of the iron hull, the "hole" was separated from the rest of the lower

Royal Mail Line Steamboat General Schematic

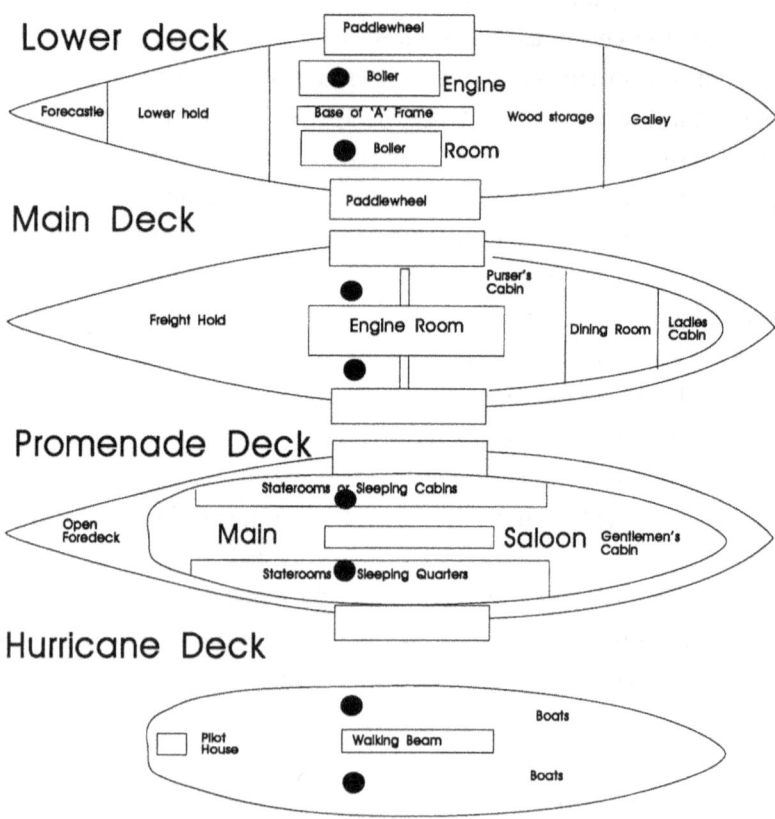

deck by two sheet-iron, water-tight bulkheads. The forward hold was largely used for freight, with some of the crew's quarters right in the bow. The forecastle housed the mess boy, firemen, deckhands, and probably the wheelsmen. Small portholes pierced the iron hull in the first ten to fifteen feet, shedding some light into this area. The kitchen (or galley) was probably in the after hold, where the cooks and waiters slept. In later years it was on the main deck just inside the port paddlewheel, and partly warmed by the heat radiating from the port boiler.

The main deck was flush with the top of the hull. Fore and aft of the paddlewheels it was, in fact, much broader than the hull. This extension of the main deck, known as the guards, was supported by sponsons, or struts, braced firmly against the iron hull just above the water line. Rising up from the lower deck, above the "hole" where the firemen stoked the furnaces, was the engine room. On the level of the main deck the chief engineer and his assistants monitored the pressure gauges and manipulated the few controls for the engine. Directly above the furnaces, it reeked of wood smoke, and the grease and tallow used to lubricate the machinery. Looking into the engine space from the observation window on the promenade deck, the passenger's eye was first drawn to the gleam of polished brass and the massive cylinder, encased in highly polished dark wood, with the long piston rod driving up and down its ten-foot length. The rod stretched up through the hurricane deck to the walking beam. There a second rod rhythmically plunged down through the vessel to the crank room, (just ahead of the engine room) where it turned the massive cranks on the shafts about twenty-eight times every minute. These stretched across to the paddlewheels just below the next deck, allowing the crew to duck underneath them in the passageways on either side of the engine room. The engine room opened aft into the main deck saloon.

It was into this saloon that the first class (or cabin) passenger stepped after climbing aboard through the after gangway. Close by the entrance was the purser's office, the business centre of the steamer, where the purser kept the cargo manifests, accounted for the fuel being taken aboard, and checked the tickets of passengers. The *Kingston*'s safe was probably also in this office. The main deck saloon was the principal area for serving meals, being able to accommodate some seventy people at a sitting. The odour of smoke and grease drifting back from the engine room mingled with the smells emanating from the galley or kitchen in the after hold below. Behind it was the ladies' cabin (which had a ladies' maid assigned to it). In the first generation of steamboats this had been both communal sleeping quarters and dressing room. But the "modern" steamer of the 1850s had staterooms, and the ladies' cabin served principally as a place where the women could congregate away from the smoking, drinking, and card-playing in the gentlemen's saloon on the deck overhead.

Those passengers boarding the *Kingston* on her forward gangway entered a very different world. The main deck forward of the engines was a more open space, barren of furniture, where second class (or "deck") passengers slept on the bare deck with their luggage, sustained only by the food they had brought aboard. People were the most valuable paying "cargo," not the least because they were "self-unloading."

As the number of immigrants entering Canada diminished in the 1850s and 1860s, and most of those travelled by train, this space was increasingly occupied by packaged freight. Especially in the spring and fall this hold would contain boxes and barrels of goods: the products of Canadian firms, artisans, and farmers being shipped east to Montreal and European goods moving west into the heart of the continent. The forward hold had the advantage of being close to the level of most of the wharves at which the *Kingston* called, reducing the time and cost of loading and unloading cargo. Alternatively cargo could be lowered through a hatch into the forward hold on the lower deck. This hatch was the cause of more than one injury:

> A gentleman going on board at mid-day on some business, was suddenly precipitated into the hold of the vessel. After getting on board, his eyes had not become accustomed to the change from the dazzle of the sun without, to the subdued light within, and therefore did not perceive the hatch to be uncovered. Fortunately in his descent, he did not come in contact with anything but the flooring and was but slightly hurt.[25]

Two forward gangways were the means of transferring cargo on board. The deck was also lit by six windows to each side. At least a couple of these would have lit the engineers' quarters, opposite the engine room on the port side.

Cabin passengers spent most of their time aboard on the promenade deck, which provided the best view forward, with the deck clear for the

The Iron Steamboat

Sir Henry Acland, "Interior Kingston": *The only interior illustration of the* Kingston, *this sketch offers hints of three important details. First, there is the styling and placement of the chairs in the main saloon. Compare these to the chairs shown in the photograph of the* Montreal *from the same period on the next page. Even the placement is similar. Second, note the lines of the door and wall treatment along the saloon. While the detailing of the cornices is not apparent, they represent a key point in the interior trim. Again compare the styling to the doors leading from the saloon of the* Montreal. *Finally note the relatively low ceiling. It is evident that the* Kingston *featured a clerestory ceiling for the greater part of the length of the main saloon. Either this is an error in detail of the artist, or at night the whole ceiling felt closer.*

Interior of Steamer Montreal: *This photograph is half of a stereoview of the saloon of the* Montreal *and sets Acland's sketch of the interior of the* Kingston *in a larger context. Like the* Montreal *the* Kingston *carried marble-topped tables. Unlike the* Kingston, Montreal *had an additional deck with staterooms and long balconies.*

first thirty feet or so, part of it sheltered by the hurricane deck above. Walkways stretched around the exterior of this deck, interrupted in the middle by the paddleboxes. The photographs of the *Kingston* do not suggest access to the staterooms (or private sleeping accommodations) from these walkways. Each stateroom, however, does appear to have had an exterior window. A long "main saloon" (not to be confused with the main deck saloon) stretched down the centre of this deck, perhaps twelve or fourteen feet wide, with stateroom doors leading off to both sides. The saloon was described in 1855 as "finished in white and gold, with carved mouldings and pilasters, lighted with richly stained glass."[26] A second account described it as:

> 160 feet in length, [an exaggeration] profusely furnished with sofas, lounges & chairs, luxuriously cushioned & gorgeously covered after the manner of the most handsome drawing rooms. Tables with marble tops, mirrors of the largest dimensions, a piano of superior quality, stained and ornamented glass lights, and the richest carpets, go to make up the *tout ensemble* of this magnificent saloon.[27]

The ceiling of this saloon was raised and arched in the style of a church clerestory, with glass windows set into the sides of this raised section to admit light and fresh air. Rising up through the middle of the saloon was the housing for the "A" frame and the connecting rods. A glass window in this housing provided a marvellous vantage point for passengers to watch the motions of the engine in operation. Indeed government regulations required a steam gauge to be visible to the passengers at all times. The smoke stacks of the *Kingston* were carried up through two cabins just inside the paddleboxes, one of which, at least, was used in 1872 as a storage room for laundry.

Towards the stern, the long saloon opened up into the "gentlemen's saloon," described in 1855 as "finished aft with a circular roof, with two dome lights filled with stained glass, and forward with a rich fanlight of the same."[28] This contained a number of tables, at least one stairway down to the main deck saloon on the port side, and doors to the after deck.

Each stateroom or cabin contained, among other furnishings, four life preservers. Other preservers were stored in the saloon near the paddleboxes. The staterooms were described as:

> unusually large, some having double beds,... in keeping with the rest. By the by, we ought not to omit noticing the BRIDAL ROOM, which has been fitted up with all imaginable care and comfort for the especial benefit of newly married couples.[29]

While a few might have had double beds, at this stage in her history most of the cabins were still equipped with berths.

Although the newspapers may have considered it too delicate to mention, the Gentlemen's Cabin was served by a bar, without which no passenger steamboat was considered complete.

All that remained was the hurricane deck. This was much shorter than the promenade deck leaving an opening for passengers to enjoy the weather. Forward on the hurricane deck was the pilot house, with its big double wheel. The gearing ran down to the lower deck and 140 feet aft to the rudder. When running down the rapids of the St. Lawrence an auxiliary tiller was attached directly to the rudder in case anything went wrong. Just behind the pilot house rose a tall mast that carried the ship's running light and bell. There is no evidence that *Kingston* ever ran under sail, although there were probably some aboard for emergencies. Most of the hurricane deck followed the arch of the clerestory roof of the saloon, raised just far enough to light that interior passage. The most striking feature of the deck was the massive, ponderous iron walking beam. Weighing tons, the beam swung up and down every two to three seconds while the vessel was underway. These beams were perhaps the most distinctive feature of the North American river steamer. Flanking the beam were two tall, black, smoke stacks, with fancy iron grillwork stretching between them. Like the mast they were also supported by a spray of ropes attached at various points on this deck. Finally, the ship's boats were carried aft of the engine equipment. Government regulations required three, at least one of which was to be fireproof, all to be capable of seating a minimum of twenty, with as many more people clinging to hand lines.[30]

In short, as she entered service, *Kingston* was both typical of the Canadian steamboats on the upper St. Lawrence and Great Lakes, and a showcase for the latest refinements. Her iron hull, her upper deck cabins, her elegant appointments led more than one to bestow on her the description: "floating palace."

2

John Hamilton's *Kingston*

Before the new steamer could return to Montreal from her shakedown cruise, she was pressed into service. A break in the Beauharnois Canal caught some of the River Mail Line steamers on the lower end of their route. The *Kingston* came to the rescue. She delivered passengers to the upper end of the canal and returned to Kingston. A couple of weeks later, after the canal repairs had been completed, she was shifted into the Lake Mail Line in the place of the *Passport*, which required some mid-season servicing. With a month of trials and emergencies passed, she settled into her own regular schedule on the river, returning to Montreal on 16 September 1855 carrying passengers and nearly 200 barrels of flour and potash.[1]

It was customary for a senior captain to take command of a major new addition to the fleet. John Hamilton, however, defied tradition: he appointed his second son, Clarke (the eldest was a lawyer). Approaching twenty-two years in age, Clarke was both young and relatively inexperienced. Certainly, he had never commanded a steamboat. Still, it was also true that he was only a year or two younger than his father had been when he entered the steamboat business.[2] And he was probably surrounded by veterans like Samuel Kinlock, his chief engineer, who, unfortunately would die before the end of the season at the age of forty-two.[3]

The River Palace

"*Kingston, Canada West, in 1855*" *by E. Whitefield: This is, more or less, how the* Kingston *would have seen her home port when she first came up the St. Lawrence. The Grand Trunk locomotive on the main waterfront in the centre of the picture is a couple of years ahead of the tracks in that part of the city. The Cataraqui Bridge separates the relatively shallow inner harbour from the action on the main waterfront. The artist has crowded a host of schooners, a pair of fully rigged ships, and a number of steamboats into the busy waterfront.*

Having begun her regular route on the river, the *Kingston* finished the season with one trip up the length of Lake Ontario for the *Passport*. She was hauled off in late November and the *Magnet* and *Arabian* finished the season.[4]

While thousands of pounds had been spent on the *Kingston*, millions were being spent on the Grand Trunk Railway. As winter approached and the schooners and steamers began laying up, railway officials were preparing for a celebration. On 17 November a special excursion set off from Montreal to spend the day in Brockville. Two days later the railway was open on this stretch for regular business.[5] All involved were confident that the following year would see the completion of the line to Toronto. The effect on shipping remained to be seen.

When the steamboat arrangements were made for the 1856 season the three iron-hulled vessels, *Passport, Magnet*, and *Kingston*, combined with *Arabian* to form the Lake Mail, Line. They would run from Hamilton down to Brockville. As additional sections of track

John Hamilton's Kingston

Kingston *at Hamilton's Wharf, Kingston, Ontario, 1856: Although the other vessel in this photograph is not identified, she is probably the* Passport, *which in 1856 was also owned by Hamilton and would have wintered at his wharf. That the Passport's outfit was not complete is evident in the fact that her smokestack was not yet up and the name was not repainted on the paddlebox. A platform appears to be suspended outside the main deck forward of the freight hold, probably for the painters to use on that part of the hull.* Passport's *scroll figurehead is clearly evident.*

Kingston, *on the other hand, is ready to sail — indeed she was the first steamer out of the harbour in 1856. Note that the port lifeboat is suspended at the level of the promenade deck. Typically, it would not have been carried at this level while underway. The dark sponsons are clearly visible on both these hulls, supporting the "guards" on the main deck. Only on* Kingston *are the much lighter fenders also visible.*

were opened the run was shortened to Kingston. A connecting line, consisting of four wooden-hulled steamers, extended the Mail Line's service down the river to Montreal.

For the first time, the label "Royal Mail Line" became a misnomer, as the Grand Trunk Railway took over the carriage of the mail. Despite this, the name stuck. Forty years after they had stopped carrying the mail between Hamilton, Toronto, and Montreal, the steamers on this route were still popularly known as the Mail Line.

In one of the earliest surviving photographs of Great Lakes shipping, taken of Hamilton's new Kingston wharf in the spring of 1856, the ice appears to have cleared the harbour. *Kingston* gleams in her full "suit" of white paint (at least down to the waterline). Some of her crew are standing about: at the pilot house, on the open promenade deck, and at the stern. No doubt aware of the photographer's presence, they stand and await his signal. The men on the *Passport,* by contrast, appear a blur as they paint her sides and scrub her decks.

Not surprisingly, in late April the *Kingston* preceded the *Passport* out of their Kingston winter quarters, the *Magnet* and *Arabian* still being trapped by ice in Burlington Bay. Despite the early start to the season, some sixty or seventy passengers climbed on board for a 4:00 a.m. departure on April 22, on a passage to Toronto. The stoves at either end of the main saloon attracted a crowd, for the lake was not clear of ice. According to "A Traveller,"

> the high winds of Saturday and Sunday had broken up the fields [of ice] or driven them toward the south side of the lake, and with the exception of some collections near Kingston harbour, which had been pounded up pretty small, and some still more minute in the bay of Toronto, the good steamer did not come in contact with ice enough to scrape off a particle of paint from her white and glittering sides.[6]

She made the passage in thirteen hours including stops in Cobourg, Port Hope, and Port Darlington (Bowmanville's harbour).

John Hamilton's Kingston

The railway was still not yet open to Toronto so the usual crush of emigrants began to make their way aboard the steamboats. On one passage a Kingston newspaper noted a "crowd of German emigrants bound to different ports in Western Canada and the Western States."[7] A small group of British emigrants described their accommodations as "very comfortable, being well sheltered from the weather...."[8] Still, the spartan accommodations of the freight hold were worlds apart from the "bridal room" on the deck above.

The sympathetic editor of the *British Whig* offered encouragement from a recent trip into the western part of the province:

> Oh! the delights and comforts of a handsome and clean steamboat after the jigging, jolting, dirt, dust and turmoil of a Railroad Car. Here one may talk, walk about, eat, drink, sleep, laugh and play, and sing, and yet be travelling onwards at the rate of twelve miles [twenty kilometres] an hour.... So men and women should travel, instead of apeing the lightning, and idly striving to annihilate time and space.[9]

The same editor reprinted some travellers' stories making the rounds of the English papers. These cited "satisfactory testimonials from passengers with regard to comfort, economy, and speed," and said that they "preferred the steamers to Grand Trunk Railway — the charges being fewer, the accommodation better & cheaper, the luggage of passengers being carried free, and only a few hours difference in time."[10]

While all this might be true, there were other aspects of travelling on the Great Lakes that many travellers preferred to avoid — particularly storms and seasickness. Of the former it was claimed that the *Kingston* "stood the heavy gales of 1855 and 1856 as bravely as any boat on the line."[11] Moreover, the Grand Trunk found its ride unfavourably compared with "a comfortable night's rest" on Lake Ontario![12]

3

The Floating Palace

Style and comfort were the key elements in the marketing of steamboats in competition with the railway. Despite some complaints, railways attracted most of the regular passenger business and the express trade (mail and package freight). They actively pursued a share of the bulk cargoes carried by schooners and freighters. Vessels like the *Kingston* increasingly catered to the "carriage trade," wealthy travellers to whom expense was less an object, and speed less a consideration. No better description could be offered than "floating palace," and no better passengers than royalty.

The royal tour of North America by the Prince of Wales in the summer and fall of 1860 provided a perfect opportunity to showcase the *Kingston*. She joined the tour at Quebec City (as noted in the Introduction) and the first night was spent at the wharf at Trois Rivières in the company of the *Quebec*, which had been chartered to bring down the members of Parliament and the legislative councillors, among whom John Hamilton may have numbered. Estimates ran as high as 25,000 for the number of people crowding the waterfront to see off the royal party. The next morning, freshly decorated with branches of evergreens, the *Kingston* set off for Montreal with the *Quebec* in her wake. One Montreal party on board the *St. Lawrence* caught up with the royal steamers while a crowd of other steamers waited in the rain off Verchères.

The Floating Palace

Matthew Brady, The Royal Party: The eighteen-year old Prince of Wales, the future King Edward VII, is perhaps the shortest member, standing in the centre of the royal party in this photograph from Matthew Brady's Washington, D.C. studio.

While the *Kingston* passed them there were numerous passengers cheering as heartily as if the weather had not obliged them to wear water-proofs and shelter themselves under umbrellas, when the whole of them fell into line, or at least followed in some way, and the sight of so many white floating houses covered in boughs and flags, crowded with passengers needed only sunshine to make it the most perfectly picturesque sight that could be conceived.[1]

Among the flotilla were the *Passport, Mayflower,* and *Bowmanville* from the upper river fleet, and the *Caledonia, Terrebonne, Hochelaga, James McKenzie, Salaberry, L'Aigle, John Redpath, Topsey, Bonaventure, St. Marie, St. Helène, Victoria, Napoléon,* and *L'Assomption*.[2] A crowd estimated at

The River Palace

"Escort to Montreal": The artist for the Illustrated London News has captured the mob scene as a host of steamers escort the "Raining Prince" and the royal party aboard the Kingston into Montreal harbour. The artist wouldn't win any awards for technical detail (the Kingston's pilot house is wrong and the walking beam is too far forward), but he was probably just trying to keep his paper dry as he sketched.

some 40,000 to 50,000 was impatiently waiting in the rain at Montreal for the arrival of the *Kingston* and her passengers. But the deluge that had followed the "Raining Prince" had ruined the city's decorations. A delegation begged for a delay so that they might replace the sodden finery. Consequently, the royal party spent a second night in the staterooms of the *Kingston* anchored off St. Helen's Island. Just after nine o'clock the morning of Saturday, August 25, the weather cleared. The scene from the approaching steamer was "quite striking," according to those on board, as tens of thousands turned the Montreal waterfront into a sea of hats and bonnets. Some muttered about the "awkwardness" displayed in bringing the *Kingston* alongside the wharf. The great crowd waited impatiently for the vessel to be secured, the gangway to be set in place, and the praying and speechifying to begin.[3]

From Saturday to Monday the prince was ushered about Montreal, opening the Victoria Bridge, viewing an exhibition at Montreal's version of the Crystal Palace, and attending more balls, concerts, and parties. Meanwhile, the *Kingston* quietly steamed up the St. Lawrence canals to Dickinson's Landing at the top of the Long Sault Rapids. After Monday night's ball (where the prince was kept dancing until 4:00 a.m.), the royal entourage was allowed a few hours of sleep before being hauled off on the Grand Trunk to Cornwall and on to the top of the rapids. There

The Floating Palace

Landing at the Bonsecours Wharf, Montreal: Vessels crowd the scene as the Kingston *discharges her passengers at the end of the Bonsecours wharf. This scene was engraved from a Notman photograph that has not survived.*

Victoria Bridge: Ships, steamers, yachts, pin flats, and even timber rafts were dwarfed by the Victoria Bridge, completed the previous year and officially opened by the Prince of Wales in 1860.

they boarded the *Kingston*. The steamer then ran down the Long Sault, the Coteau, Cedars, Split Rock, and Cascades to Lachine. The late start combined with more official fussing at Cornwall meant night was falling as they approached the Lachine Rapids. Consequently, the *Kingston* docked and let the royal party return by train to a private dinner (where the

The River Palace

Above: *The Laying of the Cornerstone, Parliament Buildings, Ottawa:* The second major reason for the royal tour was this ceremony, laying the cornerstone of the new Canadian Parliament Buildings. The cutline in Leslie's described it as the seat of government of the British Provinces in North America, anticipating the Confederation movement by a few years.

Right: *Baptiste:* From the 1840s, the Royal Mail Line vessels had used First Nations pilots to take the big steamboats down the Lachine rapids. Baptiste was one of the most famous of these, and had the honour of taking the royal party down the Lachine Rapids. This portrait was probably posed in the Montreal studios of Notman, with a big double wheel imported especially as a prop.

The Floating Palace

exhausted eighteen-year-old Prince of Wales was reported to have fallen asleep at the table).[4] The next day was more relaxing with a picnic on Île Dorval and a visit to the Native village at Caughnawaga (Kahnawake). While some daylight remained the prince boarded the *Kingston* and was taken down the Lachine Rapids.

For the next few days the *Kingston* was "off." The royal party set out by rail to Sherbrooke and the Eastern Townships and then spent one final night in Montreal. Next they journeyed up the Ottawa River using both the steamer *Phoenix* and rail connections. In Ottawa the prince performed the other major ceremonial function of the trip, laying the cornerstone of the new Parliament Buildings. In another exhausting day of travel the party came down to Brockville by rail, where the prince was greeted by another crowd of some 10,000 people. There on the evening of 3 September the royal party again retired to the comfort of their staterooms aboard the *Kingston*. A quick tour of Brockville the next morning preceded a passage through the Thousand Islands.

Kingston was the most controversial stop on the royal tour. The previous few days had seen local worthies bustling about informing all and sundry of the appropriate protocols. The Marine Reception Committee published a programme in the local papers that said:

> All steamers are requested to leave the harbor together at half-past one p.m., to proceed down the river as far as the head of Howe Island to meet the steamboat *Kingston* with the Royal party on board.
>
> The steamers will round to, to allow the *Kingston* to pass, and follow close astern in equal numbers on either side.
>
> On meeting the *Kingston* all steam vessels are to salute by dipping ensigns, blowing whistles, and ringing bells, &c....
>
> The steamer conveying his Royal Highness the Prince of Wales and suite will land at the railroad track opposite the Market Battery, consequently no other craft will be permitted to land at the same place.[5]

The River Palace

Sixty years later James P. Gildersleeve, the youngest brother in the famous shipping family recalled the reception:

> All the steamers in port on the fine summer day in 1860 formed a flotilla and went down the river some ten miles [sixteen kilometres] to escort the S.S. *Kingston* to port. The S.S. *Bay of Quinte,* owned by my brother, Overton, afterwards mayor of Kingston, and which plied up and down the Bay of Quinte from Kingston, was fortunate enough to get the first position after the *Kingston.* I had a position on the hurricane deck and

G. H. Andrews, "Kingston, 1860": *This engraving was published in the* Illustrated London News *just before the royal visit. The Market Battery and the Shoal Tower stand ready to defend the magnificent City Hall. Timber rafts in the foreground and to the right symbolize the role of timber forwarding in the economy of the city, or more precisely, of Garden Island, which stood well out into the harbour. A few schooners lie to the right of City Hall while the main forest of masts and spars stands off to the left. Dominating that portion of the waterfront is a large Royal Mail Line steamer with the profile of the* Kingston. *On arriving at the city, the* Kingston *laid just off the Shoal Tower while the politicians tried to resolve the "Orange" crisis.*

all the way up my eyes were glued on the Prince of Wales and I noted his every movement during the ten miles run to port.⁶

The guns of Fort Henry boomed out signalling the approach to an estimated 30,000 spectators. Shortly afterwards the *Kingston* rounded Point Frederick followed by *Walter Shanly, Bay of Quinte, Mayflower, St. Lawrence, Hercules, Pierrepont,* and *Traveller.* The *Kingston* drew close to the Market Battery, but dropped anchor offshore. The restless crowd fidgeted as "several boat loads of sundry civil and military authorities" hurriedly made the short crossing. Politics had caught up with the tour.

Gathered in the city were representatives of some fifty-four Orange lodges from as far afield as Toronto and Cornwall — some 4,000 Orangemen. They had erected two arches along the parade route and decorated them with traditional slogans of the order. The Orange Order, an ultra-Protestant, anti-Catholic Irish group, had been outlawed in Great Britain; however, it remained a perfectly legal entity in Canada West. The prince's official consort was the Duke of Newcastle, a Catholic, who made it abundantly clear that the royal tour could not recognize the Orange Order in any form. The Orangemen made it equally clear that they were determined to demonstrate their loyalty to the Crown and no Catholic, no matter how aristocratic, was going to dissuade them. Intense negotiations got underway between John A. Macdonald (the Member of Parliament for Kingston as well as Attorney-General for Canada West), the Kingston city council, the Orangemen, and the duke. No compromise could be found.

Meanwhile, the *Kingston* had taken a short tour of the harbour until the winds got up so high that "the motion of the waves was decidedly uncomfortable."⁷ She settled down in the lee of an island where another steamer brought out the dinner intended for the official reception ashore. At the same time a few other dignitaries had a private opportunity to be introduced to the Prince of Wales. One of those so honoured was American-born Dileno D. Calvin, the head of a lumber forwarding firm on Garden Island, some of whose steamboats had participated in the

The River Palace

Sir Henry Acland, "Cabin window & my View on Kingston": While the *Kingston* lay at the wharf loading wood, the curious struggled to catch a glimpse of the major actors within, especially the prince. Acland, as one of the royal party, here captures that sense of the rest of the party's wonder at this spectacle.

marine escort into harbour. According to one of Calvin's long time employees, "Calvin was taken aboard the *Kingston* and John A. Macdonald introduced him to H.R.H. as 'an old Vermont Yankee.' In good humour Calvin replied 'Why do you call me a Yankee? I can holler for the Queen as loud as you can.' At this retort the Prince laughed heartily."[8]

Not everyone made such a good impression and nothing was resolved that night or the next morning. Consequently, at three that afternoon the Duke of Newcastle ordered the *Kingston* to leave for Belleville.[9] Behind them the festivities carried on in gloomy spirits. A Toronto yacht, the *Rivet*, won the local regatta, and later the disappointed officials sat down to the warmed-over feast at Kingston's version of the Crystal Palace.[10] Meanwhile, the Orangemen took advantage of the superior speed of the railway and were waiting in Belleville. Here the plans had called for a procession through the town to the Grand Trunk station from which the tour was to proceed by rail. Again the duke would not permit the prince to land and the *Kingston* steamed back out of the Bay of Quinte and set a course for Cobourg. Back to their train went the Orangemen.

At this point in the proceedings a mysterious ecumenical spirit overcame their locomotive — a Catholic engine driver perhaps. The train

The Floating Palace

Sir Henry Acland, "Wood wharf or Orange bitters, Kingston, Sept. 4, 1860": Only something as absurd as the crowds struggling to catch a glimpse of the Prince of Wales could have induced a nineteenth-century artist to sketch something as humble as Doyle's wood wharf. Most of Kingston's steamer wood (and indeed the fuel supply for the city's stoves and fireplaces before the age of coal) came from the hinterlands of the Rideau Canal. The vessel to the right may well have been among the humble barges of the "mosquito fleet" that brought the wood down to the city's waterfront.

and its disgruntled, if patriotic, passengers never did make it through to Cobourg. Although the loud protests of the Orangemen threatened to taint the rest of the tour, less parochial heads succeeded in preventing them from disrupting the rest of the itinerary.

The breathless anticipation of the prince's arrival at Cobourg kept things astir for hours.

> It was generally expected that the Grand Trunk, opened from Toronto to Montreal four years before, would be the means of approach, so the station was richly decorated. In fact, when the train from the east approached, a large

choir of schoolchildren were singing "God Save the Queen" in the belief that the Prince was aboard. Later it became known that the steamer *Kingston* would carry the party to Cobourg, and the crowd hastened to the harbour. Home-owners and storekeepers rushed last-minute decorations, and the town was a mass of flowers, flags and bunting. Ladies fortunate enough to be invited to the ball were assembling their accoutrements, and cabs were reserved for those who had not carriages and coachmen of their own. False alarms continued throughout the day. A shout that the boat was coming caused a crush on the wharf, but it turned out that the ship was sailing east from Port Hope!

The crowds in Cobourg waited till nearly 9:30 p.m. before the running lights of a steamer appeared on the eastern horizon. A procession through the brilliantly illuminated town led to Victoria Hall, the new town hall, whose dance floor was propped up by a large quantity of cedar posts. An estimated 20,000 milled around as another tedious series of addresses were presented and formalities exchanged. The dancing commenced at midnight and carried on till daybreak with an intermission for supper at 2:30 a.m.[11]

A brief rest at the Postmaster General's estate was followed by a side excursion to Peterborough from which the party returned to Port Hope and Whitby. There the prince boarded the *Kingston* again for another triumphant entrance, this time into Toronto harbour.

At six o'clock the *Kingston* was seen from the platform outside the island, and at half past six approached the landing-place, accompanied by the *New York*, the *Cataract*, the *Zimmerman*, and the *Peerless*, all crowded with excursionists, who had gone down the lake to meet the approaching visitor. The *Fire-Fly* came through the eastern channel and was soon close to the landing-place. The other island steamer was near, and numerous yachts with flags displayed lay at their moorings, while row-boats darted about in the neighbourhood of the wharf. The water as well as the land was full of celebrators.[12]

The Floating Palace

Detail from William Armstrong "The Prince of Wales visits Toronto, Sept. 7, 1860": Tens of thousands of spectators merge into a vast sea of blue in Armstrong's view of the arrival of the Kingston *at Toronto. Dominating the harbour are the vessels of the Royal Canadian Yacht Club, their pennants competing with those of the official arch as the most colourful displays on the waterfront. Trailing a short distance behind the* Kingston *are the* Peerless *(foreground) and* New Era *(background), their decks crowded with well-wishers. Although Armstrong was an active artist over an extended career, there seem to have been some strange winds in Toronto this day — The flags on the steamboats and those on the yachts are blowing in opposite directions!*

The prince's entourage spent several days in Toronto and visited Niagara Falls and Hamilton, before crossing into the United States at Windsor-Detroit. The work of the *Kingston* was done and a few days later she was back on her regular route. The bridal suite could now be legitimately marketed as the Royal Suite.

As a footnote to the extravagant tour of the Prince of Wales, his brother, Prince Alfred, took a turn through Canada West the next year. Alfred, however, had already been in Canada with his regiment for an extended period. In June 1861 the *Kingston* was chartered to take him down the St. Lawrence accompanied by the governor general and a small entourage. So low key was the whole affair that at Kingston, "there was

The Landing and Reception of the Prince of Wales and Suite at Toronto: Another of the great "scenes" of the royal tour, as the worthies of Canada West gathered to pay court.

no Royal Salute, no Guard of Honor, and a very small assemblage, which however, soon became very lazy."[13]

4

The *Kingston* and the Canadian Navigation Company

For the Honourable John Hamilton the great royal tour of 1860 was an exhausting triumph amid a series of disasters. For several years he and his few surviving associates in the Royal Mail Line had been in direct competition with railways over their entire route. The sharp "crash" of 1857 meant that he and all the other shipowners on the lower Great Lakes had to cope with reduced demand for their services just when the Grand Trunk Railway had vastly increased the competition. Both railways and ships were in serious financial trouble. The shipowners quickly became incensed as the Macdonald-Cartier government sustained their arch-rival with a generous range of concessions and subsidies. Regardless of the railway's advances over traditional modes of transportation, one fact was obvious to its competitors: the railway company was playing with a loaded pair of dice. No matter how poorly it fared in the marketplace, both the current government and two of London's major banking houses had a vested interest in keeping the railway out of receivership.[1]

Although the Grand Trunk would not be allowed to go bankrupt, many of the region's shipowners were doing just that. Hamilton, legislative councillor and president of the Commercial Bank of Canada, seemed well positioned to ride out this storm. By 1858, Hamilton had tried rate-cutting and retrenchment. All but one of his former partners were dead, retired, or bankrupt. The following season he started sending the *Kingston*

Upper Canada Steamers at Montreal: The Canadian Navigation Company steamboats Corinthian and Kingston are moored by the quay in Montreal.

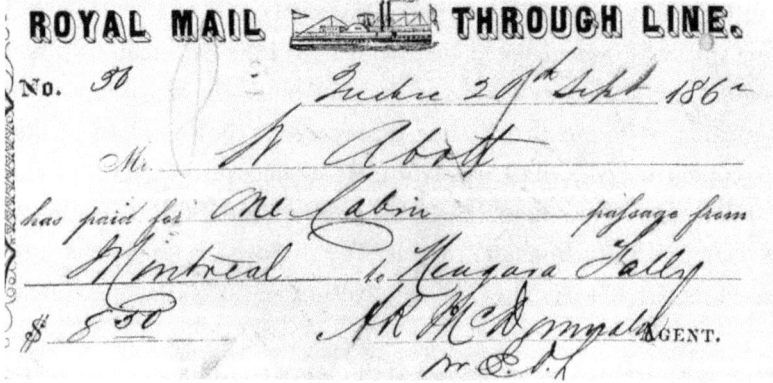

Royal Mail Through Line ticket issued Quebec, 26 September 1862: Note that this "ticket" was issued by an agent in Quebec and appears to have left a stub behind it to the left. It is more in the character of a receipt than what we have come to think of as tickets.

and other Royal Mail Line vessels further down the river to Quebec City in a desperate attempt to grab some of the immigrants before they could board the Grand Trunk's coaches.[2]

In 1860 Hamilton chartered the vessels of the failing, Ogdensburg-based Lake Ontario Express Line and came to terms with the Grand Trunk Railway. It was a three-year agreement that excluded the Royal Mail

Line from all the north shore ports between Toronto and Kingston. The steamboat fares for both passengers and freight rose to those of the railway. Hamilton agreed to carry passengers who had only bought railway tickets. In return, the Grand Trunk's agent, General Manager Walter Shanly, consented to the division of the profits or losses on Hamilton's two lines.[3]

To have concluded such an accord, Hamilton must have already been prepared to write off the next three years of business. With higher rates the steamboat lines could expect to lose even more passengers, especially in the immigrant trade. The charter of the Ogdensburg Express Line brought it into line with the Grand Trunk's rate policy without improving its competitive position. However, the agreement did offer Hamilton $4,000 in management fees and $35,000 for the "charter" value of the eight steamers in the line. Although the agreement would not come directly to the point, Hamilton had chartered the entire line to the Grand Trunk on a profit/loss-sharing basis.

Despite the prestigious voyages with the Prince of Wales, the 1860 season was a financial disaster. Between them the two lines lost over $75,000, a sum that included both charters and management fees. The *Kingston* held the dubious distinction of losing less than any of the rest thanks largely to the princely $7,760 charged for the transport of the royal entourage.[4]

Not only had the profit-sharing proven unprofitable but it had also become a major political embarrassment. A select committee of the Legislative Assembly, chaired by the acerbic George Brown (the powerful owner of the Toronto *Globe* and a leader of the reformers in the opposition), denounced the arrangement as monopolistic. The committee argued that the Grand Trunk had never been authorized to engage in such proceedings.[5]

As it turned out, the company's lawyers had anticipated this. They hoped to sidestep the issue by making the general manager personally liable, inserting a provision allowing him to assign his rights to any successor.

Such manoeuvres scarcely impressed the subsequent Commission of Inquiry (which today might be termed a Royal Commission), which aired this and other problems of the Grand Trunk before concluding the whole experience was "unfortunate."[6] Although the principal partners contemplated the dissolution of the agreement, this decision was pre-

The River Palace

Left: *Sir Hugh Allan (1810–1882): Second son of Scottish sea captain Alexander Allan, Hugh ran the Montreal end of what developed into the Montreal Ocean Steamship Company and was better known as the Allan Line. Although centred in shipping, Allan's business interests included railways, banking, and a variety of manufacturing concerns.*

Right: *Alexander Milloy (1822–1899): At the age of eighteen, Milloy began working for John Hamilton's Montreal agent. He later took over the office becoming secretary-treasurer of the Canadian Navigation Company and later traffic manager of the Richelieu and Ontario Navigation Company.*

empted by Hamilton's bankruptcy in 1861.

Within weeks Hamilton's son Clarke, his Montreal ticket agent, Alexander Milloy, and several of his steamboat captains set about establishing a new company to operate the vessels of the Royal Mail Line. Milloy recruited Hugh and Andrew Allan of the Montreal Ocean Steamship Company (popularly known as the Allan Line). The Allans, in turn, were connected to an ever-widening range of transportation, financial, communications, and manufacturing firms.[7] Hugh Allan possessed something else the promoters prized greatly: an act of incorporation for

The Kingston *and the Canadian Navigation Company*

a company called the Canadian Inland Steam Navigation Company. Although nominally created four years earlier, it had never functioned.[8]

The trustees of Hamilton's bankrupt estate delayed disposing of the steamers until it was legally possible to sell to the new firm. In the meantime, in preparation for this they arranged that the *Kingston* and the *Passport* would be registered for the first time.[9] After the sale the Canadian Inland Steam Navigation Company hired Hamilton as general manager. So the firm started operations with the same vessels, captains, Montreal agent, and general manager as the Royal Mail Line had had the previous season.

Fresh capital and a strong economic recovery made the Mail Line as profitable as it had ever been. From 1861 until its amalgamation with the Richelieu Company in 1875, the company grew five-fold, from a paid-up capital of $118,800 to $576,000. Better still, it declared dividends ranging from 5 percent to 22 1/2 percent in years when the Grand Trunk Railway failed miserably in attempts to meet the payments on its bonded debt. During the same years Canadian Inland Steam Navigation acquired the American-owned Lake Ontario Express Line and began running excursion steamers from Quebec City to the burgeoning seaside resorts on the lower St. Lawrence and the Saguenay.[10]

During this expansion the company built and purchased a variety of new vessels, most of them iron-hulled after the pattern of the *Passport, Magnet*,

Toronto Public Library, Baldwin Room, Broadside Collection.

The River Palace

The Canadian Navigation Company Fleet

Passport: *Assembled on the Marine Railway of Fowler and Hood at Kingston in 1846 from materials shipped out from Scotland, the* Passport *was the first iron-hulled merchant vessel built above Montreal. She served in the Royal Mail Line for the rest of the century. Renamed* Caspian *in 1898, she was converted into a barge in 1921. This picture shows her in her home port of Kingston. She appears to be at James Swift's wharf, just west of the Shoal Tower.*

Banshee: *Photographer H.E. Sheldon captured the wooden-hulled* Banshee *in Kingston in the spring of 1856, with the* Champion *lying just of her stern. Launched in 1854, a few weeks after the* Kingston, Banshee *was chartered to the Canadian Navigation Company along with the* New Era. *In the winter of 1865, she was sold to American interests, a transaction that was abandoned with the end of the Civil War. The Navigation Company finally purchased her outright after* Kingston's *1865 encounter with Split Rock. She served as a spare boat before being sold out of the fleet in 1874.*

The Kingston *and the Canadian Navigation Company*

Magnet: *Launched at the Niagara Harbour and Dock Company in July 1847, the* Magnet *was also built of iron acquired in Scotland. Her construction costs heavily subsidized by the British Admiralty, she was to be immediately available in the case of war with the United States. In 1868 the Canadian Navigation Company made her available during the Fenian crisis, and then charged handsomely for her "charter."* Magnet *had a more varied career than the* Passport. *Not only did she work the Royal Mail Line, but spent time on the run from Quebec City downriver to the Saguenay, serving resorts like Cacouna, Murray Bay, Tadoussac, and Ha! Ha! Bay. She is shown here in the mid-1880s when she and* Spartan *were chartered to the Owen Sound Royal Mail Steam Ship Line. Seriously rebuilt in 1894–95, she was renamed* Hamilton, *after her home port for most of her career. Rebuilt in 1910 as an oil barge, she was abandoned in the late 1920s.*

Champion: *She was another wooden-hulled steamboat, built originally for John Hamilton's brothers-in-law, John and David Macpherson and their partner, Samuel Crane. In 1857, Hamilton bought a half interest along with one of the owners of the* Banshee, *William Bowen.* Champion *came to the Canadian Navigation Company along with the rest of Hamilton's fleet in 1861. She was operated on the main route until the new iron steamboats were built, after which she ran in services like the one that brought her, in this photograph, down the St. Lawrence to Tadoussac. She was sold out of the fleet in 1873 and broken up about three years later.*

The River Palace

E. Whitefield, "Grecian": *Unlike most of the fleet of the Canadian Navigation Company,* Grecian *had a short life. Iron-hulled like most of her linemates, she had a number of scrapes in the rapids between her launch in 1864 and her wreck in May 1869 in the Split Rock Rapids. The hull was pulled out of the channel and her engines salvaged for the* Corsican. *For some time she lay on the edge of the river, her paddles still idly turning in the current.*

Spartan: *The* Spartan *came out a year after the* Grecian, *giving the Canadian Navigation Company a fifth iron-hulled passenger steamboat. Like the* Passport *and* Grecian, *she was fitted with a horizontal rather than a vertical steam engine. Consequently, travellers missed the otherwise common sight of the overhead walking beams sported by* Kingston, Magnet, *and most of the other paddlewheelers of the era. Earlier pictures show* Spartan *with two smokestacks, rather than the single one that dominates this profile. Renamed the* Belleville *in 1905, she was rebuilt into a rather graceless freighter in 1920 and abandoned two years later.*

The Kingston *and the Canadian Navigation Company*

Corinthian: *Built for the Gildersleeve interests of Kingston,* Corinthian's *hull plating followed that of* Spartan *across the Atlantic in 1864. O.S. and C.F. Gildersleeve were successively vice-presidents of the Canadian Navigation Company and sold* Corinthian *to the firm in 1868. She ran on the Royal Mail Line between Toronto and Hamilton until 20 September 1892 when she caught fire just after running the Cedar Rapids, and was destroyed.*

Bohemian *in the rapids: Launched in Montreal in 1873, the* Bohemian *was the only wooden-hulled vessel built for the Canadian Navigation Company fleet. Lengthened to 195 feet in 1900, she was renamed* Prescott *five years later. In August 1908 she burned in a spectacular fire on the Montreal waterfront.*

The River Palace

Corsican *in Toronto: Built at Montreal in 1870,* Corsican *took the engine and the place of* Grecian *in the line. She was renamed* Picton *in 1905 and burned in Toronto on 21 September 1907.*

Abyssinian: *Built in 1847 at Clayton, NY, and was originally launched as the* Ontario, *this steamboat operated between Ogdensburg and Lewiston on the American equivalent of the Royal Mail Line. The American lines were in financial trouble in the late 1850s and again in the 1860s, before the Canadian Navigation Company bought up the three remaining steamboats. Along with* Ontario, *there was the* Bay State *(1849, renamed* Athenian*) and* Cataract *(1847, renamed* Columbian*).* Abyssinian *appeared in this photograph after she had been sold to the Union Navigation Company in 1874 (her paddlebox spells this out in French: "Co'e de Nav'n Union").*

and *Kingston*. To fill out the line the first years of the company, they acquired the wooden-hulled *Champion* and *Banshee*, and briefly leased the *New Era*. Following the lead of the Allan Line, the firm used a theme for its new ships' names.[11] The *Grecian* was launched in Montreal in 1863, the *Spartan*, a year later. *Corinthian* was built to the same general dimensions by the firm's vice-president, C.F. Gildersleeve, and was sold to the firm in 1868. That same year the steamers *Ontario, Bay State*, and *Cataract* were purchased from their American owners and renamed, respectively, *Abyssinian, Athenian*, and *Columbian*. When the *Grecian* was wrecked in the rapids in 1869, her engine was placed in the new iron-hulled steamer, *Corsican*. Finally, in 1873, the firm built the new composite-hulled steamer, *Bohemian*.[12]

The heart of the operations of the Canadian Navigation Company (as it was renamed in 1868), remained the Royal Mail Line and its daily service from Hamilton to Montreal. Although passenger service remained the core of its business, the company did offer some facilities for the movement of freight. Any goods shipped by rail between Hamilton and Montreal required transhipment at Toronto in the early years, a complication that the steamboat line avoided.[13] One list of freight on board the *Kingston* in the spring of 1861 offers a sense of the range of goods carried in her career. Three different consignments of flour totalling 659 barrels filled the bulk of the freight holds. There were also 111 barrels of apples, 43 barrels of potash, 7 barrels of eggs, 7 barrels of whiskey, and 11 barrels of pots. Besides barrels, there were 35 firkins of butter, 1 box of tiles, 14 hogsheads of cattle (presumably beef), 24 bundles of trees, 4 bags of seed, 1 box of furniture, 18 boxes of medicine, 1 hogshead of brandy, 12 bundles of shovels, 12 bundles of hoes, 20 bundles of forks, 4 pairs of springs, and 32 puncheons of high wines. In addition, the hold contained a piano, a desk, a case, a printing press, and two horses. All of this was directed to twenty-four different consignees at Montreal.[14]

Along the route the Canadian Navigation Company steamboats made many stops. The deal Hamilton had made with the Grand Trunk, which kept his vessels out of the north shore ports, was dead. Instead, the *Kingston*'s ad from 1861 noted that on her trip upriver from Montreal the "Magnificent Iron Steamer" called at Beauharnois, Coteau, Cornwall,

The River Palace

H. Walker, Kingston: *This fine engraving appeared in an 1870 travel book. The* Kingston *is shown steaming past what, for most of her career, was her major port of call: Montreal. Her paddleboxes still carry the six-pointed star that was the most dominant symbol in her earliest photographs. The most unusual detail of this image is the aft lifeboat being carried at the promenade deck level.*

Williamsburgh, Prescott, Brockville, Gananoque, Kingston, Cobourg, Port Hope, [Port] Darlington, Toronto, and Hamilton.

This same ad stressed that immigrant "families with their Luggage moving West [were] not … subject to Cartage or Transhipment."[15] Numbers of large parties of Norwegians were noted aboard the *Kingston* in various seasons, and on other occasions members of the "English Operative class."[16] The *Kingston* and her linemates also transported troops and their gear to and from the British garrisons in Canada West. Although railways would prove their worth in responding to crises like the Fenian raids, in the normal course of events moving the soldiers by steamer made perfect sense. For example, in 1870, when the batteries were finally withdrawn from Kingston and Toronto, they sailed downriver in the *Magnet* and the *Spartan*.[17]

Passage down the St. Lawrence was not without its thrills and hazards. Leaving Kingston about 4:00 a.m., dawn found the steamboat among the rocks and trees of the Thousand Islands. Stops at Brockville and Prescott provided an opportunity to embark passengers who had come up from Montreal by rail for a day excursion through the rapids

The Kingston *and the Canadian Navigation Company*

The Lachine Rapids: This image is from one panel of an engraved stereoview, which might account for some of the fuzziness of the smoke stacks. It is among the earliest "views" of steamboats in the rapids of the St. Lawrence. There is no particular evidence to suggest that this was *Kingston* or any of her line mates. Indeed, the fact that there is no cabin forward of the paddlewheels would pretty much preclude that identification. On the other hand, stereoviews like this one were among the first commercially supplied "souvenirs" of the trip, probably sold on board as well as in shops in Montreal. As such it is, in fact, a fairly common survivor of the era.

of the St. Lawrence. The first few rapids were merely flat shelves as the river dropped a mere fourteen feet in the seven miles (just over eleven kilometres) between the Galops Rapids and Iroquois Point. A few miles below appeared the Rapide Plat, literally the "flat rapid," where the river dropped another eleven-and-one-half feet in four miles (over six kilometres). Another ten miles (sixteen kilometres) of open water carried the steamers past Morrisburg to the last of the short, low rapids opposite Farran's Point. Here the river dropped four feet to the level at Dickinson's Landing, one of the villages along the river drowned in the 1950s in the creation of the St. Lawrence Seaway. Eventually bypassed by canals (collectively known as the Williamsburg canals), the rapids were so gentle that from the early 1830s steamboats had routinely steamed back up through them from Dickinson's Landing. The *Kingston* offered the same, unusual experience. Below the landing stretched over ten miles (sixteen kilometres) of rough water, the Long Sault Rapids. With a total drop of forty-eight feet this section of the river offered several channels around the islands in the river. Vessels climbing the Cornwall Canal — which huddled against the north bank — had an excellent view of those vessels running down as they were separated only by a large levee. The town of Cornwall, at the bottom of the Long Sault, was one of the major ports of call along the river. Below it, the river widened into a long open stretch known as Lake St. Francis, at the other end of which lay the village of Coteau-du-Lac or Coteau Landing. The Beauharnois Canal offered a safe bypass on the southern side of the river, but downbound the Royal Mail Line steamers took the north channel, plunging in quick succession through the Coteau, Cedar, and Cascade or Split Rock Rapids. The last offered a spectacular thrill as the forty-five-foot wide steamer shot through a swift narrow passage between two rock outcroppings to emerge onto Lake St. Louis. In this eleven miles (eighteen kilometres) the river had dropped yet another eighty-three feet. Soon the muddy brown waters of the Ottawa River could be seen swirling far out into the clear waters of the St. Lawrence and the village of Lachine was approached. In the spring or fall this might be where the tour ended — the Lachine rapids were much too dangerous to be run in twilight. A train could run the passengers into Montreal, while the steamer made her way down the Lachine Canal. But if enough light remained, the Mail Line steamers would stop at the village of Oka. There they took on Baptiste, a Native pilot, who took almost all the steamers through a safe channel in the Lachine Rapids (with a drop of forty-five feet), then under the Victoria Bridge into the harbour of Montreal.

 Making daily passages down these rapids, the fleet was scarcely immune to the dangers of the river. Over the years just about every vessel in the Royal Mail Line fleet had to be rescued. Part of their problem was that the river was used by a variety of other shipping — towboats with barges, great rafts of lumber, as well as the Royal Mail Line steamers.

The Kingston *and the Canadian Navigation Company*

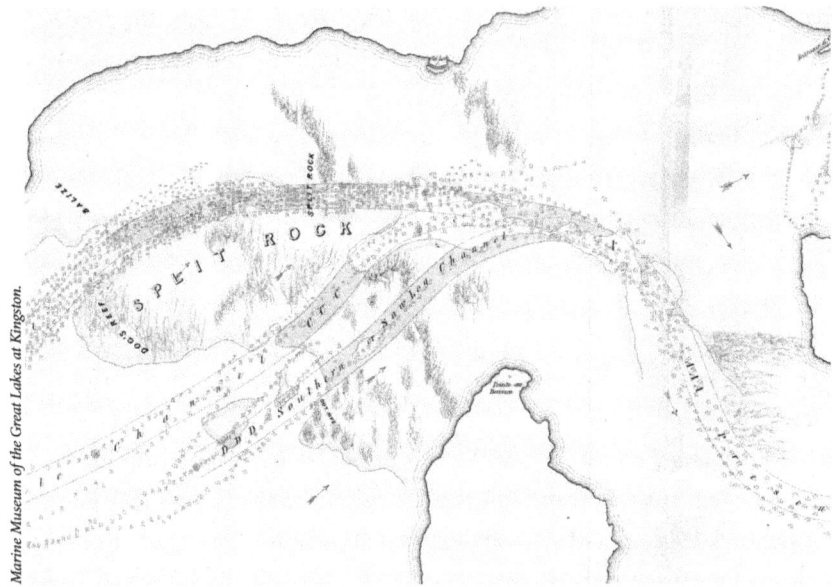

Detail of the Split Rock section of the St. Lawrence rapids showing, from top to bottom, the main steamboat channel, the middle channel and the southern, or saw log channel: From "Survey of a portion of the River St. Lawrence between Pointe an Moulin and Lake St. Louis, including the Cascades Rapids" in Maps, Reports, Estimates, &c., Relative to Improvements of the Navigation of the River St. Lawrence; and a Proposed Canal Connecting the River St. Lawrence and Lake Champlain: *Laid before the Legislative Assembly during the 2nd Session, 5th Parliament, 1856.*

About 4:45 p.m. on 3 June 1865 the *Kingston* was approaching Split Rock, perhaps the most dangerous section of the river. On board were a number of passengers and a cargo of flour, lard, and ashes. Andrew Dunlop, the captain, John Montgomery, the first mate, John O'Donell, the river pilot, and the wheelsman occupied the pilot house. After O'Donell committed the *Kingston* to running the channel, several timber rafts were sighted ahead. In attempting to avoid the large, slow-moving obstructions, the pilot immediately gave the order to stop the steamer. The bell was rung. The engines stopped. The immediate effect was to lose steerage way, and the vessel was rapidly drawn down the river where she smashed against the rocks. There was no turning back. She had to run downstream several miles before she could safely be run ashore. The passengers and their baggage were quickly removed from the vessel.[18] Thirty-four of the relieved passengers offered a testimonial to the captain, absolving him from blame. Nervous company officials rushed this into the hands of the press. Twelve of the passengers gave Montreal as their address, two more Toronto, two London, two Quebec City, while others were from Windsor, Kingston, Perth, and Point de Bisser. Ten were from the United States. The group is roughly representative of the distribution of the company's business.[19] As to the blame, it did not belong to the captain in any event; the river pilot had the command of the ship and was the one who took her into the passage before being sure the way was clear.

The passengers might have pronounced absolutions before climbing aboard the Montreal train, but the Canadian Inland Steam Navigation Company still had a very valuable property half-submerged in the St. Lawrence.

After the purser was dispatched to Montreal to report to the secretary-treasurer of the company, the crew struggled to get as much of the cargo from aft as possible, expecting the ship to completely submerge or go to pieces at any moment. A telegram was sent to Calvin & Breck, whose Kingston area firm not only operated a timber rafting and towing business, but ran a salvage outfit as a sideline. Ironically, their rafts had inadvertently caused the trouble. Three days later their wreck master, Captain John Donnelly, arrived with the steamer *Pierrepont*, twelve men, and some pumps. The next day the *Hope* arrived from Montreal with a barge to lighter the cargo. The process of "lightering" involved the transfer of *Kingston*'s cargo into the lighter, in this case the *Hope*'s barge. At the same time, a representative of the marine insurance firm arrived and authorized the building of a pier next to the bow to prevent the force of the current from further shifting the stranded vessel.

This done, hard hat divers placed the pumps on board and went to work trying to seal the windows in the Gentlemen's Cabin. More pumps arrived from Oswego on the 10th, but it would be two more days before all was in place. When the combined pumps could make no headway, the divers went back down only to discover that the window casing had given way entirely. After another day of futile pumping, on the 15th the divers were again on the wreck. This time they tried closing the stairway leading to the Gentlemen's Cabin from the saloon below and fitted temporary bulkheads around the engine. This too failed. The pumps were taken out, and some men and the Oswego pumps were sent off upriver.

Meanwhile, the *Hope* had returned from Montreal, towing two barges filled with timber. Timber was passed across the decks while Calvin's divers manoeuvred a chain under the *Kingston*'s bottom. On 1 July, the ship was finally raised, her holes plugged, and the bilge pump started, to keep the ship afloat. Passage to Montreal took seven hours, presumably through the Lachine Canal.

On 3 July, fully one month after the accident, the *Kingston* entered dry dock for the necessary repairs.[20] It was thought that it would take a month to put everything back to rights.[21] Meanwhile, the company purchased the *Banshee,* a ten-year-old wooden-hulled steamer, which had served some seasons in the Mail Line. She filled the *Kingston*'s place in the line until the *Kingston* was ready to sail again. She was then held in reserve against the possibility of other accidents.[22]

Other accidents there would be. Within a few weeks the *Kingston* struck again at Split Rock and had to have the Ladies' Cabin refitted once more.[23] The following season she had a fire in the "linen room," while at the wharf in Port Hope. It was quickly doused.[24] The 1867 season was one where particularly low water led to an unusual number of bumps and scrapes involving the Royal Mail Line vessels. In November the *Kingston* was deliberately run ashore below the Galops rapids after striking a rock. One of her linemates, the *Magnet,* had used the same shoreline for similar purposes already that season. The occasion prompted discussion of a proposition to put a six-inch "sheathing" of planking outside the company's iron hulls to protect them.[25] Some years later a survey of the hull revealed three inches of elm planking covering the single layer of iron plating on the ship's bottom.[26] Using three inches rather than six reduced the weight of this accretion to the hull and helped preserve the *Kingston*'s shallow draught. Four years later she spent time both on Split Rock and aground above the Galops rapids. On the latter occasion the *Spartan* was able to pull her off with no apparent damage.[27]

The River Palace

Apart from the visits to the dry dock necessary to recover from her mishaps in the rapids, the *Kingston* received general, regular repairs. It was June 1870 before the *Kingston* lost a trip because of a major mechanical breakdown — a broken connecting rod. She was laid up in Port Darlington until a replacement could be brought up from Montreal and fitted.²⁸

Nothing in the history of the Royal Mail Line had prepared either its crews or the public for the events of 11 June 1872. The *Kingston* left

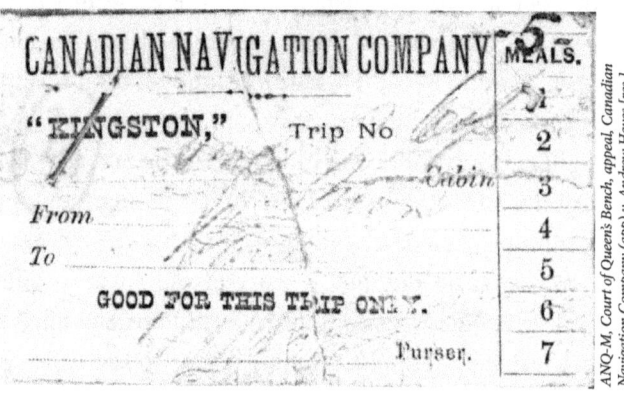

Ticket: This waterlogged ticket was saved from the 1872 burning by passenger Andrew Hayes who later entered it as evidence when he sued the Company for his losses in the fire.

Brockville on her way up through the Thousand Islands at 1:30 p.m. As they passed Grenadier Island, some eighteen miles (just short of thirty kilometres) above Brockville, the cry of "fire" echoed through the ship. Captain Charles Carmichael interrupted the conversation he was enjoying with two ladies at the stern and ran forward. Flames licked at the lattice work above the doors of staterooms 17 and 19, both of which opened onto the starboard side of the saloon on the promenade deck. Room 17 was occupied by a family, while 19 was generally used for holding dirty linen. It was rarely used for passengers because the smoke stack ran up through the room from the boilers below. Carmichael raced below and ordered the hose attached to a fire pump. While some of the crew began to fight the fire, the captain hastened to the upper deck where a bucket brigade was formed to pass some twenty-four pails kept on the hurricane deck for this purpose. Meanwhile the pilot had ordered the vessel stopped so that her motion wouldn't fan the flames. It was a mistake. Realizing how futile the firefighting efforts were proving, the captain quickly ordered the vessel run ashore on a nearby low, marshy patch of land.²⁹

The Kingston *and the Canadian Navigation Company*

Wreck of the Kingston: *Not long after the accident the curious began investigating the wreck of the* Kingston. *Here the steamer* Bruce *has brought out an excursion party. One of the members of that group was a fairly gifted photographer.*

Wreck of the Kingston, *port profile: Curiously, the flames that gutted the hull of the* Kingston *left the port paddlebox virtually untouched. Remembering that she was run ashore (and so her bow sits higher than her stern), this photograph gives a profile of her iron hull. The paddlewheels tower over the tiny figures on the remains of her afterdeck.*

The gutted interior of the Kingston: One of the most remarkable steamboat photographs of the period, this picture takes us inside the gutted hull of the Kingston looking aft. Framed by the two paddlewheels is the engine room. The two smoke stacks or chimneys (never funnels on this class of vessels) stand just inside the hull, the one barely held aloft by various wires. They rise out of the boilers that filled the entire depth of the hull. Reaching across the boilers are the two shafts, from the centre of the paddlewheels to two cranks. The iron "A" frame reaches up between the stacks supporting the walking beam. Other details evident from this photograph include one of the midship bulkheads, stretching across the hull immediately forward of the boilers. The lines of rivets are clearly visible, holding the sheets of iron together. To the left of the image the debris outside the hull is on the "guards," which stretched outside the line of the hull, supported on struts (or sponsons), until they appeared to enclose the paddlewheels. The lower deck was enclosed by the hull. The main deck rested on the edge of the hull and incorporated the guards; the men standing in the engine space would have been on the main deck. The promenade deck was just above the shafts of the paddlewheels, while the stacks have flanges at the hurricane deck level.

As the wheels lurched back into motion one of the three lifeboats was being lowered with its precious cargo of women and children. It swamped as soon as it touched the water. By now the fire was a roaring inferno. No time was left to launch the other two boats.

Instead, passengers and crew leapt into the river wearing life preservers or clutching pieces of debris they hoped would carry their weight. Most owed their lives to the fact that the water towards the bow was shallow and relatively warm in the late spring. With forty or fifty passengers and upwards of thirty crew, it is astounding that only two people drowned. One of the deck hands was missing. Remarkably, no one knew his name or anything about him. One newspaper account almost savoured the pathetic details: about twenty-three years old, five-feet, six-inches tall, clean shaven, with the figure of a girl with a skipping rope tattooed on his left arm and a star and a half-circle on his right. His surviving effects consisted of one American penny, a piece of tobacco, and a silver ring. Of course, like many others on board, his gear or luggage had been destroyed. By contrast, many recognized the body of Dr. Walter Jones' widow who had jumped from the stern wearing a poorly adjusted life preserver. According to the testimony of John Madden, the wheelsman, "it was too low on the body, and the large part was on the back in place of the breast; this kept the body on its face ..." Madden's attempts to resuscitate her failed. Shortly afterwards the propeller *Dominion* came upon the scene. By 8:00 that evening she had returned the exhausted passengers and crew to Brockville.[30]

While the passengers bemoaned the loss of their baggage and sought alternate ways to their various destinations, rumours began to fly.[31] How much had the fire cost? The loss was estimated at between $75,000 and $80,000, although the preliminary report of her insurance was $60,000. Of this, $32,000 had been held by the Citizens' Insurance Company of Montreal.[32] Did Canadian steamboat crews ever perform fire drills? Had there been a fire on board earlier on that same passage?[33] Had the regular hands struck for an increase of wages, been discharged, and a fresh, inexperienced crew put aboard?[34] The last speculation was fuelled by the mysterious anonymity of the drowned crew member.

Both in Ontario and Quebec, the courts would have an opportunity

Canadian Illustrated News, 29 June 1872

Burning of Kingston, *June 1872: Flames engulf the* Kingston *in the shallow waters off Grenadier Island. Only two people were killed: the widow of a Montreal doctor who put on her life preserver backwards, and one of the crew whose name no one would remember. In this image the gangplank is presented as significantly longer than it would usually have been in this class of steamboat.*

to review the events surrounding the fire. In February 1873, a Kingston judge concluded that the Canadian Navigation Company was not liable for damages to passengers' goods resulting from an accidental fire at sea.[35] That fall a Quebec court came to the opposite conclusion. It refused to accept that the fire had been "fortuitous," or that the fire had occurred "at sea" and awarded one of the passengers, Andrew Hayes, partial compensation for the loss of his personal luggage.[36]

Meanwhile, almost a month had passed before a party of wreckers was dispatched to raise the machinery and hull of the *Kingston*. In charge was Captain Howard, former captain of the vessel, and now the superintendent of the line.[37] He and his crew arranged to have the gutted hull towed down to Montreal.

5

The *Bavarian*

Plans were in place for the overhaul of the wreck even before the wrecking crews arrived at Grenadier Island. Specifications for building two new boilers for the *Kingston* were circulated to interested parties. They required the work to be completed, tested by the government inspector, and placed on board the hull at Cantin's shipyard by 1 December 1872. The connections with the engine and erection of the smoke stacks were to be finished by the beginning of March. On 3 July, W.C. White, a leading Montreal boiler maker, tendered $10,850 for the job. His securities were signed on 9 July, and two days later the salvagers were dispatched[1] (See Appendix B). *Kingston* might be missing for the balance of the 1872 season, but her owners wanted her back for 1873.

Some years ago historians argued whether the *Bavarian* should be considered something other than a rebuild of the *Kingston*.[2] As the boiler contract indicates, W.C. White was to provide new boilers for the old hull of the *Kingston* in Cantin's shipyard. A report in the Montreal *Evening Star* followed the launch the following spring:

> The remains of the steamer *Kingston,* which took fire and was stranded last Fall [*sic*], have, at Cantin's dock, been made the foundation of quite an elegant boat, which will be ready for travel in about three weeks. She will be known as the *Bavarian*.[3]

The River Palace

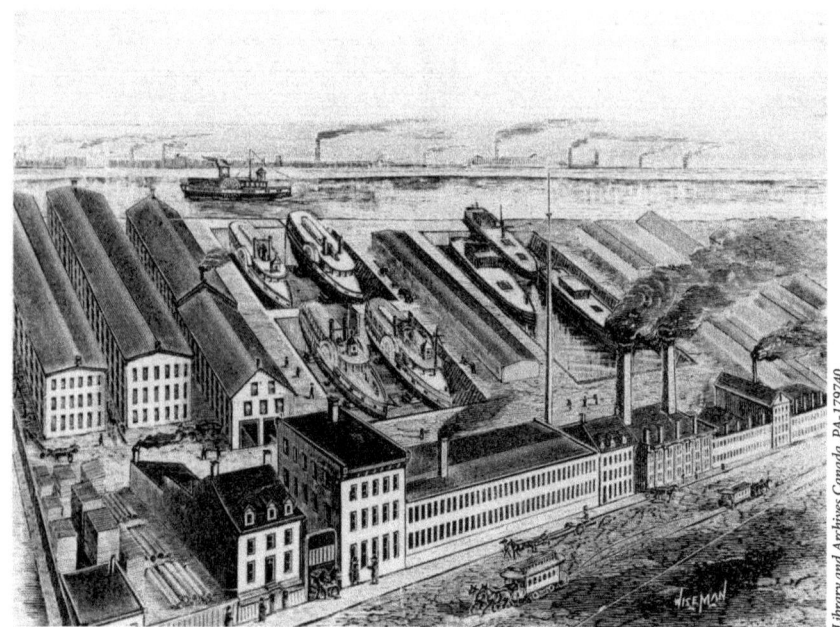

Augustin Cantin's Canada Marine Works: One of the leading shipyards in central Canada, Cantin's was located on the Lachine Canal in Montreal. In 1872–73 the hull of the Kingston *was rebuilt into the* Bavarian *at this site.*

The trials of the renovated and reconstructed hull proved a dismal failure. In the twelve miles (twenty kilometres) between Prescott and Brockville, on her first trip up the river, she had a half-hour lead on the old *Bay State* (then known as the *Abyssinian*). Despite this she was overtaken, and reached Brockville in the neighbourhood of two hours. If this rather jaundiced account is correct, the *Bavarian* scarcely achieved a mere six miles (ten kilometres) an hour.[4]

The Canadian Navigation Company made a significant departure from traditional Royal Mail Line scheduling. Instead of running through from Lake Ontario ports to Montreal, the *Bavarian* and the other new Canadian Navigation Company steamer, the *Bohemian,* began the summer on a route from Montreal to Prescott. There they connected with the American Express Line that served the south shore of Lake Ontario.[5]

By late summer the *Bavarian* was running further up the lake. As she rounded the pier entering Rochester's harbour, Charlotte, on 25

The Bavarian

August 1873, she swamped a boat carrying a party of four young people, drowning one young woman.[6] The superstitious might have taken it for an omen of troubles to follow.

The vessel was bound down the lake for Kingston on the night of 5 November 1873. Rather than the 100 to 120 passengers known to have been aboard during some of her summer passages, only six could be found rattling about the saloon this late in the season. The freight holds were full, packed with a thousand barrels of apples, nearly a hundred barrels of flour, nine bushels of potash, and twenty-two casks of high wines or spirits. When they had been brought aboard in Hamilton earlier that day, the wines had been stowed, rather injudiciously, just forward of the crank room. This put them between the smoke stacks passing through this deck from the boilers below.

The crew numbered thirty-four, including two men who were working their passage. Some of those gathered around the stove in the saloon might have been discussing the latest news out of Ottawa, where Sir John A. Macdonald's Conservative government tottered on the brink of defeat over the Pacific Scandal. The crew might have taken a special interest in the news, for the *Bavarian* was owned by the Canadian Navigation Company, whose president was Sir Hugh Allan. And Sir Hugh's suspiciously generous contributions to the Conservative cause in the election of 1872 were in the eye of the national political storm. Meanwhile, the *Bavarian* steamed into a storm of her own making.

About 8:00 p.m., she was three hours out of Toronto and standing twelve to fifteen miles (roughly twenty to twenty-five kilometres) out into the lake opposite Whitby. Ten minutes later, the quiet of the evening was shattered by a series of loud crashes. First mate John Henderson, standing in the wheelhouse, heard "a crash of breaking machinery. An explosion and fire followed instantly." James Finucan, the watchman, was standing in the deck saloon, heard "a report which he supposed was the steam chest blowing up." Finucan made it all the way up to the hurricane deck before he heard a second crash and noticed the fire. Sound asleep near the kitchen young Obadiah Dixon, the black cook, didn't wake up until the second explosion. Head waiter John Rivier

The Burning of the Bavarian*: The four following illustrations are details from the engraving presented by the* Canadian Illustrated News, *22 November 1873, and were conceived "from particulars furnished by a survivor."*

of Cornwall thought the floor was breaking in as he heard the crash. Chatting with the captain and the three women passengers, Napoleon Dufour, the pilot, thought he heard a very loud, long rumbling and was convinced they had struck a schooner.

By the time most had heard the second explosion, those in the main saloon could see the flames leaping up around the engine enclosure, which rose like a chimney from the hull to the hurricane deck. One of the passengers, Jonas J. Parmenter of Toronto, rushed into his nearby stateroom to grab a life preserver. The steam from the boiler was billowing out into the saloon. So thick was the smoke and steam that he had to feel his way out along the walls.

Meanwhile, most of the crew were actively engaged in abandoning ship. Unlike the fire in the Thousand Islands the previous summer, on this occasion they were twelve or more miles (about twenty kilometres) off Lake Ontario's north shore where there were no convenient islands. They were almost an hour off shore steaming at their best speed, an impossible hope with the engine room a flaming inferno. But even in a dead calm or light swell, there was little hope for anyone who sought safety in the bone-chilling November waters.

The Bavarian

The pilot had rushed out onto the starboard promenade deck expecting to see a schooner. There was none. He then raced up the ladder and confronted the flames leaping up around the engine. The *Bavarian* carried four boats on her hurricane deck. The wheelsman abandoned his post. With Dufour, he put the small dinghy overboard. Small help it proved to be. It caught fire and promptly sank.

Joined by the two mates, the pilot lowered one of the larger boats. Even before it struck the water one man had clambered in. Dufour found his way on board it. He was quickly followed by the ladies maid. Maddeningly, at least two minutes were lost trying to disentangle the tackle and get the boat clear. To the utter astonishment of those who thought they had escaped to relative safety, water began pouring in through the drain hole (a feature expressly intended to let water out because the boats were carried upright)! They frantically bailed while a makeshift plug was found. The water stopped rising inside the lifeboat but were they really saved? Those few in the boat immediately began pulling for the distant shore.

At the same time on the hurricane deck, the two mates persisted in launching another boat. It fell, end on, into the water. It too immediately began to fill to the thwarts. The mates and a few others scooped and bailed the frigid waters out of their craft.

Around them, others plunged into the near-freezing water clinging desperately to life-preservers. Still more clutched pieces of furniture they prayed would keep them afloat long enough for the boats to reach them. Few of their prayers were being answered that night.

Canadian Illustrated News, 22 Nov. 1873.

The three female passengers appear to have followed the captain from the stove in the main saloon outside onto the forward promenade deck. As the wheelsman brought the vessel around to run for the shore the breeze was in their faces, forcing the fire aft. Their quick exit, however, proved a fatal one — it took them past none of the life preservers. Captain Charles Carmichael, apparently the only member of the crew to pay them any heed, returned with only two preservers and promptly plunged into the icy water clutching both of them. There he seized a pail rack floating about in the debris to which the mess-room boy also clung. Pleading with the second mate, Charles Bradley, who was in the second lifeboat with Henderson, the captain called, "Charley! Charley! Save me!"

The Bavarian

Still desperately bailing out the lifeboat, Bradley replied, "Captain I am not able to save myself!"

As the mess-room boy lunged towards the life boat, the pail rack tipped up and the captain slid under the water. According to those in the last boat, he was never seen again alive.

No one in the boats ever admitted to paying any attention to the women at the bow of the burning ship. One member of the crew dismissed them as the "captain's passengers." Passenger safety was not acknowledged as any of their concern. Instead, the second lightly-crewed lifeboat pursued the other away from the burning steamer, ostensibly to persuade the first to turn about. Either boat, according to the evidence, could have carried twenty to thirty people. In the light swell that evening either was capable of carrying those it saved and all of those lost in the disaster.[7]

Meanwhile, a crowd was gathering on shore. On the pier at Port Darlington "the lurid flames from the burning vessel, which was considerably west of the port, lit up the scene." A tug was dispatched to the burning vessel, and several boats set out for the site.[8] The two lifeboats landed near Oshawa and the survivors were rapidly bundled into shelter. Damp and barely dressed, some were suffering severely from hours of exposure to the frigid November night air. They were the lucky ones.

Overall, fourteen people never made it ashore. Some, like the captain had plunged quickly into the near-freezing waters and struggled towards the safety of the lifeboats. Others, like Mrs. Sibbald, her daughter and Miss Ireland, waited until it was too late. The Chief Engineer, William Finucan, reached the gangway and could have gotten clear but was last seen running towards the engine room, possibly in an ill-fated attempt to stop the engine. His son James had urgently searched what he could reach of the vessel before making his escape in the mates' lifeboat.[9]

The immediate news of the tragedy was lost amid the fall of Sir John A. Macdonald's government. But his successors promptly ordered an inquiry into the loss of life on one of Sir Hugh Allan's steamboats. As the long columns of testimony began appearing two weeks later the cries of indignation began to rise. Perhaps none of the published commentary better captures the scathing contempt for the company and the crew than a letter from "Sir Herbert," a Montreal correspondent of the Kingston *Daily News:*

> This boat runs all the season, and carries between 100 and 120 passengers sometimes, and sometimes greater, it has in all [four] boats, that will only hold 49 people; it has a lot of French Canadian deck hands, that according to Mr. Girouard's (a French Solicitor of the company) translation become "half-cracked fools" in case of an emergency, it promotes pursers to be captains "as they are more gentlemanly" according to Mr. Milloy; although according to Mr. Macpherson (the purser on this *Bavarian*), "he did not know anything about boats, and was not likely to learn anything as he had nothing to do with the sailing of the vessel." This boat we say starts from Hamilton — takes a large cargo — takes six passengers on a calm night on Lake Ontario — the old walking beam of the old *Kingston* breaks, smashes in a lot of spirits, sets fire to the boat and the deck hands go for it, *sauve qui peut*, each man for himself, takes the largest boat and leaves a lot of people to perish in the flames and water.[10]

"Sir Herbert" raised the major issues stemming from the inquiry. At the height of the season the number of passengers carried frequently surpassed the capacity of the life-saving equipment. Although it was testified that some 200 life preservers were on board, many were stored in the staterooms. Few who survived reported wearing them. This might be true, contended the company's lawyers, but the Canadian Navigation Company had exceeded government regulations in the number of preservers and the size of lifeboats provided on the *Bavarian*.[11]

Utter contempt for the French Canadian members of the crew was displayed by the English-speaking officers. The purser testified that he had never heard the captain "make any complaint of the crew on the vessel, except that 'Those Frenchmen were not of much use.' I don't think they were of much use either."[12] On the other hand, F.X. Poirier, the wheelsmen, said that "he did not know the English language sufficiently to understand the order of the captain who could not speak French."[13] Small wonder that most of the French Canadians in the crew responded by following the only one of their number with any authority, the river pilot. The pilot, however, felt himself to be utterly without responsibility in any matter outside the navigation of the vessel on the St. Lawrence River. In the meantime, excoriating the French Canadians for abandoning the scene in the first life boat, served to disguise the fact that the "English" boat, commanded by two of the ship's senior officers, had hastily pulled off with little or no care for those left struggling in the water.

The testimony of wheelsman Poirier graphically revealed the sham that was the reputation of a Royal Mail Line captain. So irrelevant was he to the navigation of the vessel that he need not communicate with a number of the hands, including those at the wheel. That would have to be done through the mates, whose years of service vastly outnumbered Captain Carmichael's. When pressed on the issue, the secretary of the company, Alexander Milloy, admitted that "Captains were chosen from the pursers who had shown themselves to be active and capable men.... Formerly it was thought necessary that captains on the lakes should be sailors, but lake was now quite different to ocean navigation, and since [Milloy] had been connected with the Company the captains have been selected from the pursers."[14] On salt water this would have been illegal. British shipping regulations required the commander of every vessel of British registry to possess a master's ticket, proof of some level of competency. Not so on the Lakes.[15]

Although it is merely speculation, there may even be a darker side to Charles Carmichael's death. Neither of the mates would directly admit it, but the captain had practically reached the second life boat before they pulled away from him towards the distant shoreline. Carmichael's body drifted up on the American shore of the lake several weeks later.[16] In the subsequent inquiry, the first mate, a man of some twenty-five years' experience in steamboats, found it convenient to shift responsibility onto the captain for permitting the stowage of the wines so close to the engine.[17]

The only independent evidence indicated that the second mate, a man of some nineteen seasons on the Lakes, had been in charge of stowing the cargo there.[18] There is no evidence that the captain had earned sufficient respect from any of his officers to make them want to save him.

The commissioner for the inquiry, Samuel Risley, made some serious recommendations to the Minister of Marine and Fisheries: amend the law so that passenger-carrying steamers "be provided with as many boats as they can find place for, and of the largest capacity the crew can handle," with a minimum number to be decided by the Board of Steamboat Inspection; hang the boats on the davits ready for lowering; assign responsibility for lowering the boats to specific members of the crew, and then drill them in the task. These issues would be addressed for the first time by Parliament in an amendment to the Steamboat Inspection Act passed the following spring. Regular life boat drills, life boats hung on separate davits, the posting of instructions in the use of life preservers, and where to find them, are shipboard routines that in Canada are directly attributable to the fourteen lives lost on the *Bavarian*.[19]

The act also demanded that "inflammable matter … shall invariably be stowed as far as possible from the boiler." This was a response to the conclusion of the board of inquiry that the walking beam had broken. As Risley described the scene: "that portion of the beam attached to the [connecting] rod made its way through the roof and deck of the saloon down to the main deck, where the casks of spirits … were stowed — breaking through them, and their contents, running down upon the fronts and into the furnaces of the boilers, at once ignited."[20]

Finally, Risley pleaded the "urgent necessity for a Marine Law for the examination and granting of certificates to properly qualified officers, and for regulating the discipline and management of Steamers."[21] Unlike the prompt action on his other recommendations it would be 1883 before the Masters and Mates Act would be amended to lift the exemption for the Great Lakes and other inland waters. As the contradictory decisions in the Ontario and Quebec courts came down over liability from losses by fire in the *Kingston* disaster, Parliament passed an act confirming the exemption from liability for losses occurring by fire on the Lakes.[22]

6

The *Algerian*

The fires still smouldered the next day when the iron hull of the *Bavarian* was towed into Whitby harbour.[1] A couple of weeks later the blackened wreck docked in Kingston where some small boys were caught stealing roasted apples, remnants of the thousand barrels stowed in the forward freight hold.

In an era dominated by rail travel, and in an economic climate that was worsening, the directors of the Canadian Navigation Company might have been expected to retrench, save money and sell the burnt out hull to whomever would have it. Like their retired general manager, John Hamilton, in 1853, there is no evidence that they gave this strategy a passing thought. They would rebuild. Initially it was announced the wreck would be towed down to Montreal, but on second thought it was decided to do the reconstruction at Power's shipyard in Kingston.[2]

William Power was a relative newcomer to the Kingston waterfront. However, his Kingston shipyard, the Kingston Marine Railway, was by this time almost two generations old. Built for a syndicate of Kingston investors in 1837, the Marine Railway had had a chequered financial career. When the courts put it up for sale in 1862 the property included not only the Marine Railway, but a steam saw mill, workshops, offices, sixteen stone cottages for the men, the Ontario Foundry, Fenwick's Hotel, five stone warehouses, and extensive wharfage.[3] By 1870 it was in

The River Palace

Algerian: *Upbound in the Thousand Islands on a fine day in the 1880s or 1890s.*

H. Brosius, Bird's Eye View of Kingston *[map], 1875: This detail from the Bird's Eye View of 1875 features a sketch of the* Algerian *steaming up the lake in front of William Power's Kingston Marine Railway (number 25 behind wharf number 47). The burned out hull of the* Bavarian *was transformed into the* Algerian *at this site over the winter of 1873–74.*

the hands of Power, a marine architect. Power had been born on Prince Edward Island, and raised at Quebec City. There and in New York he had learned his trade. For a time he had even superintended the shipyard operations of the St. Lawrence Engine Works, although not during the period when the *Kingston* had been assembled. At the same time as his men were sifting through the debris in the scorched hull of the *Bavarian*, Power was launching a campaign for public funding for a dry dock to complement his shipyard.[4] Another fifteen years would pass before the Dominion government would build the works that have since become the home of the Marine Museum of the Great Lakes at Kingston.

Although the decision was quickly taken to let Power rebuild the gutted iron hull, another set of specifications was circulated to Canadian engine and boiler makers. Tenders were due at the Canadian Navigation Company's offices on 17 December, less than six weeks after the disaster. The specifications called "for the taking out and reconstruction of the Engine of the Steamer *Bavarian* now lying on the ways in Power's shipyard in the Port of Kingston, Ont." The contractor could take no more than twelve working days to remove "the present engine shafts and cranks, part of Walking Beam, the connecting Rod and Engine Frame and bolts." Why the rush? They needed to shift the boilers to repair the hull! Apparently, despite the public outcry over recycling the walking beam and other engine parts after the Kingston fire, the company had no intention of ordering a new set of boilers. Instead contractors could recondition the boilers whose furnaces had touched off the inferno that had gutted the vessel. The word "reconstruction" suggests that the company cared not that parts of the engine might find their way into the "new" engine. Indeed, later evidence suggests that the shafts that turned the paddlewheels remained in place until they snapped two years later. The engine frame, bedplate, condenser, shafts, and cranks were to be in place by 1 March 1874. The beam, cylinders, steam chests, and pipes would follow in a further three weeks. All was to be ready for testing by 20 April.[5]

The company awarded the contract to E.E. Gilbert, of Montreal's Beaver Foundry, for $14,850. (See Appendix B) About mid-century, Gilbert, along with W.P. Bartley, had founded the St. Lawrence Engine Works. He had left, having been replaced by Dunbar by the time the

Kingston was built. Several financial embarrassments could not diminish his success as an engineer.[6] In 1873, Gilbert patented his own improvements in valve arrangements in both Canada and the United States — improvements probably implemented in the work on the new engine for the fire-blackened iron hull.[7]

The work was seriously behind schedule. Consequently, the launch was planned for seven o'clock on the evening of 16 April 1874 "so as not to interfere with the workmen engaged on her." Three hours later they gave up on the effort for reasons no one cared to explain publicly. The job was finished the next morning. It was the ship's third launch in her nineteen-year career: first as *Kingston*, a year before as *Bavarian*, and now as *Algerian*. It would not be her last name change, nor would it be the last time she endured a major rebuild.

The newly-named *Algerian* was towed around to a finishing berth where the press noted she only presented "a part of her upper works." A large gang of carpenters and a small army of McMahon's painters failed to get her ready for an announced excursion on Dominion Day, 1 July. The

Tourist Rates/Time-table: The 1897 rates and time-table as they appeared in From Niagara to the Sea.

The Algerian

trials finally came off five days later and the *Algerian* set off for Montreal where she would be re-registered. She was accompanied by descriptions of her as "superior to the finest floating palaces of the line."[8]

A few years later some accountants added up the "costs" of the *Algerian*. They set the cost of the hull at $15,185.53, the engine and boilers at $26,691.45, the carpenters' and joiners' work at $23,564.01, and the furniture at $10,379.89. The grand total was $75,820.88. It is unclear how they arrived at these numbers, considering the hull had been built in 1854, the boilers in 1872–73, and the rest of the work in 1874. Nevertheless, they concluded that the new vessel "cost" almost as much as she had in 1855.

She measured 914 gross tons under the new Canadian tonnage regulations. After deductions for engine space, the *Algerian* was registered at 576 tons. But what did that really mean? Tonnage is perhaps the most frequently misunderstood measurement in marine history. These numbers have nothing to do with weight or displacement of sea water, but some arcane, frequently revised formulas for measuring most of the volume of an irregularly shaped and very large object. Most people link its name to a medieval container for shipping wine, the tun. How many of these you could get aboard a sailing vessel in one cargo really

Picturesque Canada, 449, Walter Lewis.

Burlington Bay and the approach to Hamilton: The western end of the Royal Mail Line's route until the early 1880s was Hamilton.

did matter. While the tonnage calculations allow very loose comparisons of size in this era, the principal application of the figure was to assist in assessing various classes of taxes and fees. Because of her tonnage, in 1884 *Algerian* was paying $173 in American customs fees and nearly $58 each time she landed in Montreal.[9]

In response to the outcry surrounding her late "purser" captain, the company placed one of the most experienced navigators available to them, John Trowell, in command of the *Algerian*. Born in 1813 in Milford, in south Wales, Trowell had gone to sea at the age of fourteen. He had sailed the coast of England, as well as to the Mediterranean, Ireland, France, Germany, and Spain before crossing to Quebec on the brig *Columbus* about 1833. Jumping ship, Trowell made his way to the Lakes where he sailed in a variety of schooners, earning his first command about 1838. His first steam vessel was the legendary propeller *Vandalia*, which was wrecked on Lake Erie in 1851 while under his command. For a few seasons, he alternated between schooners, propellers, and the sail-making profession. Starting in 1855, he served seven years on his first paddle-wheeler, the *Passport,* probably as first mate. After a few years in other commands, he returned to the Royal Mail Line for nine years as first mate of the *Magnet*. In 1874, the company assigned a "real" sailor, whose forty-seven years at sea and on the Lakes were expected to reassure passengers of the competence of the man in charge.[10]

So how safety-conscious were the owners of the twice-burned *Algerian?* In the summer of 1881 the steamboat inspector in Kingston detained Trowell and the *Algerian* for carrying undersized lifeboats. The telegraph wires between Kingston, Montreal, and Ottawa hummed. The Minister of Marine and Fisheries overruled his officials and sent the *Algerian* on her way, with the demand that she quickly conform to the requirements.[11]

The career of the *Algerian* offered several real tests of Captain Trowell's mettle and the ship's safety equipment. In August 1875, she again struck on Split Rock. Some newspaper editors were astounded to learn the pilot was the same Napoleon Dufour whose actions in the *Bavarian* disaster they had so thoroughly excoriated two years before. The passengers had just concluded dinner and the forward decks were crowded with people

The Algerian

F.M. Bell-Smith, *Yonge St. Steamboat Wharf, Toronto: Crowds of summer travellers bustle aboard the* Algerian *at the R & O's Yonge Street wharf about 1882. Deckhands carry the "steamer" trunks aboard.*

waiting for the run through one of the most notorious parts of the St. Lawrence rapids. A strong south wind caught the vessel as she entered the narrow passage, swinging the stern against the rock. As the *Daily British Whig* reported the scene:

> All at once the vessel bounded heavily and rebounded again and again. The timbers strained as though they were going to part; the saloon lamps were thrown from their places and crashed heavily against the walls and ceiling, and the passengers hitched from their seats and mixed in the greatest confusion. There was great excitement for a few moments. A rush was made for life preservers, [a] woman fainted, children cried bitterly and as may naturally be expected a great many men turned very pale. It was probably fifteen minutes before the Captain could get a boat lowered. A crew were despatched with the purser to obtain assistance and returned after a long

time followed by several habitants in their scows. The other life-boats were lowered and manned with a crew of six men in each. The Captain acknowledged that the remaining boats were unseaworthy.[12]

Women and children were quickly ferried ashore. Then, as night fell, Captain Trowell refused to allow any more boats to leave the stricken steamer, pointing out "the risk incurred in rowing against a very swift current, dark at night, with a succession of boulders and seething waters a few hundred yards below...." The pumps were keeping up with the water seeping into the hull so the remaining passengers should have been safer on board. But the fuel ran out. At 2:00 a.m. the pumps stopped. Water rose to the bottom of the furnace ... but no further. Before this occurred, one passenger, insisting he would not leave the women in his party ashore unprotected, hired local folk to ferry the men ashore. The offer was extended to as many others as wished to go. Between forty and sixty took the chance.[13] This group groused about the discipline of the crew but several others described Trowell as a "jolly old cricket" who had acted precisely as an old "sea dog" should. Despite all the fuss the accident proved only a minor one. Quickly rescued, the *Algerian* was repaired for about $1,000 and was back in her station on the line in a week and a half.[14]

A few lessons could have been learned from this experience. It took much too long to lower the boats. If the crew were drilled in this at all, it was not done well. Although there may have been some extenuating circumstances, the boats they carried did not perform well, and there were still not enough of them.

Appendix C contains a summary of the various misfortunes of the iron-plated and riveted hull shipped across the Atlantic in the 1850s. But not every incident ended in a collision with rock, boat, or wharf. In the fall of 1880 the *Algerian* sought shelter from a gale in South Bay (off Prince Edward County) and spent nearly a day at anchor. The trip was remarkable, not for the storm, but because the passengers had the opportunity to watch a waterspout sweeping down the lake.[15]

Nor should this vessel's record of misfortune be considered out of the ordinary. Of her line mates, the *Spartan* came dangerously near being

The Algerian

Algerian at Bowmanville: Canoes paddle out to greet the Algerian as she stops at Port Darlington, the harbour for Bowmanville.

Midnight at the Harbour, Port Hope: Somewhere around Port Hope on the trip down the lake it started to get dark. It was unlikely that one of the R & O steamers would have still been in Port Hope at midnight. But not as unlikely as this coloured postcard with the moon carefully added in the northern sky!

The River Palace

a total loss while chartered to the Owen Sound Transportation Company in 1883. And the *Corinthian* was destroyed by fire in September 1892 just after passing the Cedar Rapids.[16] These and the rest of the line experienced the same litany of bumps and scrapes in the rapids, canals, and ports of the upper St. Lawrence and Lake Ontario as had the *Algerian*.

During the first few months after the launch of the *Algerian*, Sir Hugh Allan, president of the Canadian Navigation Company, had orchestrated a series of manoeuvres designed to persuade the ever-profitable Richelieu Company to merge with his firm. They concluded terms that winter and the Richelieu and Ontario Navigation Company was formed. Before long, Allan was at the head of the enlarged concern, often known simply as the R & O.[17]

For the next quarter century, the *Algerian* would be one of the vessels featured in the R & O's promotional literature, especially the pamphlet featuring the company slogan, "Niagara to the Sea." Arrangements were made with the Milloys of Toronto to forward the R & O passengers who wished to cross to Queenston and Niagara Falls on vessels like the second *City of Toronto*. Before 1881 the Royal Mail Line ran from Hamilton, departing at 9:00 a.m. every morning.[18] From then until the end of the

Swift's Coal Wharf at Kingston: Early on the second day of the downward passage, the Algerian would be found in Kingston. When the R & O's western fleet converted to coal in the 1880s, Swift's Wharf become one of the major coaling stations.

century the R & O boats would turn in Toronto, making connections with the Hamilton steamboats, including the *Macassa* and *Modjeska*.

In Toronto, the *Algerian, Corsican, Bohemian, Corinthian*, and *Passport* were a familiar sight in fair weather, setting off through the eastern gap on their way down the lake. Stops might be made at Port Darlington for Bowmanville, Cobourg, Port Hope, and Kingston. In August 1890, the *Algerian* became the first of the line to take advantage of the newly constructed Murray Canal at the head of the Bay of Quinte. This added stops at Belleville and Picton to the cruise up the lake to Toronto.[19] Except in rough weather, downbound, the steamers kept to the open waters of the lake on the overnight part of the passage.

Passengers joining a vessel in Kingston had to be early risers for departure had to be around 5:00 a.m. to reach Montreal in daylight. Quick stops were made at the major Canadian towns along the river: Brockville, Prescott, and Cornwall. However, the first major attractions were the Thousand Islands stretching for miles down the St. Lawrence

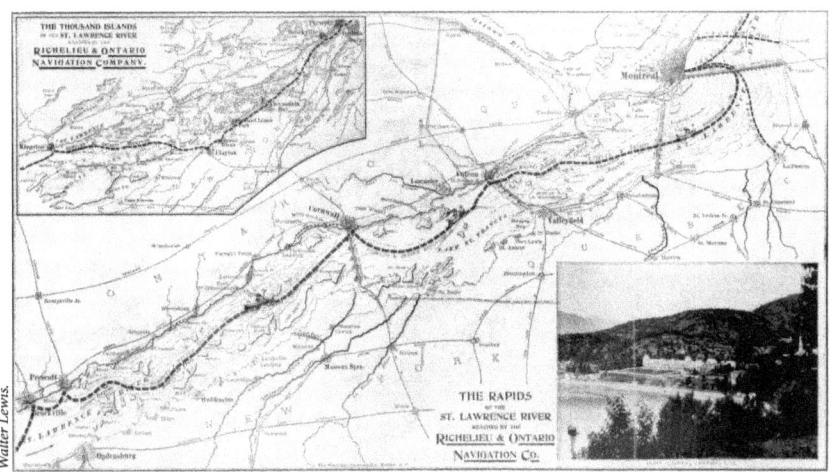

The Thousand Islands and the Rapids of the St. Lawrence River: This map shows the increasing importance of the resort communities of the Thousand Islands to the business of the R & O steamers. The company scarcely bothered to note that its vessels had to use most of the St. Lawrence canals on the upward voyage. Tucked into the corner of the map is a photograph of the Hotel Tadoussac, the ultimate destination of many of the voyagers seeking to escape the heat of an Ontario summer.

The River Palace

The Algerian

Algerian *in the Long Sault Rapids:* The Algerian *is well into the rapids as she approaches the position of the photographer, her smoke trail drifting off to the south.*

As quickly as the photographer can set up for another photograph, the onrushing steamer has doubled in size.

The steamer may be making 20–25 mph as she plunges down the river. The passengers are all gathered forward to help the pilot with his task. Those at the stern on the hurricane deck are not thrill-seekers; they are standing by on the auxiliary tiller, which could be handled manually should something go amiss with the main steering mechanism.

Rapidly, the Algerian disappears down the river bound for her next stop at Cornwall.

Although rarely seen as a set, these Notman images number among the most frequently reproduced images of the Algerian, being printed by more than one competing firm, well after she no longer looked as she did here, even after she had been renamed, again.

River. As the summer population of the islands grew, the R & O steamers began adding even more stops at Clayton, Round Island, Thousand Islands Park, and Alexandria Bay.[20]

Below Prescott, the rapids of the St. Lawrence began. The *Algerian* and her linemates ran all the rapids, including the 10 miles (16 kilometres) of the Long Sault and the steep drop of the Lachine. The sensation of running rapids in a vessel as large as the *Algerian* was fully exploited by those marketing the Richelieu and Ontario Navigation Company. Nowhere else in the world would first class excursion steamers run the risks associated with the Royal Mail Line steamers. Few travel accounts of the period were complete without a passage through either the Thousand Islands or the rapids. One, from the travels of "Captain Mac," a Confederate veteran, will have to stand for the rest:

> We reached Prescott in time to take the steamer *Algerian* for Montreal and soon are running through the Galop Rapid, thence through Long Sault, a continuous rapid of nine miles [about fifteen kilometres] in length. The sensation experienced in descending the rapids is a very pleasing one: steam is shut down and the vessel glides silently along at the rate of 14 or 15 miles [22 to 24 kilometres] an hour by the force of the current alone. Great accuracy has to be observed in steering the craft, and in order to accomplish this object the steering gear is of the best, and the steering wheels are double, and in descending the rapids a tiller is placed astern so that it can be manned as well as the double wheels, and when the little steamer strains, labors and pitches into the boiling cauldron at Lachine the feeling is a peculiar one, being akin to the notion that the boat is settling down; but under the guidance of old Baptiste, the Indian pilot, we were soon through and came in sight of the bronzed dome of the Bonsecours Market and the great Victoria tubular bridge, that connects the island of Montreal with the mainland.... Then under

The Algerian

the bridge, and in a few moments we were moored alongside the wharf and landed.[21]

It is unlikely that steam was routinely shut down. To maintain any steerage way the steamer would have had to be going faster than the current. Note the photographs of *Algerian* in the rapids. The air is thick with thick black smoke.

Algerian *at Thousand Islands House in Alexandria Bay, NY: One of the most popular of the resort communities on the upper St. Lawrence was Alexandria Bay, and one of the most popular hotels in Alexandria Bay was the Thousand Islands House, immediately behind the* Algerian *in this photograph.*

Although the hull that plunged down the rapids all those years remained the same, the *Algerian* went through many changes in her career. During the winter of 1871–72, a wooden sheathing had been attached to her hull. On the steamers of the Richelieu and Ontario Navigation Company, this sheathing was supposed to reduce the risk of rocks puncturing the hull in the rapids.[22]

When rebuilt in 1874, the *Algerian* had been equipped with a new engine, though the boilers were still the ones built by White for the *Bavarian* the previous year. They consumed cordwood in vast quantities. Almost as soon as the Richelieu and Ontario Navigation Company was formed in 1875 the former Richelieu Company directors began questioning the use of wood. Engine builder George Brush, of Montreal's Eagle Foundry, hired to examine the western fleet four years later, "found them all in a less or more bad condition and for many reasons unfit for the use of Coal." The furnaces were too large; the iron too light and insufficiently stayed or braced; and the water spaces too small. Except the *Passport*, the furnaces had all been patched.[23] After considering the costs, the board decided to do nothing. Three more years would pass as the cost of wood continued to escalate. The entire fleet was finally converted to burning coal over the winter of 1882–83.[24] The smoke pouring from the stacks grew thicker and blacker.

Repair work was almost constant as the fleet aged. *Algerian* received general engine repairs in the winter of 1890–91 and yet another major boiler overhaul the following winter.[25]

For years the managers of the Royal Mail Line (and most other Great Lakes vessel owners) had resisted the movement towards improved paddlewheels. Straight-bladed or "radial" wheels were notoriously inefficient but they were also cheap to build and easy to repair. The alternative was a feathering paddlewheel in which a fairly ingenious set of gearing kept the blade vertical as it entered the water. Although feathering paddlewheels had been around in some form since the 1840s, they would not become a common sight on the Great Lakes until the 1880s.[26] In 1894, the general manager recommended feathering paddlewheels to improve the speed of the *Algerian*. Six years later his directors agreed.[27] The first season the *Algerian* sported her new, lower profile, and more compact wheels was 1901. It was also her last regular season on the Toronto-Montreal route.

Electricity came on board as late as 1895 when all the western steamers were equipped with electric chandeliers.[28]

Niagara to the Sea, 1901.

The Algerian

Algerian *in Lachine Rapids: One of the most dangerous of the St. Lawrence Rapids was the Lachine, a fact ignored by the crewman with his feet hanging out of the forward hatch. Well above him, in front of the pilot house, the captain leans on the railing. Unlike the images of the Long Sault Rapids, here there isn't much smoke coming from the boilers.*

Algerian *at Swift's Wharf, Kingston, 1902: In 1902* Algerian *came out sporting a rather sleeker profile. Her new 19-foot feathering wheels did not even clear the hurricane deck. Such views are rather rare for it was in 1902 that she dropped back to the status of spare boat. Three years later her name had been changed again.*

The River Palace

The R & O was never particularly happy with the number of staterooms available on its western steamers. Their overall hull size was constrained by the locks of the St. Lawrence canals, which had seemed generous when construction had begun on the Cornwall Canal in the mid-1830s. In that era most first class or cabin passengers slept on berths attached to the walls of the ladies' or gentlemen's cabins. Now, everybody wanted the privacy of their own stateroom.[29] Some, like the newlyweds and others using the *Kingston*'s bridal room, or the Prince of Wales's entourage, may even have insisted on beds rather than berths in those cabins.

Government passenger licencing, when finally established, proved extremely permissive. In 1882 *Algerian* was allowed to take 642 passengers aboard! Her linemates were permitted between 610 and 676. Over the course of the eighties and nineties this number was lowered to 400. Near the end of her passenger career in 1904, it was further reduced to 325.[30] Even so it would take the *Titanic* disaster almost a decade later before this lesson was properly learned and, in the meantime, the lifeboats remained hopelessly inadequate for these numbers of passengers. Instead, it was assumed that in the season in which large numbers of passengers were aboard, the water was warmer and life preservers would suffice. Anything like her licenced capacity would only have been carried on day excursions where the vessel would not be far out from shore. Other accidents would prove the folly of these assumptions, but they did not involve the R & O fleet.

Many of the crew of the company's steamers would not have looked or felt out of place in a major hotel of the era. The *Algerian*'s crew included one steward, one porter, eight waiters, three cooks, and a ladies' maid. They represented fourteen of the crew of forty. Usually the steward was held accountable for the profits from the bars.[31] The head cook, however, was by far the best paid of this group, earning $50 a month in 1884. This was just five dollars less than the first mate and ten dollars less than the chief engineer. By contrast, the second cook made one dollar a month more than a common deck hand and the balance of the meal's department were the poorest paid staff on board. Perhaps none of the "hospitality" crew were more familiar to the travelling public than "old Ben Parker,"

The Algerian

Algerian *in the Lachine Canal: Perhaps the most unglamorous part of the* Algerian's *weekly routine was the passage up the canals of the St. Lawrence, particularly the heavily industrialized section of Montreal through which the Lachine Canal passed. Indeed, the vessels of the line often slipped up the canal during the night. This view probably dates from the 1890s given that* Algerian *still has her original paddlewheels, but telephone and electrical poles line the canal.*

the elderly porter of the *Algerian*, nicknamed "Bismarck" for his general resemblance to the German chancellor. A veteran of thirty-three years on steamboats and fifteen with the Royal Mail Line, Ben was renowned for his story telling.[32]

A second group included those in charge of the engines. The chief engineer was usually the best paid member of the crew after the captain and purser. In 1884 he would earn $60 a month. Under his command were a second engineer and seven firemen. The engineers had to hold certificates of competency from the Board of Steamboat Inspection. To qualify required literacy, a basic grasp of arithmetic and several years of practical experience on a steam vessel or in a shop that made or repaired steam engines. In addition, they had to convince the board's examiners that they understood the workings of various types of steam engines and boilers and could respond to a variety of emergencies. For up to $25 a month the firemen mostly heaved wood or shovelled coal into the boiler furnaces.

The River Palace

Crew list, 1884: The staffing complement for the Algerian in 1884 from an internal company publication.

STEAMER "ALGERIAN."

J. Troweil	Captain		$900
G. W. Comer	Purser		500
J. Lefebre	First Mate	$55	
D. F. Mills	Second Mate	28	
Elezear Arcand	Engineer	60	
F. Beford	Second Engineer	35	
D. Prevost	Steward	40	
One	Porter	22	
One	Watchman	16	
Four	Wheelmen	25	
Six	Deck Hands	19	
Seven	Firemen	25	
One	Second Waiter	14	
Seven	Waiters	12	
One	Head Waiter	16	
One	Cook	50	
One	Second Cook	20	
One	Third Cook	10	
One	Message Boy	10	
One	Ladies' Maid	10	

Queen's University Archives, Canada Steamship Lines Coll., Vol. 183.

General navigation of the ship was in the hands of the two mates. The first mate, especially before the passing of the Masters and Mates of Inland Vessels Act in 1883, was usually the most experienced seaman aboard. John Henderson of the *Bavarian* had had twenty-six years on steamers. After 1883, the rank of first mate became the stepping-stone to command. Of *Algerian*'s captains after 1883, George Batten, John McGrath, and Daniel F. Mills all rose from the rank of first mate. In 1884 the *Algerian* also carried a second mate, a watchman, four wheelsmen, six deck hands, and a message boy. Like the engineer's crew, this group almost never dealt with the passengers. Instead they stowed freight and baggage and navigated the vessel. Although not assigned to any particular vessel five pilots were also employed for the Mail Line steamers, one for each vessel normally running. A very special employee was the pilot, Baptiste, who came aboard specifically for the run down the Lachine rapids.[33]

One of the striking things about the wages is how few of the crew earned a dollar a day. The position of the company was undoubtedly that they were supplying room and board, however crowded the "rooms" might be. We have not quite arrived in the era when college students filled out the ranks of the waiters and maids, but the service was very seasonal and the Royal Mail Line service had gradually shrunk into operations from early June to the end of September.

Salaried senior management consisted of the purser and the captain. The purser's duties were generally focussed on the business ledgers of the vessel, being directly accountable to the head office on St. Paul Street in Montreal. In 1877 he earned $500 a year. The purser was responsible for collecting tickets and payment of passage, as well as accounting for the freight and fuel brought on board. Apart from the vessel's ledgers, the purser's cabin was also the location of the ship's safe, containing not only the steamer's cash but also any valuables the passengers wanted to keep secure. The operation was not unlike that of a hotel safe. Apart from these qualities a good purser was one who could establish a comfortable relationship with the travelling public.

The captain's duties, as senior manager, were less specific, although one general manager recommended:

> that the Captains on the Western Steamers have charge of the office business on their respective Steamers, the Pursers being directly under their instructions, and that the Captain be not expected to take charge of the sailing or to stand watch on deck on these steamers, but have power to do so where they have Masters papers and in the event of their assuming charge they immediately take responsibility for the safety of the vessel.[34]

This remarkable statement implies, first, that not all R & O vessels were under the command of captains with their master's papers. This was still possible in cases like Andrew Dunlop who had commanded a vessel for years before the passage of the Masters and Mates of Inland Vessels Act and thus qualified under its "grandfather" clause. What it also suggests is that head office preferred that the captain be a businessman rather than a sailor, and that only if they "assumed charge" would they be held responsible for errors of navigation. Occasionally the captain would have hired the crew, but often the other officers were appointed by head office in Montreal and the Mechanical Department at the Sorel yards. In turn, these officers often hired their own teams within the company's general wage guidelines.[35] Nevertheless the captain reported to the general manager and more than once was held accountable before

The River Palace

Cornwall Canal: The passage back upriver through the canals attracted fewer passengers. By the turn of the century, the St. Lawrence canals were being seriously rebuilt on a grander scale. In the new locks two of the older paddlewheelers could fit. Richelieu and Ontario Navigation Company officials began planning for larger vessels to replace those built between 1847 and 1874.

the board for the performance of his vessel. In 1884 Captain Trowell was paid $900 for this service.

At various times the Canadian Navigation Company and the Richelieu and Ontario Navigation Company leased certain facilities on board to outside contractors. For example, experiments were made in the eating arrangements aboard ship. Traditionally, the meals had been served on tables set up the length of the main deck saloon. After the 1882 season, the R & O decided to convert the Ladies' Cabin into a dining room and then offer the meals on the "Restaurant System." To do the renovations they retained James Shearer who twenty-seven years before had done all the carpentry and joinery on the *Kingston*.[36] Victor Olivon of Montreal was then contracted to operate the bars and restaurant on all five Mail Line vessels. The company was to retain 25 percent of the gross earnings and prices were fixed for feeding all the crew except the captain and purser. Neither crew nor passengers were happy with the experiment and Olivon was quickly in financial trouble. The following season, the company resolved once again to manage the "Meals Department," and advertised the hours and prices of meals "so ... as to resume the popularity of the Steamers ..." Breakfast and supper would be fifty cents, while dinner was seventy-five cents. Considering the crew's wages these were still substantial sums.[37]

Although sub-contracting food services was less than a success, leasing the bar was an option often used on Canadian steamers. Beginning in 1869, Martin Finn of Montreal had leased the bars on the eleven vessels of the Canadian Navigation Company fleet for $7,300 a season.[38] The contractor had to provide the spirits and wines. His employees were subject to the authority of the captain, were required "to assist at table at Meals on board of said Vessels," and were entitled to berths and meals (one per steamer).[39] By the mid-1880s the Canadian Railway News Company held a contract for selling books and fancy articles on board.[40]

Of the labour movement on the Great Lakes only small echoes can be found in the records of the Richelieu and Ontario Navigation Company. Three of the crew of *Algerian* were hauled up before the Montreal Police Magistrate and sentenced to two weeks imprisonment in 1877. Apparently they had refused to eat bread or rolls they claimed were mouldy. Captain Trowell had said that they should either eat the bread offered them or go ashore, after which they were charged with refusing duty. The superintendent of the line, Captain Howard, claimed it was the same bread being served the passengers and of the finest quality.[41]

The principal disturbance came early in the 1881 season when the hands struck on the Mail Line. The board promptly sanctioned "the action of the Manager in increasing the wages to keep the line in regular running order."[42] Those increases were up to $2.00 a month and followed the 1880 season when wages had been reduced between 5 percent and 20 percent.[43]

Trouble of a different sort was brewing with the engineers when the new restaurant system was tried in 1883. The engineers were among the senior officers of the vessel. The new scheme no longer permitted them to eat in the saloon with the other officers. Instead it relegated them to the mess room with the crew. A letter from the five chief engineers of the Mail Line steamers was dispatched to the board of directors protesting the new rule. The board "after deliberating and considering that Mr. D. McLean was the promoter of this opposition to the new scheme,... resolved to dismiss him at once from his employ, and to continue the others if they agree to have their meals in the Mess Room."[44] In the expanding Canadian steam fleet in the 1880s, an experienced engineer like McLean would not have had much trouble securing a new berth. This reflex on the part of the board may well have backfired as not many years later, acknowledging the difficulty of keeping good engineers, the company found itself increasing the salaries of the chief engineers by 25 percent to $75 a month.[45]

When an ailing Sir Hugh Allan left the board of the Richelieu and Ontario Navigation Company in 1882, the first plan of his successors had been to dispose of the Mail Line altogether, or, in effect, to undo the merger. Opposition was being offered by the *Rothesay*, which had just been driven off the Toronto-Niagara route. Her owners expressed serious interest in acquiring the Richelieu and Ontario's Main Line West (the Mail Line). When it became known that the R & O was entertaining proposals, another syndicate came forward headed by William Mitchell of Ottawa. While the bids ranged from $250,000 to $280,000, the terms proved difficult to settle. Mitchell, for example, wanted to pay $75,000 in cash and the balance in annual payments of $15,000! This being unacceptable the R & O immediately sponsored negotiations with the St. Lawrence Navigation Company and the Grand Trunk Railway "relative to Western Traffic." A five-year agreement with the Grand Trunk was concluded in June 1882. A senior vice-president of the Grand Trunk, William Wainwright, served several years as vice-president of the R & O.[46] In an interview with the president of the Canadian Pacific Railway, Cornelius Van Horne, he was reported as saying that CPR management "had the impression that [the R & O] was almost entirely Grand Trunk."[47]

It was not until new leadership took over the R & O in the early nineties that attention really turned to improving the accommodation on the western line.[48] In 1891 the board contracted with the Morgan Iron Works of New York to build a new, canal-class, twin-screw, iron-hulled steamer.[49] But the *Columbian* would not prove to be the answer.

The Algerian

The search for a better solution led to one of the most misunderstood moves in the history of the Richelieu and Ontario Navigation Company. Business had been poor in the early nineties as passenger traffic tailed off in a major economic downturn. The company was quarrelling with its bankers about overdrafts and had trouble paying a dividend. Some have viewed the transfer of the fleet to the Montreal Safe Deposit Company in 1894 as a move to cover failing incomes and near bankruptcy.

It was true that the company desperately needed working capital. Besides the Mail Line they were operating a variety of steamers between Montreal and Quebec City, on runs to the Saguenay, and on ferry routes about Montreal. Many of these vessels were seriously aging: of the western steamers in 1894 only the *Columbian* was less than twenty years old and *Magnet* and *Passport* were nearing fifty. In 1894 the company dismissed General Manager Julian Chabot and replaced him with a member of one of the oldest shipping families on the Lakes, C.F. Gildersleeve.[50] At the same time, plans were laid for an amendment to the act of incorporation that would allow them to raise $500,000 in bonds.[51] Ownership of the fleet was placed in trust as security for the bond issue. The shareholders approved the plan in a special meeting on 15 August and the directors appointed the Montreal Safe Deposit Company as trustee. In all these manoeuvres the directors of the R & O were in complete control. So successful did they feel they had been that in January of 1895 they declared a dividend of 3 percent on the previous year's earnings (the first dividend in some time). General Manager Gildersleeve received a $1,000 raise.[52]

The purpose of all this was to raise capital for major improvements. In the fall of 1894 Gildersleeve recommended the acquisition or construction of two new, larger steamers to run from Toronto to Prescott. There they would rendezvous with "observation" steamers that would carry the passengers down to Montreal.[53] The idea was scarcely new; the American lines had been doing precisely this when the *Kingston* was first launched in the 1850s. The *Bavarian* had tried the route in the summer of 1873. The key to the scheme was vastly expanded accommodation for the overnight passage on the open lake, while the "observation" steamers would be enlarged to the standards of the new fourteen-foot St. Lawrence canals. Approved in principal, the plan was delayed until

The River Palace

The new steamboat Kingston: *One of the two new steamers built at Toronto to serve the growing passenger traffic at the turn of the century,* Kingston *was too large even for the enlarged St. Lawrence canals. Instead it ran down to Prescott and rendezvoused with one of the smaller river vessels and later the* Rapids Prince, Rapids Queen, *and* Rapids King.

the economy saw a major upswing and the canals neared completion. New opposition from the Folger interests in the summer of 1897 added a sense of urgency. Before that the Folgers had largely confined their operations to the Thousand Islands excursion trade in connection with the New York Central Railroad.[54] In November of that year, Bertram's in Toronto signed an agreement to build a new paddle wheeler for the R & O for $244,000.[55] Launched in 1899, the *Toronto* was joined two years later by a new *Kingston*.

How then to reorganize the balance of the fleet? No longer would five canal class steamers be necessary to handle the daily service through from Toronto to Montreal. By the turn of the century the canals had outgrown them. The long painful process of enlarging the St. Lawrence and Welland canals to minimum dimensions of 270 feet by forty-five feet,

The Algerian

The barefooted paperboys stand ready to intercept passengers on their way to the wharves at the foot of Yonge Street, Toronto. Across an expanse of railway tracks, stands the entrance to the Geddes Wharf which served the R & O as well as the Niagara Navigation Company. Below the main sign is the "team entrance" used by the freight wagons as well as the cabs and omnibuses. Alongside in the entrance to the Toronto Ferry Co.'s wharf promising a 5 cent ride to the Toronto islands.

with fourteen feet of water over the sills, was nearly complete. Although work had begun in 1873 to enlarge the Welland Canal, it would be 1901 before the last of the critical locks was operational on the St. Lawrence.[56]

As the launch of the new *Kingston* was anticipated, the question arose as to which of the existing steamers should meet her at Prescott. Gildersleeve recommended the *Algerian*. But she would need to be lengthened and have her speed increased with new feathering paddlewheels. These two moves, in turn, required the complete reconstruction of her cabins. The board balked at the $25,000 price tag and decided to renovate the newer *Columbian* instead.[57]

The River Palace

The last chance had passed for the aging *Algerian* to see a major overhaul at the hands of the Richelieu and Ontario Navigation company. Although mooted in 1899, it was not until the following year that she joined *Hamilton* (ex-*Magnet*) back on the route from Hamilton to Montreal.[58] While this was the route she had been designed for in the 1850s, it was now a distinctly less glamorous line. Despite this the crew probably appreciated the longer working season. Instead of first appearing in Toronto by mid-June, the *Algerian* arrived on 10 May in 1900 and 8 May the following year. Instead of laying up in late September, her last departure from Toronto was 3 November 1900. Apart from her new wheels, the 1900 overhaul was only to be "the necessary repairs" for this more humble posting.[59]

By 1902 she had sunk to the status of spare boat, running up to Toronto only twice in August, once in September, and twice in October. In 1903 she appeared nine times in Toronto between June 24 and August 20. Two more passages in 1904, one in 1905, and a final appearance on 11 October 1907 completed her service as a spare boat on the "Through" western line.[60]

Toronto Harbour: Along with the new **Kingston**, the Toronto *served the overnight passage from Toronto to the top of the rapids. Here she is seen in the increasingly industrial Toronto waterfront with the* **Chippewa** *of the Niagara Navigation Company. The older Mail Line (or "through" or "western" line) steamboats arrived at the same Toronto wharf until the First World War.*

7

The *Cornwall*

For some years the Richelieu and Ontario Navigation Company's board of directors had idly speculated about changing the names of the western vessels. On its Quebec routes, the company's practice was to name steamers after the communities served by the vessels. As early as 1895, *Magnet* had been renamed *Hamilton* following a major refit. In a single reversion to the old style, *Passport* was finally given an old "Allan Line" style name, *Caspian*, in 1898. In December 1904, the board met and debated a wholesale set of changes. A remarkable document surviving from this discussion shows that of the seven directors polled, there was no consensus. For *Algerian*, various directors suggested *Cobourg*, *Prescott*, *Port Hope*, or *Deseronto*. One voted not to change the names at all. An attached paper showed the majority then wanted *Belleville*. However, president L. J. Forget suggested *Cornwall* and *Cornwall* it would be. Among the other alterations *Spartan* was changed to *Belleville*, *Bohemian* to *Prescott*, *Columbian* to *Brockville*, and *Corsican* to *Picton*. The new names received government approval early in the new year.¹

Some historians have speculated about another major fire about this point in the career of what was now the *Cornwall*. Erik Heyl asserts she burned in 1906.² The biography of the vessel in *Scanner* hints at a fire in 1904, but carefully notes that the authors failed "to find any documentation in this respect."³ One would expect to find confirmation

The River Palace

in the minute books of the Richelieu and Ontario Navigation company. In September 1905 they refer to a fire in an unnamed steamer that caused "slight damage."[4] Twice before her name had changed after a fire; perhaps Heyl and others simply expected the pattern to continue.

For several years the *Cornwall* lay in Sorel, the winter quarters and repair depot for the R & O fleet. Late in 1904 (while still called the *Algerian*) she had assisted in towing the *Canada* from Sorel down to Lévis where she would be lengthened and renamed the *Ste. Irenée*.[5] Two years later, staff complained that men had to be stripped from several departments at Sorel if they needed to crew *Cornwall*.[6]

From 1906 to 1908, she ran twice a week between Montreal and Chambly. This was a market boat route that led down the St. Lawrence to Sorel and up the Richelieu river to Chambly. Like her predecessor, *Chambly*, she was too large to go higher up the Richelieu by way of the Chambly Canal. The stops on this route had probably not changed since the 1880s when they had included Chambly, St. Mathias, St. Basile-

Cornwall *at Beloeil: Much of* Cornwall's *career as a passenger vessel was spent slowly rusting in harbour at Sorel. For three seasons, however, she ran on the Chambly route, from Montreal up the Richelieu River. Here she lies at the Grand Trunk bridge at Beloeil (site of one of Canada's worst railway disasters).*

The Cornwall

le-Grand, Pont de Beloiel, Beloeil, St. Hilaire, St. Marc, St. Charles, St. Antoine, St. Denis, St. Roch, St. Ours, Lanoraie, Lavaltrie, and St. Sulpice, besides calls at the regular R & O wharves at Sorel and Montreal.[7]

Throughout the Great Lakes region a surge in the construction of electric, interurban railways or trolley lines was taking place. They were more convenient, faster, and cheaper than the market boats. When the Montreal and Southern Counties Railway Company tracks connected Montreal to Chambly, the end was in sight. The declining profitability of the route led the board to resolve that:

> in view of the company's policy adopted some time ago to develop high class through lines and where advisable to withdraw from small local lines, it was decided that if any satisfactory offer was obtained for these steamers [the *Cornwall* and the *Terrebonne*] that they might be sold and the routes abandoned, as the railroads were cutting into the trade very heavily.[8]

The Richelieu and Ontario Navigation Company Fleet at Sorel: The Richelieu Company's origins were in the vicinity of Sorel and after its merger with the Canadian Navigation Company the combined fleets often wintered there. By the turn of the century a number of still serviceable, but recently replaced, older vessels lay in the river awaiting repairs or reassignment.

The River Palace

The principal tug operation in the Montreal region was the Sincennes-McNaughton fleet, which shared berths along the Richelieu with the R & O. Much later in her career, Cornwall *would find herself in the expanded Sin-Mac company.*

Nevertheless, under Captain L. Valois, the *Cornwall* was out longer in 1907 than she had been in years and didn't lay up until 21 November.[9] The next year, the board were prepared to dispose of the Hamilton-Montreal line if $90,000 could be obtained for the good will, the *Belleville* (formerly *Spartan*), and the *Cornwall*. When negotiations failed, the *Belleville* remained on the route for 1908.[10] The *Cornwall* remained on the Montreal and Chambly route, grounding at the latter point that July.[11] For 1909 the company effected an insurance of only $10,000 on the *Cornwall*. Even this appeared excessive when the board seriously considered an offer for a total of $2,000 — with payments spread over five years! They would have preferred cash but couldn't get it.[12] Later that summer the general manager was authorized "to advertise and dispose of the older boats which were no longer of any use to the Company, and which were a continued expense in the up-keep." These included the *Beaupré, Cornwall, Chambly, Chicoutimi,* and *Hamilton*. A mere $3,000 secured two of these for the Empire Refining Company, which then cut them down into oil barges.[13] As late as May 1910 the general manager was still lamenting the cost of the *Cornwall*'s maintenance as a burden on the company.[14]

The Cornwall

Cornwall *at Saint Roch de Richelieu: Another rare image of* Cornwall *in one of her final seasons as a passenger vessel.*

Between 1911 and 1913 the directors of the Richelieu and Ontario Navigation Company were deeply immersed in the negotiations and mergers that culminated in the formation of Canada Steamship Lines (CSL). The fate of an ancient hull like the *Cornwall* must have seemed inconsequential.[15] However, her remaining life was full of a variety of challenges. Some of her most interesting days lay ahead.

8

The *Cornwall* and the Calvin Company

In March 1912 *Railway and Marine World* announced that the *Cornwall* had been acquired by the Calvin Company and was going to be used for wrecking.¹ This publicly confirmed the negotiations conducted after the close of the 1911 season. J.D. [Jack] Calvin and John Mullen, one of Calvin's marine engineers, had gone down to Sorel on 4 December to look over the vessels that the R & O was still trying to unload. They returned to Garden Island three days later to discuss the matter with other members of the family firm. The next morning Jack's father, Hiram A. Calvin, wired Captain Johnston of the R & O with an offer of $3,000 for the *Cornwall*.²

The Calvin Company was primarily known as a timber forwarding firm. Vessels from all around the Great Lakes had been delivering timber to its Garden Island headquarters (across the harbour from Kingston) since the 1830s. There the timber was made up into rafts and towed down the St. Lawrence to Quebec City where it was loaded into ships and carried across the North Atlantic to markets in Britain.³ Along with the rafting and towing business, the Calvins had developed a side business providing wrecking and salvage services. We have already encountered them raising the *Kingston* in 1865. For years Calvin's salvage business had been managed by Captain John Donnelly Sr.⁴ Although the Donnelly family defected to set up their own salvage business a few years after the

The Cornwall *and the Calvin Company*

Chieftain III: *Built at Garden Island by the Calvin Company for their towing and salvage business, the* Chieftain III *was sunk in a collision with the Norwegian freighter* Hero *on 20 August 1911 off St. Antoine, Quebec. There were four killed.* Chieftain III *is seen here with* Parthia *engaged in the salvaging of the* George T. Davie, *in 1911.*

death of the senior Calvin, the next generation of Calvins had also kept their hands in the trade. For some years the *Parthia* had been one of their principal wrecking vessels, although any of their other steam tugs might be enlisted under the appropriate circumstances. The *Cornwall* would replace the *Chieftain III*, which had foundered near St. Antoine, Quebec in August 1911.[5]

While the *Chieftain III* had been designed for towing, the *Cornwall* was still a passenger vessel. Before they would take delivery, the Calvins required she have major alterations. Jack Calvin left for Sorel again in the spring. With him went Thomas Brian, the man who would superintend all *Cornwall*'s wrecking jobs for the firm. Brian was to oversee the alterations planned at the R & O's Sorel yard. Calvin returned to Garden Island and dispatched three men to assist Brian, who a couple of weeks later reported on progress:

> In reply to your letter of the 14 I might say we ar not geting a long very fast. we cant get men. we have got 2

The River Palace

Cornwall *in full wrecking gear by 1919: For a number of years this photograph was used in the ads for the Donnelly Salvage and Wrecking Company. The most noticeable difference between this and the early photographs of the* Cornwall *as a wrecker is the dominating presence of the steel girders that supported the clamshell rig. An extension has also been added at the back of the pilot house.*

carpenters and 3 goiners 4 Labers. we have got lean[?] posts or qarters posts all right and a cuple of days more the stering and wheel House will be down. I am riging up a dining room and a ctichen on the port side. [ ] the same as the Chiefton. and caping that Big Room aft for pumps and such[?]. I dont in tend to tuch them rooms on the uper deck for I think when your father [H.A. Calvin] seas them he will take them all down. we cant get the sakes[?] on to we get down tower [t'other?] ther is ondley one dun yet. thea promes to give us men to cover the deck on tuesday and tom gray is going to get men on monday. we will have to get a stove for the galley. You will want 2 spares [spars] about 50 feet long and about 16" in side. we can make them at home.[6]

The Cornwall *and the Calvin Company*

The surviving bills for the conversion provide some insight into the kind of work done. Between 1 and 25 April, almost $170 was spent on parts for the engines and boilers. Each piece was itemized, from three cents for one 1" x 1/4" bushing to $14.40 for 1,500 bricks. Over the same period they built two new smoke stacks ($62.96), demolished and rebuilt the cabin ($282.54), and laid down canvas decking ($225.93). In addition, she was outfitted with everything from twelve bars of soap (fifty cents), to salt shakers (twelve cents), to a collection of flags including the Dominion of Canada flag, the Union Jack, the French flag, and, (for $3.00) the R & O house flag![7] In all, the Calvins paid the Richelieu & Ontario Navigation Company $3,000 for the *Cornwall* and over $1,200 for the alterations.[8]

Cornwall *approaching Garden Island, c1912: Very early in her wrecking career,* Cornwall *lacks the steel girders that supported her clamshell. The cabins on her promenade deck have been completely removed, as has a section of the main deck cabins at the stern.*

Cornwall was delivered to the Calvin Company's Garden Island headquarters by Captain James W. Phelix on May 16. There her particulars were entered into the company's vessel Character Book (see Appendix B). Her overall length was 175 feet. The hull was only 28 feet wide but the guards added 15 feet over the paddle wheels. The hold was 9 feet, 9 inches deep but the removal of the forward cabins reduced her

The River Palace

draught to 4 feet, 6 inches forward and 6 feet aft when light. Her decks and deck beams were pine, while her iron hull was sheathed in 3-inch elm planking. The single cylinder, walking beam engine built by Gilbert in 1874 was still working. She was registered as having 61.5 nominal horse power, or 400 indicated horse power. At 28 to 30 rpm it was still capable of moving the *Cornwall* about 13 to 14 miles (21 to 23 kilometres) per hour. Her walking beam towered 36 feet above the water line and was framed by two smoke stacks. The 12.5-inch-diameter steel shaft and her 19-foot feathering wheels were those installed in the 1901 refit at Sorel. A Beauchemin steam steering engine and an electric light engine and dynamo were also aboard.

It is not clear from the surviving correspondence just when the steel derrick was erected on the forward deck of the *Cornwall*. In early May, H. A. Calvin wrote the mechanical superintendent of the R & O declaring that "we wish to have these [masts or derricks] as lofty as possible, this to ease as much as we can the strain on the peak-halliards …" Ultimately the height of these would be determined by the lowest bridge over the St. Lawrence, the new Victoria Bridge at Montreal.[9] But

Parthia: *Another of the products of the Calvin Company shipyard on Garden Island, the* Parthia *was a particularly graceless tug, driven by a recycled walking beam engine that was probably a half-century old when installed in 1896. She was retired about 1916 and kept at Portsmouth harbour for the following decade.*

The Cornwall and the Calvin Company

before the derrick could be built the Calvins had to follow Brian's advice and ordered the staterooms taken off the forward promenade deck. The 18-inch imbalance in her trim noted upon her arrival at Garden Island was swiftly corrected by the massive weight of steel placed forward. At the same time a pair of davits were placed abaft the wheels on either side for the lifeboats. A cabin for the captain was added behind the new location for the wheelhouse.[10]

The alterations in Sorel reduced her tonnage from 575.84 to 303.78 registered tons, largely by the complete removal of her promenade deck.[11] The cabin space had been reduced to only the captain's quarters (15.6 feet x 13.5 feet), the machine and windlass areas and the mess (27 feet x 6.6 feet). The result was a vessel on which they effected $5,000 worth of insurance.[12]

Surprisingly, the value of the *Cornwall* was small when compared to the gear she carried. A year-end inventory of her wrecking plant included one centrifugal pump and boiler valued at $2,500, and three

Details of Certificate of Survey, 1912: Cornwall.

rotary pumps that, with their boilers, were worth $2,000 each. To this were added nine Norton Jacks at $100 each, six steel girders at $250 each, and miscellaneous wires and hawsers worth $500. Finally, the diving apparatus was valued at $300. In total, Calvin's placed a value of $11,700 on their gear, more than twice as much as the *Cornwall*.[13]

The final acceptance of the vessel was delayed until mid-July. A special meeting of the board of directors of the Calvin Company, H.A., S.C., and J.D. Calvin was held to confirm by resolution the purchase of the vessel in order to effect the transfer of the registry back to Kingston.[14]

The shipping world in which the *Cornwall* would be salvaging was in transition. Sailing ships had proved remarkably durable. Up to the 1880s, schooners still carried an appreciable portion of the freight on the Great Lakes. The development of the marine triple-expansion engine back in Scotland on the Clyde had proved the beginning of the end for working sail. Coal, the dirtiest of all the bulk cargoes, was just about the limit of what the few remaining schooners were hauling after the turn of the century. Ironically, some of this was being shovelled back into the boilers of the steam vessels that had pushed them out of most of the bulk trades. In a final indignity, many sail vessels had been "cut down" — their masts and rigging removed — to serve as barges, unceremoniously towed about the Lakes by tugs or older, smaller steam freighters. Even barges were less and less efficient, requiring more men relative to their cargo carrying capacity than the new vessels designed for the fourteen-foot canals. Under construction were considerable numbers of their replacements, the classic canallers. They were all about 259 feet long, 43 feet wide, and with a 14-foot draught. Many canallers were being built in British yards and steaming across the Atlantic.[15] The first motorships had also arrived. As yet a cranky, unreliable new technology, the motorships were equipped with huge internal combustion engines that burned oil. Wireless radios reduced the isolation of ships out of port. Consequently, the next wrecking job offered the *Cornwall* might be a schooner, a tug

The Cornwall *and the Calvin Company*

with a barge in tow, one of the new canallers or motorships, or even an old-fashioned, paddlewheeled excursion steamer such as she herself had been for over a half-century.

Even before the Calvins paid the final purchase price of $3,000, the *Cornwall* had begun to prove her worth as a wrecker. From 9 to 11 June 1912 her new linemate, the *Parthia*, had been engaged in the salvage of the barge *Winnipeg*. Cornwall made a brief appearance and the bill included two hours of her time, billed at $10.00 an hour.

Just one week later she was dispatched on her first solo wrecking job: the barge *Hiawatha*. With her wrecking gear (pump, hawser, and the diving apparatus) aboard, she cleared Garden Island at 11:20 on the morning of June 18. Thirty-seven hours later she returned from Prescott. The invoice ran to $646, including the services of the steamer at $10 an hour and the pump at $45 a day. The times of foreman Thomas Brian, Chief Engineer John Mullin, and Diver Rawley were all billed at $5 a day.[16]

There is no question that as a wrecking vessel the *Cornwall* was an instant success. In her first two years the *Cornwall* quickly paid back her purchase price and the money spent on her improvements. By late 1913, this had attracted the attention of a couple of business interests. In October H. A. Calvin offered the *Cornwall* and the four wrecking pumps to J.W. Norcross of Toronto for $20,000. For an additional $20,000 he was prepared to throw in the tugs *Frontenac* and *Johnston*. The offer seems to have been made to Norcross on his own account and not as managing director of the newly formed Canada Steamship Lines. By the end of the month Sandford C. Calvin was talking to John Donnelly. The offer of sale to Norcross was withdrawn and Calvin bought the *Cornwall* and her pumps for $17,000 on his own account.[17]

Calvin had little specific interest in running the company's wrecking operations. On the morning of 9 November, he met with Donnelly again. Over the next few weeks, as they worked out the details, *Cornwall* went to the aid of the *McKinstry* and the *Hecla*. At 3:30 p.m. on 6 December 1913 the Calvin Company journals note the departure of the *Cornwall*. The Kingston paper that Monday announced that Calvin had struck a deal with John Donnelly and the estate of his late brother, Thomas:

The River Palace

> The *Cornwall*, though an old vessel, has a steel [*sic*] hull, and is in splendid condition. She makes a valuable acquisition to the outfit of the Donnelly Salvage and Wrecking Company.... Four steam pumps of the Calvin company are included in the transfer of the wrecking property which was effected on Saturday.... The Donnelly concern is better equipped than ever to handle all wrecking jobs.[18]

The next day the paper noted that the *Cornwall* was getting ready for another salvage effort.[19]

9

The *Cornwall* and the Donnelly Salvage and Wrecking Company

By the beginning of the First World War Donnelly Salvage and Wrecking was one of the most important salvage firms on the lower Great Lakes — certainly on the Canadian side of the border. John Donnelly Sr. had commanded the salvage operations of the Calvin Company since 1860. Not many years after the death of D. D. Calvin, the founder of the Calvin Company, John Donnelly and his sons had struck out on their own, enhancing their reputation with some of the most spectacular salvage jobs on the Lakes. Since John Sr.'s death, the firm had been managed by John Jr., the equal of his father in many respects. Not the least of his exploits had been the salvage of the *William Nottingham* and *Hurlbut W. Smith*, two huge freighters that had been carried a quarter mile (a third of a kilometre) inland by a wild storm on Lake Erie in January 1907.[1]

In the small Donnelly fleet, the *Cornwall* took pride of place. At 175 feet, she was 33 feet longer than the *Saginaw* and almost twice as long as the *William Johnston* or the *Frontenac,* both of which were acquired from the Calvins in 1915.[2] Moreover, the Donnellys were proud of her heritage and never missed the opportunity to loudly proclaim that one of their fleet had carried the Prince of Wales in 1860. Nevertheless, they would often add, the *William Johnston* was even older. She was a reincarnation of the *Raftsman,* built for the Calvins on Garden Island in 1839–40. As we have seen, the *Cornwall*'s hull was about all that remained of the vessel graced

The River Palace

Donnelly: *Almost as old as the* Cornwall, Donnelly *was launched in Augustin Cantin's shipyard in Montreal in 1863 as* Rochester. *For most of the nineteenth century she ran for the Gildersleeve interests on a Kingston-Oswego-Rochester or a Bay of Quinte route. Renamed* Hastings *(1876) and* Eurydice *(1890), she was used as a wrecking boat briefly by the Donnelly's in 1884–85. From 1886–98 she ran as an excursion steamer out of Toronto, before being sold to the Donnelly's again. Renamed* Donnelly *she was cut down to the vessel in this picture. Rebuilt several times in her fifty year career,* Donnelly *was finally abandoned shortly after the acquisition of the* Cornwall.

by the Prince of Wales. How much might remain of the original, wooden-hulled *Raftsman* would be even more difficult to tell.[3]

The equipment carried by the *Cornwall* represented the latest in salvage gear. According to the company advertisements she was outfitted with:

> a 40-ton steel derrick, fitted with clam shell outfit; 3 12-inch rotary steam pumps and boilers; diving outfits; air compressors, lifting jacks; 11-inch wrecking hawsers; syphons, 2 6-inch, 1 4-inch, 12 1/2-inch; steam connections and steel hose for steam pumps.[4]

The Cornwall *and the Donnelly Salvage and Wrecking Company*

Green's Marine Directory of the Great Lakes, Cleveland: Fred W. Green, 1916, 11.

Moreover, she could carry 350 tons of lighterage, goods removed from a wrecked vessel. She also carried full outfits of lumber and canvas for patching. When not in action the *Cornwall* was usually berthed with the rest of the Donnelly fleet in Portsmouth harbour in the shadow of the Kingston Penitentiary.[5]

One eyewitness account of a salvage operation comes from the reminiscences of William P. Palmer, who as a young lad was spending the summer of 1920 near Iroquois. On 17 August the *T.P. Phelan*, a 241-foot twin-screw steam cargo barge running in the service of Canada Steamship Lines, stranded on a shoal in the river. Claims Palmer:

> for me, the big star in the whole show was the old *Cornwall*. With her huge sidewheels and two smokestacks, she was quite a sight arriving from downriver pulling a couple of scows…. The grain was clam-shelled up out of the wreck using *Cornwall*'s big crane, and was dumped into the barges which were lashed in turn along the outer side of the *Phelan*…. Why they didn't take all the grain out of the boat is a mystery to me. The grain was wet, there's no doubt about that, and the stink was getting stronger

The River Palace

The Donnelly Fleet at Portsmouth, 1917: In the background of both photographs is one of the towers of the Kingston Penitentiary. In the foreground of the top photograph, rising out of the harbour is the wreck of the Parthia. *Behind, roughly from left to right, are the* Harriet D. *(with the* Cornwall *barely showing behind her), the* William Johnston, Rideau King, Saginaw, Frontenac, *and an unidentified yacht. In the lower photograph, a woman seated on the government pier at the hull of* Cornwall.

The Cornwall *and the Donnelly Salvage and Wrecking Company*

The wreck of the T.P. Phelan at Iroquois: Some of the Donnelly fleet wait at the lower entrance to the locks while the lightering takes place.

and stronger as each day passed. But that would hardly have been sufficient excuse to leave 10,000 bushels of it still in the holds. When the barges were filled *Cornwall* pulled them the half mile [nearly one kilometre] or so down to the lock of the Cardinal Canal, and then up and away to Kingston.

For the next three days other Donnelly tugs tried to work the lightened *Phelan* off the rocks before abandoning her for some other work. Meanwhile the *Cornwall* was upriver rescuing the *Stormount*, which had broken her propeller shaft.[6]

The 1920s saw a steady decline in the salvage trade. The age of the sailing ship and its successor, the cut-down wooden tow barge, had decisively come to an end. So also had ended the era of the wooden-hulled steam canallers like the *Simla* or the *Mapleglen*. Built for the previous generation of canals and requiring constant maintenance on their aging wooden hulls, dozens of these vessels were rotting in places like Kingston's inner harbour. New shipping was appearing in the mold of the *Lemoyne*, 621 feet long, steel-hulled, and equipped with wireless.[7]

At the same time the Donnelly Salvage & Wrecking Company was improving its salvage plant, adding the tugs *Mary P. Hall* and the *Mary Frances Whelan* (renamed *Donnelly*) by 1924. The *Mary P. Hall*

The River Palace

The Donnelly fleet in Portsmouth harbour, winter of 1926: By the mid-1920s the city fathers in Kingston were anxious to clean up those parts of the harbour congested with derelict vessels. The Donnelly fleet was both part of the solution and part of the problem. This view is from the penitentiary looking past the harbour to the asylum.

was stationed at Morrisburg to service the St. Lawrence River, while the *Frontenac, Johnston,* and *Donnelly* did most of the work out of Kingston. In addition they converted the steel barge *Cobourg* by adding a travelling McMyler derrick with a sixty-foot boom and one-and-one-half-yard Clamshell bucket. The 175-foot *Cornwall* had always been less manoeuvrable than the smaller tugs, especially for work in the river. With the steel-hulled *Cobourg* also equipped with a derrick, Donnelly assigned it most of the lighterage that had been *Cornwall*'s "bread and butter."

The post-war recession caught up with the shipping trades. Between the new arrangements and the economic troubles, the *Cornwall* found herself with little to do after 1921. In the latter part of that season the *Cornwall* was sent to the aid of the *Bessemer No. 2* at Farran's Point, but the *Frontenac* had to come to help. The *Cornwall* went back to Salmon Point to the wrecked *Aragan,* before bad weather forced Donnelly's to abandon her. (The Russell outfit, out of Toronto, finished the job in

The Cornwall *and the Donnelly Salvage and Wrecking Company*

the spring.) *Cornwall's* final job for the year involved the *Keybell*, hard aground in Kingston off the Royal Military College. It took ten days over Christmas for the *Cornwall, Frontenac, Hall,* and a lot of block and tackle to get the *Keybell* off the bottom.[8]

In the following four seasons, the *Cornwall* left harbour on a salvage job only once a year. Late in 1922 she helped the *Frontenac* to get the *Malton* off Charity Shoal. The following spring the *Cornwall* and the lighter *Harriet D.* were dispatched to Prescott, where the *Wahcondah* had run up on an old wharf and sprung a leak. Damage was slight and their job was simply to lighter some of the 60,000 bushels of grain on board. Her last two trips, both in the company of the steel lighter *Cobourg,* were to rescue the *Elmbay.* In May 1924, the *Elmbay* was stranded on Grenadier Island. After the removal of 7,000 bushels of wheat she came free and continued to Montreal. The following year, the final working excursion of the *Cornwall* was a slow trip across the lake through the fog to Fairhaven, NY where the *Elmbay* had run aground 100 feet out from the pier. Again the *Cornwall* and the *Cobourg* lightered about 160 tons of coal and the *Elmbay* came free. They reloaded the steamer and she proceeded to Montreal.[9]

In 1925, seventy years after she had started to work in the Royal Mail Line, the *Cornwall* was effectively retired.

10

The *Cornwall* and Sin-Mac Lines Limited

The 1920s were also an era of mergers, and in 1928–29 James Playfair and his associates were buying salvage and towing companies. On 12 December 1928, the Playfair interests concluded a deal for the Sincennes-McNaughton Line. Since 1849 Sincennes-McNaughton had been a family-owned business specializing in towing around Montreal and Sorel. The price was rumoured to be more than $1,000,000.[1] Shortly afterwards, a Dominion of Canada charter was taken out for Sin-Mac Lines Limited (a nickname carried by the line for years).[2] Under this corporate umbrella were merged the Sincennes-McNaughton Line of Montreal, the Donnelly Salvage and Wrecking Co. of Kingston, the Reid Towing and Wrecking Co. of Sarnia, the Dominion Towing and Salvage Co. of Port Arthur, and the towing and salvage interests of J.E. Russell of Toronto. Local managers from the Donnelly, Reid, and Russell families were kept on to manage the divisions. The Sin-Mac prospectus noted that the five businesses "handle more than 90 percent of the general towing, harbour towing and general wrecking service on the Canadian side of the international boundary from Fort William to the sea. The management will be in the hands of those who have been largely responsible for the success of these businesses in the past."[3] This was critical to the future of the new firm. The achievements of the Donnellys were much more a result of skill than the simple tools and tugs used in the trade.

The Cornwall *and Sin-Mac Lines Limited*

Cornwall *being dismantled: Looking forward along the* Cornwall *as she is being stripped of most of what was valuable. Most notable is the absence of the walking beam and the stacks that used to be immediately behind the pilot house.*

The *Cornwall* was acquired along with the rest of the Donnelly fleet. Her registration was shifted once again to Montreal, where Sin-Mac's headquarters were located.

Sailing into the thirties, Sin-Mac Lines was quickly wrecked in the storms of the Great Depression as fewer and fewer ships ventured out onto the Lakes to pursue the limited cargoes on offer. Shippers and insurers opted to abandon ships rather than pay the price of salvage. On 1 October 1931 Sin-Mac Lines defaulted on its bond payments and the Montreal Trust Company moved to manage the property for the bondholders, desperate to salvage some revenue from their sinking investment.[4] They kept the tugs and wreckers afloat, even if in a limited fashion. Finally, Joseph Simard of Montreal bought the firm in a deal that involved a mere $150,000 in cash and required the conversion of the bonds to equity. Sincennes-McNaughton Tugs Limited was formed to take over the assets of the old firm.[5]

Most of the old Donnelly fleet could still be identified among the assets of the new company. Not the *Cornwall*. As late as the summer of 1928, she had been called the "flagship" of the Donnelly fleet. Sin-Mac

Portsmouth Harbour in 1931: The wharves are rotting. An assortment of cabins salvaged from various vessels (including the Mary *to the right of the lower picture) clutter the breakwater next to the* Cornwall.

The Cornwall *and Sin-Mac Lines Limited*

management had little patience, however, with her old walking beam engine with its small nominal horse power. The smaller tugs had some value but were themselves aging and underemployed. *Cornwall* took up a berth and required too much money each year to keep her rusting hull afloat to justify her retention as a reserve vessel. Her registry was closed in 1932.

The late Vic Ruttle was one of the men who scuttled her one late December day. As he described the scene, anything of any value had been stripped from the hulk. The cylinder, piston, walking beam, and much of the other metal from the engine had been removed, though not

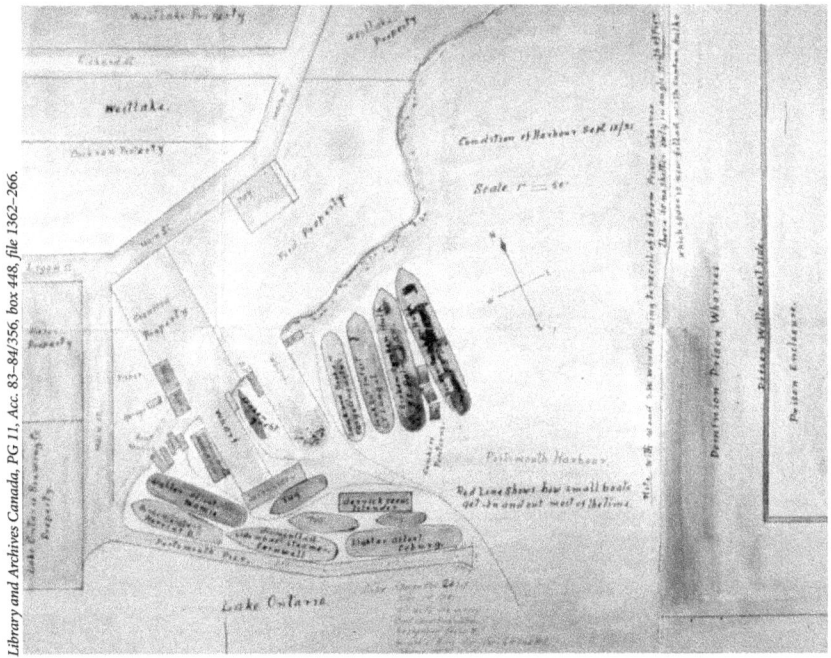

Sketch map of Portsmouth Harbour, 3 December 1931: One of the last pieces of evidence of the Cornwall *lies in this map. She is shown as the middle of the three vessels lying along the breakwater. The* Harriet D. *lies sunken ahead of her, the lighter* Cobourg *astern at the extreme end of the pier. The other lighter then afloat, the* Mamie, *lies next to the* Harriet D. *Three working tugs and a couple of "derrick scows" (including the* Islander*) make up the rest of the Sin-Mac salvage fleet. North of the fleet lie the wrecks of a yacht, the barge* Augustus, *the steamer* Simon Langell, *the* Palm Bay, *and the* Simla. *Within a decade almost all of this fleet would be lying in Kingston's ship "graveyards."*

the boilers. The cabins were bare of furniture. It was a cold, bitter day and all the men on the tug towing her out wanted to do was to go back ashore and get warm. A few years previously, in 1925, the Donnellys had had a contract to pull some old hulks out of the muck of Kingston's inner harbour. These had been towed out off Amherst Island and sunk in some seventy or eighty feet of water. Not far off this "graveyard," the wreckers detonated a charge of dynamite placed in the hull of the *Cornwall*. She was not long finding the muddy bottom.

Epilogue

The *Cornwall* is a museum, an artifact of an age when princes travelled by steamboat, and coal-laden schooners went down in storms. She is a museum open to the public 24 hours a day during the season of navigation. She has no security guards to protect her, for she carries no wealth. No hidden fortune awaits the treasure hunter. She carried to the bottom only what the salvagers could not be bothered to remove. What remains can still tell us much of the life on the Lakes in the late-nineteenth and early twentieth century. We just have to observe and learn. And if her last owners left little of interest to collectors aboard the ship they abandoned, she remains one of the most historically significant vessels to lie beneath the waters of the Great Lakes.

Appendix A

Captains

Clarke Hamilton

Born: 1833 in Queenston, son of the Honourable John Hamilton and Frances Pasia Macpherson

Married: Sara Doremus Nixon (1832–1916)

Died: 10 November 1915, Kingston

Clarke made one on his first appearances in Kingston society on New Year's day, 1853 as the secretary/treasurer of the Kingston Assemblies. He was the steward of the assemblies in 1858 and of the Cataraqui Yacht Club as well as the president of the Kingston Curling Club. About this time his father built the duplex near the waterfront that he shared with his sister and her husband.

Independent of this social life, at age twenty-two he was appointed captain of the *Kingston* for the balance of the 1855 and 1856 seasons. Command was then turned over to J.R. Kelley until Clarke's father's bankruptcy in the spring of 1861. As one of the three assignees of his father's estate, Clarke was in part responsible for the selling of his father's assets. Weeks later he was rumoured to be investing $10,000 of his own money in stock

Appendix A: Captains

Clarke Hamilton.
McCord Museum, Notman Collection, I-9645.1.

of the Canadian Inland Steam Navigation Company (CISN), and the following week to be a director of the new concern. When the company hired his father as general manager, the circle was complete.

In 1863, the first year that the CISN dividend book is available, Clarke held 140 shares, a number that dropped to thirty in 1866, and to a nominal ten in 1869. Clarke was a director again in 1862. Clarke was both director and employee, commanded the *Kingston* from 1861 through to 1863, after which he transferred to the newly built *Grecian*. A later bylaw of the company prevented employees from being directors, though the date of this is uncertain.

In 1866 a Mr. Hatch was advertising as sub-agent for Captain Hamilton "for the Commercial Union" (Fire and Life). Clarke obviously had some relationship with the insurance firm. After his father's death, on 29 June 1882, Clarke Hamilton was appointed Collector of Customs in Kingston, retiring about 1909. He had two daughters. One married Ed. J.B. Pense of Kingston, the owner and publisher of the *British Whig*. The other was Mrs. Maitland Hannaford of Westmount.[1]

John Ramage Kelley

One of the first notices of Kelley was in the Spring Walks of the *British Whig* for 1855 when he was described as a "late Purser, a very excellent young man" who had taken the place of Captain L.N. Putnam in command of the *Ottawa*. It is not clear if Kelley had served as purser on the *Ottawa* or one of the other steamboats in the region. Though owned by a Lachine consortium that included Sir George Simpson of the Hudson Bay Company, the *Ottawa* had been chartered by the Honourable John Hamilton for most of her career to this point.

When Kelley made the shift to the *Kingston* in 1857 he was described, in proper newspaper fashion as "a very gentlemanly young man and a general favourite with the travelling community."

Kelley served on the *Kingston* until replaced by the return of Clarke Hamilton in 1861, when he was transferred to the less prestigious command of the *Champion*. The demotion may have related to the fact that he had only bought fourteen shares of the stock in the Canadian Inland Steam Navigation company. Three years later he moved the *Passport* when the *British Whig* offered this fairly stock description of him: No captain, it said, "is more careful of the comfort of his guests, or more anxious to look after the Company's interests." Four years after that he moved to the *Grecian*.

The *Grecian* was a particularly doomed command. She had sunk in the Lachine rapids in 1867. She struck rocks twice in the rapids under Kelley's command in 1868 and was finally destroyed in the rapids on her first trip down in 1869. For years the *Grecian* would remain in the rapids, her bow on the shore, her paddle wheels eerily spinning in the current.

Kelley was soon after transferred to the *Spartan*, serving on her for the balance of 1869 and the following two seasons. But *Spartan*, while under his command ran on Pigeon Island with 150 passengers aboard in September 1871. A number of questions were raised in the account of this accident but the *Daily News* carefully avoided mentioning Kelley's name. *Spartan* was rescued and repaired but Kelley, after seventeen years in the Royal Mail Line, both under John Hamilton and the Canadian Navigation Company, was not given another command.

When he died in Prescott in September 1875, it was reported that he had been sick with rheumatism the last two years of his life. He left a widow and six children.[2]

Appendix A: Captains

Thomas Howard

Born: 15 September 1826, Shinroan, Queen's County (now County Laois), Ireland
Died: Easter Sunday, April 1898, Montreal

According to his obituary, Howard emigrated to Canada in 1842, when he was sixteen years old. The first newspaper reference to him is as chief officer (presumably first mate) of the *Passport* in the spring of 1850 when he was twenty-three. At the end of the season he was appointed captain of the *St. Lawrence*. The appointment was an obvious one for the owner of the *St. Lawrence*, Captain William Bowen, who had been Howard's commanding officer the previous year.

Howard kept that command until 1855 when he shifted to the *Banshee*, a new wooden-hulled steamer, in which William Bowen, Howard, O.S. Gildersleeve, and Alexander Milloy held a significant interest. Howard held seven of the sixty-four shares. Howard held the command of the *Banshee* from her launch through to the end of the 1858 season.

The following year he joined the Royal Mail Line's Montreal agent, Milloy, in a venture with the *Magnet*, which Milloy had recently purchased. Milloy and Howard took her down to Quebec City where the *Magnet* ran to the Saguenay and Gulf of St. Lawrence watering places. For the next few years he operated the *Magnet* for part of the season in the Royal Mail Line and partly in the lower St. Lawrence.

Thomas Howard.

McCord Museum, Notman Collection, I-9820.1.

After the purchase of the *Magnet* by the Canadian Inland Steam Navigation Company in July 1862, Howard became another captain in their fleet. Indeed Howard owned fifty-six shares in the company in 1863, a stake he raised to 105 shares by 1866. In addition, in 1861 he was reported to be the owner of the *Hero,* one of the smaller freight steamers on the upper St. Lawrence-Great Lakes trades.

In 1864 he replaced Clarke Hamilton in the command of the *Kingston,* then still the newest of the Canadian Navigation Company's fleet. When the *Spartan* was brought out the following season, Captain Howard was in command. He remained on the decks of the *Spartan* until the company underwent a significant transformation in 1868. At this point, a number of vessels were acquired and the Honourable John Hamilton retired. Captain Howard replaced him as superintendent. One of his more dubious duties, according to the Liberal *British Whig,* was to encourage the crews of the Canadian Navigation Company vessels to vote Conservative in the wake of the Pacific Scandal.

Howard remained superintendent of the line even after it was absorbed into the Richelieu and Ontario Navigation Company in 1875. In 1881 he was appointed harbour master in Montreal, a position he retained until his death in 1898.

He was described as "highly respected by all with whom he came in contact and was a general favourite in commercial circles." He left a widow, three sons, and two daughters. According to this same obituary he lived at 4 Beaver Hall Square in Montreal and had been a resident of Montreal for fifty-six years (i.e., since arriving in 1842.) However, for some period he had been a resident of Kingston, being described as that in the registry of the *Banshee* in 1855. As well he had been the vice-president of the Portsmouth branch of the St. Patrick's Society in 1864.[3]

Appendix A: Captains

PETER FARRELL

Born: About 1821, in Ireland
Died: 28 June 1880 in Kingston

Farrell's family emigrated to the Kingston area in the early 1830s. He served as purser on the *Henry Gildersleeve* under Captain Thomas Maxwell. This was at least for the 1849 and 1850 seasons. At his death in 1880, it was said that he had thirty-three years of service on the Royal Mail Line that, discounting the fact he did other things over his career, suggests he went on board about 1847 or 1848.

Farrell appears to have continued his business career, not in the shipping trades but as a grocer. In 1851 the *British Whig* commented that "it is seldom that a young man starts in business under more favourable auspices ..." At the same time he was serving as secretary of the building committee for completing the interior of the Catholic cathedral in Kingston. His credit rating was as a small retail grocer of "not much means." A later observation was that he had commenced business "on the Roman Catholic interest ... owns no R[eal] E[state] ... but does not h[a]ve anyth[in]g. This is hardly surprising as he was the brother of John Farrell, a priest then teaching at Regiopolis College in Kingston and in 1856 the first bishop of Hamilton. By 1855, the credit reporter noted that Peter was hard up and "sued occasionally."

In the spring of 1855 he was a partner with Captain Chambers in the £750 lease of A & D. Shaw's wharves on the Kingston waterfront. Farrell sold out his grocery business for the venture. The lease subsequently became the matter of a legal battle. At the same time he had acquired the Rideau Canal steamer *Firefly*. But this, like his other ventures, went badly and on 16 January 1857 he declared bankruptcy. By that summer he was a clerk in an insurance office. Another, particularly tangled, legal case involved his charter of the schooner *Josephine* that same year.

However, Farrell was able to land on his feet, becoming the master of John Meagher's *St. Lawrence* at a salary of $1,000 a year. The same report characterized him as "an honest, good hearted fellow but has no property & no means beyond his Salary as Captain." His financial troubles followed him aboard the *St. Lawrence* where, in November 1858, a constable came aboard to deliver a commitment for contempt of court for the non-payment of a debt. As he arrested Farrell and took him off to prison the crew "effected a rescue," (in the words of the *Whig*). Farrell was acquitted of assault but there was no question that a fight of some sort had taken place.

Replaced shortly afterwards on the *St. Lawrence*, he appeared on the deck of the *Boston* in 1859. In 1862 his legal interests in the steamboat *Protection* were disposed of by the courts although he remained in command. It was 1868 before he joined the Royal Mail Line as captain of the *Kingston*. The previous year he had acquired all of four shares of the Canadian Navigation company. By 1871 these were being held in trust. He commanded her until 1871. That season there was reported to have been some "unpleasantness" over breakfast with some of the passengers after which resolutions "were in order."

Beginning in 1872 he took command of the *Corinthian* (as Dunlop was promoted to the *Spartan*). He remained on the *Corinthian* until he collapsed from an "inflamation of the bowels" and died in Kingston at the British American Hotel on 28 June 1880. Like Captain Kelley he had suffered from rheumatism. He had a wife but no children.[4]

Andrew Dunlop

Born: 30 June 1831
Died: 20 February 1918

The first public reference to Dunlop is in a Kingston directory published in 1857 when he was living on Barrack St. and noted as the purser of the *New Era*. Other Dunlops on Barrack street included James (mariner), Robert (pensioner), and Robert (gentleman).

Like many of the other captains in the Royal Mail Line, Dunlop had begun his career as a purser. In 1854 he was hired as the purser on the propeller *Lord Elgin*. In 1856–57 he was purser on the paddlewheelers *St. Lawrence* and *New Era*. The reduction in vessels on the Royal Mail Line

Appendix A: Captains

Andrew Dunlop.

forced him back to the freight trades on the propellers *West, Banshee,* and *Avon,* as well as the freight steamer *Boston*. In 1861 he returned to the Mail Line as purser of the chartered *New Era* (then renamed *Empress*). The following year he was promoted to captain. In 1864 he shifted to the *Champion,* and the following year became captain of the *Kingston*. After three seasons on the *Kingston,* he shifted to the newer *Corinthian*. In 1871 he took command of the *Spartan,* where he remained through the 1875 season.

In 1876 he accepted a position as inspector for the Royal Canadian Insurance Company. As his obituary noted, "circumstances alter cases." The insurance company decided to forego underwriting marine risks and let Dunlop go. For a few years he worked for Edward Browne, in his Hamilton waterfront enterprises, until just before Browne's death in 1890. The previous season he returned to work for the Gildersleeves, commanding the *Norseman*. In 1890 he took command of the steamer *Kathleen,* and the following year returned to the Mail Line on the decks of the *Corinthian*. Dunlop escaped the fire that destroyed the *Corinthian* in the fall of that year. In August Captain McGrath was removed from the command of the *Algerian* after the collision with the *Tecumseh* and Dunlop was transferred to his command. Dunlop remained on the *Algerian* till 1898. Although in 1899 he would make the occasional run up the river with *Algerian* his principal command was the *Bohemian*. In the fall of 1907 at the age of sixty-six, Captain Dunlop was removed from the command of the *Prescott* (as the *Bohemian* had been renamed), after colliding with the *Havana* early in the summer, sinking the barge *Davidson* in the Lachine Canal on 12 September, and damaging both the tug *Kate* and construction work on the canal five days later. The R & O minutes regretfully noted "although in 10 days he would have finished his season and his forty years connection with this Company." Hardly coincidental was the decision of the board of inquiry into the *Havana* incident, delivered on 12 September, which censured Dunlop for not being on deck, and not insuring that the *Prescott* had adequate backup signalling devices for the pilot.

In an oddly personal note, Captain Dunlop allowed his name to be used in conjunction with Polson's ads for the patent medicine Catarrhozone, which, he claimed in 1905 had cured the bronchitis he had suffered from for over twenty years.

Dunlop left three sons, Wallace, James, and Herbert, and one daughter, Mrs. D. J. Dick, all of whom at his passing lived in Kingston.[5]

CHARLES CARMICHAEL

Married: 1864, Jane Goodall of Vaughan township
Died: 8 November 1873, in sinking of Bavarian

Shortly after his death in the *Bavarian* disaster, Carmichael was described as "having sailed in the *Champion* and *Kingston* for many years, and more recently on the *Corinthian* and *Passport*. Another account, thoroughly exaggerated, called him "an old and experienced lake commander."

Early in 1868 Carmichael had still been described as a purser, living at 44 Wood St. in Toronto.

Charles Carmichael.

Appendix A: Captains

The secretary of the company indicated that he had been several years a purser, before being promoted to the command of the *Champion* in 1868. In the winter of 1872 he was assigned to the *Passport*. He was captain of the *Kingston* when she burned in the summer of 1872. The following year he brought out the *Bavarian*.

In the midst of the crisis after the *Bavarian* caught fire, the crew seems to have ignored Carmichael whose body drifted up on the south shore of Lake Ontario about a month later.[6]

JOHN TROWELL

Born: 1813, Milford, South Wales
Married: Mary Jane Holmes of Toronto, 1836 and subsequently Jane Wilson of Port Robinson, 1855
Died: 16 October 1891, Kingston

When John Trowell was promoted to the command of the *Algerian* when she came out in 1874, he was described as someone "who has been a long time in the service of the company [Canadian Navigation], and is a gentleman of large experience and matured judgment. The concern may well have been a reaction to the perceived immaturity of Captain Carmichael, lost the previous fall in the *Bavarian* disaster.

Born in 1813 in Milford, in south Wales, Trowell had gone to sea at the age of fourteen on the coasting brig *Colstack*, ferrying ore between Swansea and Cornwall. After two years in this trade he shipped for four years on the schooner *Maria and Elisa* out of Cardiff. She sailed the coast of England, as well as to the Mediterranean, Ireland, France, Germany, and Spain. Two short stints on the *Erin-go-bragh* and the *Ebenezer* preceded a crossing to Quebec on the brig *Columbus* about 1833. Trowell jumped ship and made his way to Kingston.

For five years he sailed in a variety of schooners, including the *Kingston*, the *Farmers' Delight*, *Red Rover*, *John Watkins*, *Peacock*, and *Matilda*. About 1838, at twenty-five, he started shipping as sailing master or mate. Over the next few years his assignments included the schooners *Fanny*,

Toronto, Henrietta, and *Peacock.* He earned his first command about 1847, on the schooner *Clyde.* This stint was followed by a quick succession of commands including *Thames, Ottawa* (sunk at Port Stanley), and *General Wolfe.* His first steam vessel was the legendary propeller *Vandalia,* which was wrecked on Lake Erie in 1851 while under his command. For a few seasons, he alternated between schooners (*Elgin, Emblem*), propellers (*St. Lawrence, Banshee*), and the sail-making profession.

Starting in 1855, he served seven years on his first paddlewheeler, the *Passport,* probably as first mate. After a few years in other commands (*Walter Shanly* (1861), *Bay of Quinte* (1861), *Banshee*), he returned to the Royal Mail Line for nine years as first mate of the *Magnet.*

Before 1874 Trowell commanded, for brief periods: *City of Montreal* (1872), *Chatham, Bristol* (1873), *Hamilton,* and *R. W. Stanley.* In 1874, the company was promoting a real sailor, whose forty-seven years at sea and on the Lakes were expected to reassure passengers of the competence of the man in charge. Moreover, Trowell retained the command of the *Algerian* longer than he had any other vessel in his career. He finally resigned in 1889 following several years of poor health.

Trowell died two years later, having suffered from Bright's Disease. The children from his two marriages included Mrs. W. A. Geddes (Toronto), Mrs. James Minnes (Hamilton), Mrs. John Parrott (Watertown, N.D.), Mrs T. Richardson (Winnipeg), and Miss Belle Trowell.

His son, Captain John Valentine Trowell, was a Toronto wharfinger who a few years later would be secretary-treasurer of the Canadian Marine Association.[7]

WILLIAM GEORGE BATTEN

Born: 19 July 1854, Prescott, Ontario
Died: 28 May 1928, Kingston, Ontario

Batten was one of the first mates employed by the R & O who was able to take advantage of the change in regulations in 1883, which practically required the company to shift to promoting mates as captains. Batten's

Appendix A: Captains

career dated from 1870 when at the age of fourteen he signed on as the cabin boy of the *Athenian*. By 1884 he was first mate of the *Corsican*. At the end of that season he took the exam that led to his master's ticket. At that time he was living in Barriefield, in the Kingston area. For the 1890 season he was promoted captain of the *Algerian*. By the end of the next season he had the confidence to demand a bonus of the company directors for acting as his own pilot in the Bay of Quinte, a season he inaugurated with the *Algerian*. In 1892 he was transferred to the new steamer *Columbian*. By 1897 rather that holding a command, he was engaged for three years at $1,200 as a pilot, specializing in the St. Lawrence rapids. To that point most of the river pilots were French Canadians. As Batten later told the story, they didn't know that he understood French and inadvertently revealed the secrets of the river to the ambitious mate.

The new century brought a new approach to the service on the St. Lawrence with the *Rapids* vessels meeting the luxury paddlewheelers *Kingston* and *Toronto*. In 1908 he was appointed to the command of the *Rapids King*. By the time he retired from the command of the *Rapids Queen* in 1927, Batten had compiled a record of over fifty-seven years of service with Canada Steamship Lines and its predecessors.

His brother-in-law, Captain Henry Esford, was also a captain for the R & O, commanding *Magnet*, *Passport*, *Corinthian*, and *Corsican*. Captain Batten was survived by two sons and two married daughters.[8]

JOHN MCGRATH

Born: 26 August 1843, Lachine
Died: 5 June 1921, Montreal

John started service on the river in his teens. He started in the freight trades, on the propeller *Clyde*. From there he went to the sidewheel steamer *Osprey*, which ran on a freight line between Montreal and Hamilton. He served as a wheelsman on her towards the end of the American Civil War when she was bought by Northern interests and taken down to New York. The war ending she was repurchased and steamed back to the Great Lakes, one of the few to return. In the next few seasons he served as a wheelsman in a succession of freight steamers including the propeller *Magnet* and the *Bristol*, and finally went to work for the Gildersleeves on the *Norseman*. In 1871 he shifted to the steamboat *Magnet,* on the Royal Mail Line, leaving shortly afterwards in search of promotion, as he became first officer on the propeller *Saint Lawrence*, and later the *Bruno*. He returned to the Mail Line about 1875 as first mate of the *Corinthian,* where he was almost ten years later. After earning his Master's ticket, in 1892, he succeeded Batten as captain of the *Algerian*. The company suspended him for the amount of speed he was carrying in the fog when he collided with the *Tecumseh*. Dunlop quickly replaced him. In July 1893 he was suspended again after he grounded the *Bohemian*, and subsequently discharged. Despite this shaky start, in 1898 he was back as sailing master of the *Passport*, and the following season he was in command of the *Corsican,* in 1901, the *Spartan*, and in 1907, the *Brockville*. He served some years with the Dominion Wreck Commission before retiring.[9]

Daniel F. Mills

Mills was second mate of the *Algerian* under Trowell in 1884 and first mate under McGrath in 1892. Two years later he was described as pilot of the *Algerian*. Promoted captain in 1898, he became master of the *Algerian* the following year. Transferred to the *Corsican* in 1902, Mills still commanded the *Algerian* several times in the following couple of years.[10]

Contracts and Descriptions

1872, Steamboat Inspector's Report

1872, Steamboat Inspector's Report (from ANQ-M, Court of Queen's Bench, Canadian Navigation Company (Appellants) and Andrew Hayes (Respondent), Appellants' Factum, filed 28 May 1874.)

Kingston

Date of Inspection	23rd May, 1872
Port of Inspection	Montreal
Owner	Canadian Inland Navigation Co'y
Master	C.D. Carmichael
Engineer	Wm. Finnean.
Gross Tonnage	344 Tons
Registered Tonnage	201 Tons
Tonnage Fees	$8.00 $34.40
Inspection Fees	$42.40
Passenger, Freight or Tug	Passenger
Side-wheel or Screw	Side-wheel
Route	Montreal to Hamilton

The River Palace

Date of Certificate	
Age of Hull	17 years
Where built	Kingston [sic]
Length, ft.	174 ft.
Breadth, ft.	26 ft. 2–10
Depth, ft.	9 feet
Wood or Iron	Iron
Diameter of Cylinder, inches	44 inches
Length of Stroke	10 feet
Diameter of Boiler	9 feet
Thickness of Plate	5–16
Distance between Stays	5 inches
Stamp of Plate	Unknown
Age of Boiler	17 years
Description of Boiler	Flue
Number of Glass Water-Guages [sic]	Two, one on each
Number of Try Cocks	Four
Height of lowest Try Cock above Heat. surf.	Three inches
Description of Steam Guage [sic]: Bourdon	
Number and size of Safety Valves	Two, 5 and 6 inches
Number and size locked up	Two, 5 inches
Hydro pressure in pounds	60 pounds
Working pressure	40 pounds
Number of Boats	None
Metallic Boats	Three, 18, 20 and 18 feet
Oars to each Boat	6 each.
Number of Iron Buckets	Twenty-five
Number of Leather Buckets	None
Number of Steam Pumps	One four inches
Number of Hand Pumps	Two
Feet of Hose to each Pump	150 feet and 50 feet

Appendix B: Contracts and Descriptions

Number of Anchors	Two
Weight of Anchors	6 and 3,0,0.
Fathoms of Chain	
Size of Chains	One inch and 3/4
Number of Cork Life Preservers	224.
Number of Wood Floats	None.
Number of Lanterns	6
Number of Axes	5.

ANQ-M, J.S. Hunter, no. 18127

ANQ-M, J.S. Hunter, no. 18127, Contract & Agreement for building Boilers for steamer Kingston between W.C. White Esq. and the Canadian Navigation company stipulated for by Sir Hugh Allan, 21 Oct. 1872.

Specification for the building of two new Boilers for the steamer *Kingston* the property of the Canadian Navigation Company

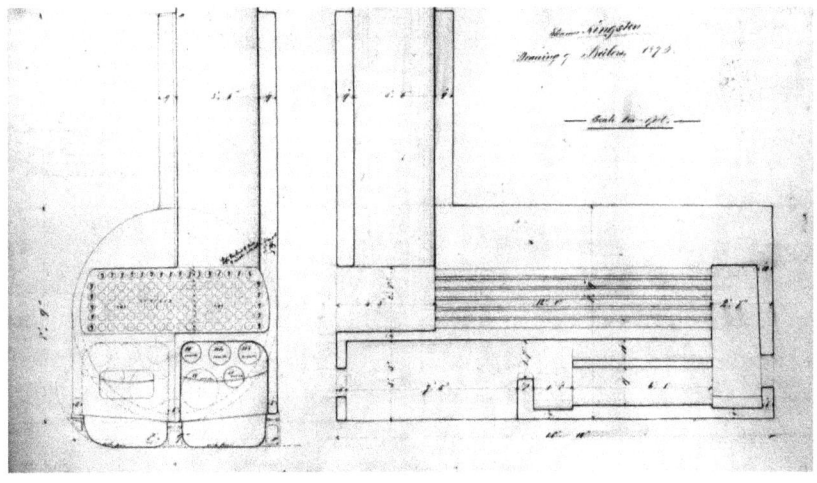

Boilers

To be two in number of the description known as the return tube boiler, and to be made according to the drawing to be seen at this office:

Thickness of iron

The shell to be of 5/16ths best Staffordshire iron, double rivetted at the seams and butts. The Boiler to be of 3/8ths iron on the outside next to the hull, for the length of the furnace, the inside of the steam Drums also to be 3/8in iron. And the whole shell and furnaces to be thoroughly caulked and to be perfectly tight and free from leaks. The furnaces spouts and all flanging and head sheets to be of 3/8 inch lowmoore iron. All iron to be stamped.

Test

The Boilers to be tested by hydraulic pressure to 80 lbs per square inch, with the guage [sic] at the ordinary water level before being placed in the steamer.

Safety Valves

Two sufficient safety valves on each Boiler one to be a lockup safety valve as required by law. The Boilers to have all required mud ports and manholds [sic] suitably and conveniently placed, and to be furnished with the necessary grate ball and Dampers. The Doors of the furnaces to be divided in the centre and to be double.

Appendix B: Contracts and Descriptions

Water Glasses and Guage [sic] cocks

Each boiler to be furnished with water glasses and three brass guage [*sic*] cocks, of a good quality and properly fitted to the boiler in a convenient place.

Steam Stop Valve

Each Boiler to be furnished with a steam stop valve, and to be so constructed that either may be shut off from the Engine similar to those of the *Corinthian* or *Magnet*.

Chimneys

The Boilers to be furnished with good & sufficient chimneys similar to those of the steamer *Spartan* with bulb iron on the Joints, and to have the necessary Dampers screens and stays, and to be made of No. 10 iron. Also a blow off pipe to each safety valve and an umbrella round each pipe.

Connections

The contractor to furnish all new pipes of boiler plate or castings that may be required to connect the new Boilers with the Engine.

The Boilers to be finished and tested by the Government Inspector and placed in the Boat in Cantin's ship yard by first day of December 1872. And all Connections made between the boilers and Engine, and the Smoke stacks erected by the first of March 1873.

… Montreal 25 June 1872.

The River Palace

ANQ-M, J.S. Hunter, no 19180

ANQ-M, J.S. Hunter, no 19180, Contract and Agreement for building an Engine Between Ebenezer E. Gilbert Esq. and the Canadian Navigation Company, Stipulated for by Sir Hugh Allan, 2 Jan. 1874.

Canadian Navigation Company
Montreal December 1873

Dear Sir
    Tenders will be received at this office addressed to the Secretary, Alexander Milloy Esqr up to Wednesday the 17th December at 10 O'clock in the forenoon.
    For the taking out and reconstruction of the Engine of the steamer *Bavarian* now lying on the ways in Power's shipyard in the Port of Kingston, Ont.

Specification

Cylinder
To be 44 inches in diameter and 10 feet stroke of Piston to be of best cast iron, cast in loam with a good head, hard and durable, with suitable strengthening Bands and brackets for the Cross-head guides.
    Cylinder to be covered with felt and lagged with reeded black walnut, polished, and brass bands for fastening same in place, bottom to be seperate [sic] Casting. Cover to be double, well finished and fitted with a deep stuffing-Box bushed with Brass, bolted onto Cylinder, flange with finished bolts and nuts. The Cylinder to be bored perfectly true and smooth, free from flaws and all the flanges faced with metallic joints. And to be one inch thick when finished. The Cylinder Cover to be filled with charcoal.

Appendix B: Contracts and Descriptions

Steam Piston
To be of the best cast iron, properly turned and bored. Follower to have a rim on the lower side, so as to be used with hemp packing should it be required, to be turned and jointed in steam tight double set of rings inside and outside, truly turned scraped and ground steam tight, and fitted with best steel springs. The whole to be a perfect fit to the bore of the Cylinder, and to allow no waste space for loss of steam.

Piston rod
To be of the best hammered steel, with tapered head and draw filed and polished, fitted perfectly in piston with nut and key, likewise in cross head.

Cross head Guides
To be of the description known as box guides, of cast iron with suitable brackets to bolt on corresponding lugs on Cylinder well stayed, also to Engine frame, plained [sic] and polished.

Beam
To be of the skeleton variety, body of the best cast iron very strong with suitable arms and heads to fit to the strap. Strop to be of lowmoore scrap, and not less than 5 inches by 3 1/4 inches in the smallest section and forged with solid ends to receive the end centres, and suitable inside projections forged on to answer the arms and heads, to be securely fastened together with best hammered scrap gibs and keys, and well secured with keys and cross straps. Main centre to be of the best hammered scrap, and not less than 8 inches in the Journals. All centres to be of best hammered scrap and to be perfectly true and fitted with best gibs and keys all polished.

Steam chests
To be of best cast iron, sound and smooth of ample dimensions and fitted with faced joints, large ports and valve seats for double beat or conic

balance valve. The valve seats well bored and the valves to be ground-in perfectly true and steam tight.

The valve spindles to be of the best cast steel, forged with collars and raised threads for jam nuts and turned and finished all over.

Bed plates

Of the best cast iron very strong, strongly bolted to Keelson with suitable faces for condenser and air pump and sent for foot valves. All perfectly faced and fitted for metallic joints. Foot valves of best brass and seats faced with brass. A suitable cover or door opening to foot valve seat. Valve seat castings well fitted in, with best hammered keys.

Side pipes

Of the best cast iron, bell mouthed, expansion joints, suitable brackets for rock shafts turned and polished all over, fitted with expansion joint. Steam connections from the Boilers to be of wrought iron and finished with suitable stop valves for disconnecting and throttle valve for admitting steam in the steam chest.

Cut off

The valves to be worked by means of two eccentrics one on each paddle shaft for steam and exhaust respectively, and long toes commonly called Steven's Cut off. All the valve gear, lifters, toes, levers, hand wheels &c. to be finished and polished bright similar to those of steamer *Magnet* as also the side pipes and brackets for connecting the rocking shafts. Rocking shafts also polished and their bearings fitted with the best gun metal Boxes.

Engine Frame

To be of the best red or white pine free from sap or shake, made very strong well bolted and kneed and of sufficient size with spurs from the top of front leg to the Keelsons. All to be well fitted and bolted.

Appendix B: Contracts and Descriptions

Missing or Defective Parts
Any part or parts missing or defective in any way to be renewed by the Contractor. The shafts and cranks and connecting rods to be properly adjusted and if found bent in any way to be made straight.

Crank Pin
To be of the best hammered steel finished bright and properly keyed and fitted.

Donkey Engine
To be thoroughly overhauled and put in first class working order with all its connections with the Boilers and feed pipes and pipes for pumping water out of the boat.

Brasses
All brasses to be new heavy and of the best quality. All connections between the boilers and the Engine to be made by the Contractor.

Safety valves
The safety valves on each Boiler to be readjusted and fitted, loaded and finished complete.

Smoke stacks
The smoke stacks to be erected and properly stayed also blow off pipes and steam whistle.

Steam Guages [*sic*]
To be finished with a steam and vacuum guage [*sic*] of the best quality.

Finish
The engine to be well finished bright and all the materials of the engine to be of the best description and sound quality. And all the workmanship thorough and substantial, so as to make the engine effective economical and durable, as it is possible to make an engine of this description.

Water wheels
Water wheels to be well fitted and put together, all the Timber and bolts and iron rims, that are good in the present wheels, to be used in their reconstruction.

Removing of the present broken Engine
The contractor will have to remove the present Engine, shafts and cranks, part of Walking Beam connecting rod, Engine frame and bolts in twelve working days after acceptance of his Tender, so as to allow the shifting of the Boilers to repair the hull.

Water Glasses
Each Boiler to be furnished with water glasses and 3 brass guage [sic] cocks properly fitted.

Omissions
Any omissions of details in the above specifications to be faithfully fulfilled by the Contractor the whole of which is to be compleated to the entire satisfaction of the company or their superintendent.

Extra work
No charge will be allowed for extra work without special written authority.

Appendix B: Contracts and Descriptions

Time of Completion
The engine frame, bed plate, Condenser, shafts and Cranks to be placed in the boat by the 1st of March 1874.

And the Walking Beam, Cylinder, Steam chests & side pipes to be placed in the boat by the 20th March 1874.

And all to be completed ready for testing by the 20th April 1874.

Castings and wrought iron
All castings and wrought iron of the present engine, also Brasses that are discarded or broken to become the property of the Contractor and to be removed at his expense from the Boat. The half of the walking Beam now lying at Swift's wharf [Kingston] to be the property of the contractor also. And to be removed by him and at his expense in 12 days after the acceptance of his Tender. After which time any charges thereon for wharfage to be paid by the Contractor.

Gunwale Bearings
Each Shaft to be provided with inboard gunwale bearings similar to those of the steamer *Spartan*.

MMGL, CC COLL., CHARACTER BOOK OF THE CALVIN COMPANY FLEET.

Character Book of the Calvin Company Fleet
Cornwall

Official No.71609
No 5, 1912, Kingston Ont.
No. 7, 1875, Montreal, Que.

British Steamship Paddle, Built Kingston, Ont. 1874
W.C. White, Kingston, Ont. Builder

The River Palace

Length 175 3/10' Breadth 17 1/10' Depth 9 9/10'
Length of Engine Room 30'

One low pressure Engine, Built 1874 by E.E. Gilbert, Montreal, Cylinder 43," Stroke 10' 88 H.P.

Gross Tonnage

Under deck	305.76 tons
Saloon	298.48
Ladies Cabin	26.05
Main Deck	283.73
	914.02 tons
Deduction	338.18 " for propelling power
Register tonnage	575.84

Remeasured after alterations

Gross Tonnage

Under deck	305.15
Space between decks	277.61
Deck houses, upper deck	5.07
	587.83

Deductions

% propelling space 37%	217.50
Crew space on deck	66.55
284.05	
Registered Tonnage	303.78

Appendix B: Contracts and Descriptions

Fitted out and partially altered at Sorel
April and May 1912
Arrived at Garden island, May 16/1912

Iron paddle steamer

Length over all 175 ft
Beam — Hull 28' — over guards 43'
Hold 9'9" [sic]
Hull of steamer 3/8" plate — frame 3 1/2 x 3 1/2 x 3/8 L spaced 2'
Engine Keelsons but no long centre Keelson
Draft light 4'6" fwd, 6' aft
Shelf plate — iron
Deck & deck beams — wood (pine)
Single bottom — iron plate — covered with 3" elm plank

Engine

Beam engine — single cylinder 44" diam by 10' stroke
28–30 revolution @ 13–14 mls/hr.
From water to top of beam about 36' feet
Crank pin 6 1/2"
Main centre 10" long bearing
1 pony pump
Inspirator
Electric Light Engine & Dynamo for 150–16 c.p. 110 V.. lamps
Feathering Wheels 19' diameter
10 buckets 40" x 5'9"
Shafts 12 1/2" steel — shafts & wheels new in 1901.
Beauchemin steam steering engine

The River Palace

Boilers

Two square fire box boilers
9' high 19' long
8'6" diam of shell 3/8" thick
Built 1874 — Flues & insides renewed about 1901
40 lbs. allowed spring 1910
lap joint double riveted
Each boiler has
2 furnaces 43" x 6'6"
5'6" grate bar
85 — 4" tubes}
15 — 3" tubes} 12' long
4 flues {2 — 27"}
{2 — 12"} 6' long 3/8" thick
2 safety valves {1 spring 4 1/2"
{1 lever
9" steam pipe (boiler plate)
L valve to steam chimney

Appendix C

Accidents

Kingston

3 June 1865, Split Rock: [details in text]

1 September 1866, Toronto: The schooner *Oddfellow* collided with *Kingston* at the Yonge Street wharf. *Kingston* lost part of her upper deck and railing.[1]

3 October 1867, Galops Rapids: Struck a rock in the Galops Rapids on her way up. The rock knocked a small hole in the forecastle. Ran into Edwardsburgh (now Cardinal, ON). According to the first reports there was no damage to either freight or baggage. Nevertheless, several pumps were shipped down to her to help her run back down to Montreal to be dry docked.[2]

7 November 1867, Galops Rapids: Almost exact duplicate of events in October. Struck in the rapids on her way up. She missed just one week, but laid up after that next run.[3]

July 1871, Split Rock

The River Palace

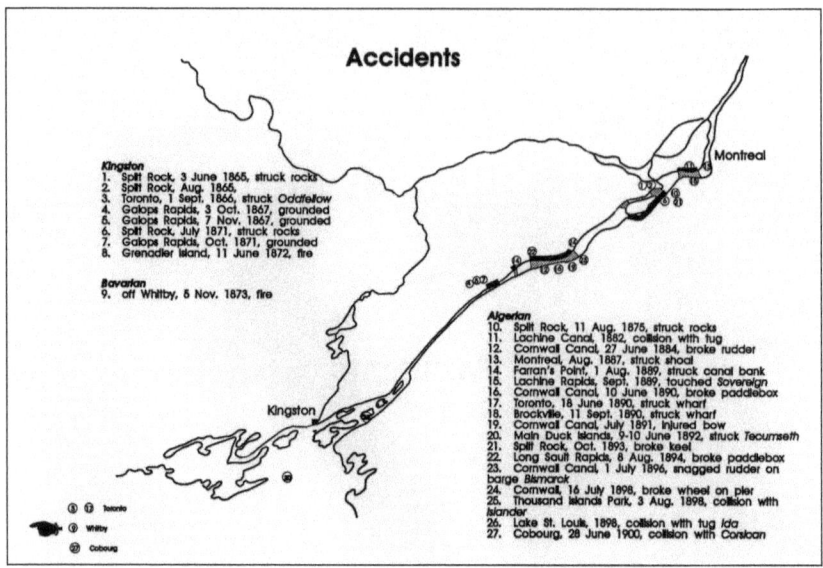

October 1871, Galops Rapids: Ran aground at the head of the Galops Rapids. Delayed 12 hours until the *Spartan* could get her off. No serious damage.[4]

11 June 1872, Grenadier Island: Took fire near Grenadier Island. One passenger and member of crew drowned. The *Kingston* was run ashore where the rest of the passengers and crew escaped. Vessel completely gutted [details in pages 76–80].

Bavarian

25 August 1873, Charlotte, NY (port for Rochester, NY): As *Bavarian* entered the harbour at Charlotte, her wake swamped a small boat containing four young people. One young woman was drowned.[5]

5 November 1873, off Whitby: Burned about nine miles (15 kilometres) off Whitby. Fourteen passengers and crew died in fire. Again the hull was completely gutted [details in pages 83–90].

Appendix C: Accidents

Passport *in the Cornwall Canal, after 31 July 1886:* Algerian *wasn't the only vessel that came to grief in her passages up and down the St. Lawrence River and the canals. Note that none of the* Passport's *lifeboats remain on the hurricane deck (the only part clear of the water towards the stern). Crew appear to have been removing the wood onto the quay.*

Algerian

11 August 1875, Split Rock: Struck just after dinner as the wind caught the hull as *Algerian* entered the Split Rock passage. Most of passengers ferried ashore through the rapids. Pump quit at 2:00 a.m. Repairs cost almost $1,000. [details in pages 96–98]

13 September 1875, Hamilton: A French Canadian deckhand named Fournier was killed when he became entangled in a rope and was strangled as it was drawn into the shaft of the hoisting engine.[6]

1 September 1876: Broke her shaft on the upper St. Lawrence and was repaired at Kingston. Almost immediately after repairs were completed she went into winter quarters in early October. Over the winter the other shaft had to be straightened as well.[7]

1882, Lachine Canal: Struck a tug in the Lachine canal in 1882.[8]

27 June 1884, Cornwall Canal: Veered and smashed her rudder in the Cornwall Canal. Taken to Montreal for repairs.[9]

25 July 1885, Clayton: Edward Kenny, a recent immigrant from England and new deckhand, fell overboard while trying to replace the "shutter" at the gangway and drowned.[10]

September 1885, Clayton: As *Algerian* arrived at the railroad dock at Clayton. The captain thought he had rung the bells to signal the engineer to back the engines. Only one bell was heard and the engine put ahead. *Algerian* struck the steamer *J. F. Maynard* a glancing blow.[11]

August 1887, Montreal: Struck a sunken reef near Allan's wharf in Montreal. This tore away her elm sheathing, which in turn started the bolts through the hull. Some water leaked into the bilge.[12]

1 August 1889, Farran's Point: On the night of 31 July-1 August 1889, the *Algerian* was running up the river. About 3:00 a.m. she ran into the canal bank at Farran's Point, smashing eight arms of her starboard paddlewheel and punching a hole through her hull. She turned about and sank up to her main deck just below the canal. On board was a "general cargo" and only about seventeen passengers. Captain John Donnelly had her afloat within ten hours of starting the pumps. Two holes were found in her hull: three feet x four feet and two feet x two feet. According to one report, "these were covered with boiler plate and the space between the wood and the iron filled with cement." This, it was averred, constituted "thorough" repairs.[13]

September 1889, Lachine Rapids: The *Algerian* was downbound for Montreal. As she approached the village of Lachine, the *Sovereign,* one of the Ottawa River excursion vessels, took a

Appendix C: Accidents

position to her stern. Both vessels plunged into the Lachine rapids. As they worked their way down, the *Sovereign* gained on the R & O vessel. Before they cleared the rough water an excited passenger claimed "the passengers could reach over the rails and almost clasp each other's hands." Both captains, according to this source were ringing and whistling their engine rooms to go ahead. Finally they crashed together and, as the *Algerian* slowed, the *Sovereign* ground her way forward until she was clear.[14]

10 June 1890, Cornwall Canal: *Algerian* broke her paddlewheel in the Cornwall Canal. One week later she ran on a pier in the canal and broke the paddlebox.[15]

18 June 1890, Toronto: The *Algerian* hit the dock . One of her boats as well as the steering gear was damaged. She was back in service within the week.[16]

11 September 1890, Brockville: Again she collided with a wharf. This time there was no serious damage.[17]

July 1891, Cornwall Canal: Her stem, the timber at the front of the bow, was injured in the Cornwall Canal.[18]

May 1892: There was a fire in a stateroom off the Ladies Cabin that was the result, company officials reported, of "spontaneous combustion [of] a lot of rags saturated with Turpentine being carelessly left there." The estimate of damage was between $500 and $600.[19]

9–10 June 1892, off Main Duck Islands: The *Algerian* was steaming down the lake towards Kingston and was just off the Ducks, a group of rocky islands cast eastward from the fingers of Prince Edward county. Despite a heavy fog the night of June 9–10 the *Algerian* was making her usual speed, constantly sounding her whistle to warn off any passing ships. Suddenly the *Tecumseh,* an iron-hulled propeller with two or three barges in tow, loomed up out of the murk. In moments the *Algerian*'s bow crashed into the freighter, smashing over ten feet of her own bulwarks. Water burst through the bow of the passenger steamer.

At this point the tales of the crew and the passengers vary wildly. The reporter from Kingston's *Daily News* interviewed Robert Nish, a Scot on a tour of Canada with his wife and two daughters:

> About 11:15 o'clock I was awakened by a terrific crash, and jumping out of bed, received the contents of a water pitcher in the face. As all was in darkness I was under the impression that water was coming in from the lake and that we were sinking. I drew on some of my outer clothing and with my wife and family, who, though badly frightened, bore up nobly, rushed out and up on to the bow deck. Here a man was running up and down crying out "She's sinking, she's sinking fast," and creating a panic among the women, one of whom fainted. I stepped up to him and shouted in his ear, "Shut up you d … fool,' and this gentle remonstrance seemed to have some effect, for he subsided at once. I walked to the starboard side and saw a dark man receding in the gloom and to my great surprise also saw one of the ship's boats with nine of the crew in her. On crossing to the other side I saw another containing three of the crew, while along the deck railing stood seven or eight others ready to jump. The confusion

Appendix C: Accidents

at the time was indescribable and a woman tried to throw herself overboard, but was prevented. My wife who stood beside me was shivering with fear, but I calmly drew a cigar case from my pocket, abstracted a weed, lit it and leaving her for a moment went to my berth. There I procured my six-shooter and coming on deck, threatened to riddle the men in the boats if they deserted the steamer. The captain called on the men to stand by him, and at last they obeyed his command and commenced to examine the damage sustained by the collision. The big holes made in her bow were stuffed with ticks, blankets, etc., and a sail lowered and fastened over them. By the time this was done, the passengers seeing that there was no immediate danger, began to recover their presence of mind, and the panic abated.[20]

This remarkable piece of puffery, condescending both to the women and the crew, was the immediate subject of rebuttals in the press. One letter praised "the self-possession displayed by the lady passengers."[21] The captain, John McGrath, claimed that he had immediately ordered a boat lowered and taken to the aft gangway in case the passengers had to be evacuated. Proceeding below, he determined that the forward bulkhead was holding and his vessel was unlikely to sink. But it had proved difficult to convince the nervous passengers when he returned to the main deck. Both McGrath, a seventeen-year veteran of the company recently promoted to command, and first mate Daniel Mills, claimed the men had obeyed orders to the letter. One expert pointed out that the crew were assigned boats to take charge of in case of accident and that they had simply followed orders. The discipline seems much improved over the *Bavarian* debacle, but then in 1892 there was no fire.[22] Despite the spirited public defence of Captain McGrath by company officials, he was suspended for the balance of the season. His replacement was one of the vessel's former "purser" captains, Andrew Dunlop, who had spent some of the intervening years working for an insurance firm.[23] The *Algerian* was docked from the 11th to 17th of June in the Kingston Dry Dock, the only time she ever appears to have spent in that facility.[24] Usually she was taken into dry dock in Montreal or Sorel. Her "air-tight bulkheads" were given credit for saving the ship and those aboard.

October 1893, Split Rock: According to a private report of company officials she broke her keel in nine places, damaged the keel plate in several other spots, and two strakes of her wooden sheathing had to be removed.[25]

8 August 1894, Long Sault Rapids: Here she broke part of her port wheel housing while running the rapids. This incident was potentially disastrous. Most of the passengers were on deck, only a few lingering about the tables in the dining room. When the wheel broke it thrust some timber through the iron hull. The *Montreal Gazette* report claimed there was a 20 foot x 10 foot hole! Water rushed in the gap, flooded the baggage compartment and spilled into the dining room. Captain Dunlop coolly placed all the passengers to starboard, while the crew frantically shifted the baggage. This altered the trim enough to raise the gash above the waterline as the *Algerian* continued to plunge down the rapids. Another steamer was engaged to carry the passengers from Cornwall on to Montreal, but most voted with their feet and found their way to the local railway station. The damage proved relatively simple to repair and the *Algerian* was back on her regular trips in a day.[26] However, this incident probably led

Appendix C: Accidents

to the breaking of her paddlewheel shaft near Brockville two weeks later.[27]

1 July 1896, Cornwall Canal: In 1896, two tugs were trying to manoeuvre the *Algerian* around the sunken barge *Bismarck* in the Cornwall Canal when the rudder snagged.[28]

August 1896, near Montreal: An accident to machinery led to one trip upriver being taken by the *Columbian*.[29]

August 1897: Allegations were made of a collision between the steamers *Algerian* and *America* as they passed under the Victoria Bridge entering Montreal harbour. Both sets of management denied the incident occurred.[30]

16 July 1898, Cornwall: She smashed her starboard paddlewheel on a pier by the Cornwall Canal and was towed to Cornwall to get six new arms and buckets for her starboard wheel.[31]

3 August 1898, Thousand Islands Park: *Algerian* ran into Folger's *Islander* at the dock of the Thousand Island Park.[32]

16 August 1898, Kingston: *Algerian* and *Caspian* collided in front of Swift's wharf. The published reports said that the wind had swung *Caspian* into the bow of *Algerian*, which then damaged some of the gingerbread ahead of the *Caspian*'s port paddlebox. *Algerian* did not appear to have suffered any damage.[33]

September 1898, Lake St. Louis: She collided with the tug *Ida* towing some barges from Lachine to Beauharnois. The tug was blamed for not having her signal lights lit. The appeal court reversed the decision, stating that *Algerian* ought to have kept to the south side of the channel.[34]

28 June 1900, Cobourg: *Algerian* was "rear ended" by her linemate, the *Corsican,* while lying at the wharf in Cobourg. Repairs were made in Montreal again.[35]

3 June 1902, Montreal: Stranded at her dock in Montreal after the propeller *Ocean* smashed No. 2 gate in the Lachine Canal. The water burst No. 1 gate and carried the *Ocean* out into Montreal Harbour where she collided with the Allan liner *Parisian.*[36]

Appendix D

Salvage Operations

Although the reports of salvage operations involving the *Cornwall* are fairly complete for 1912 and 1913, the years for which the Calvin accounts have survived, this record represents only a sampling of activity after that date.

9–10 June 1912, barge *Winnipeg*: 51 hours of work by *Parthia* and 2 by *Cornwall*. Required divers and pumps. Bill for $920.85.[1]

18–19 June 1912, barge *Hiawatha*, Prescott: Left 11:20 a.m. on 18th and returned 6:30 p.m. on 19th. Trip required work by Diver Rawley, of the Calvin Company. Bill $646.00.[2]

29 June 1912, Steamer *Alexandria*, Salmon Island: The *Alexandria* was a paddlewheel steamer ashore on Salmon Island, a small patch of rock between Collins Bay and Amherst Island. The *Cornwall* towed her off with little difficulty and sent her owners a bill for $125 for three hours steaming.[3] Three years later the *Alexandria* would not escape so lightly, stranding below the Scarborough bluffs and being abandoned in a severe mid-summer blow.

Marine Museum of the Great Lakes, 982.2.230.

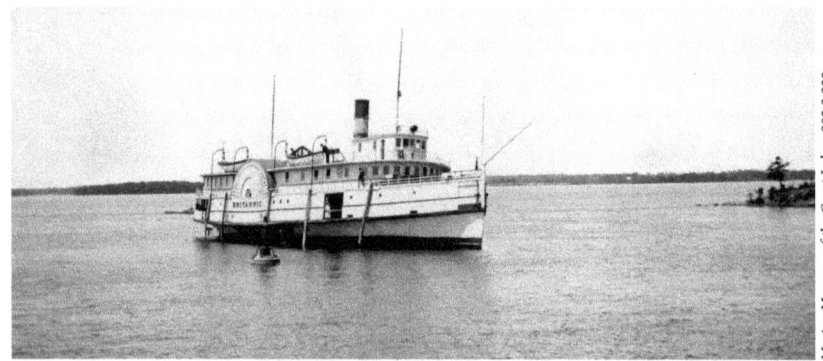

The steamer Britannic *aground off Weaver's Point.*

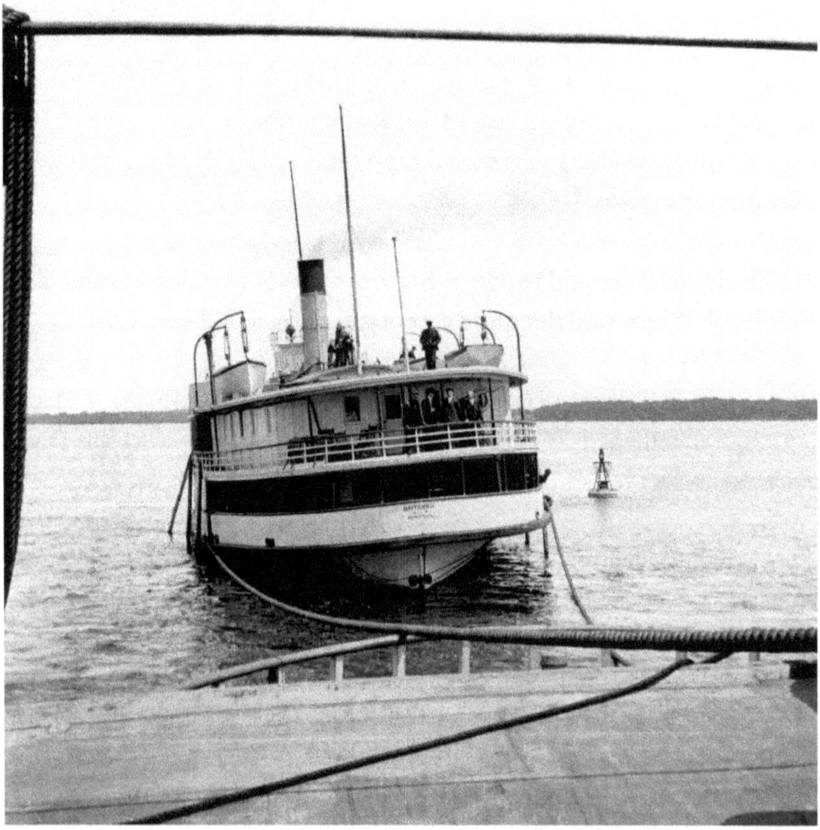

Marine Museum of the Great Lakes, 982.2.231.

Towlines on the steamer Britannic, *August-September 1912.*

Appendix D: Salvage Operations

24 August–2 September 1912, Steamer *Britannic*, Weaver's Point: The salvage of the *Britannic* illustrates that the Calvins could and did still co-operate with the Donnellys in salvage jobs. The *Britannic*, hard aground at Weaver's Point below Morrisburg, required the services of Calvin's *Cornwall* and *Frontenac* as well as Donnelly's *Saginaw*. Ten days of work failed to release the aging American wooden steamer. A second expedition from 28 September to 11 October consisting of the *Frontenac* and the *Johnston* finally freed her.[4]

9–10 September 1912, barge *Augustus*, Salmon Point: With the others the *Cornwall* temporarily abandoned the *Britannic* and returned up the river to Salmon Point, off the south-west corner of Prince Edward county, where the Montreal Transportation

Barge Augustus: *One of* Cornwall's *first salvage jobs was to rescue the Montreal Transportation Company's barge* Augustus. *At the end of her career, the barge spent a number of years aground in Portsmouth harbour.*

Company tug *Bartlett* and her coal-laden tow-barge, *Augustus,* had run on a reef in a fog. While another company steamer pulled off the tug, the *Cornwall* and a barge were instructed to lighten (or to use the salvage term, lighter) the heavy barge. The *Augustus* was released at 3:00 a.m. the same day. The Montreal Transportation Company enjoyed a special relationship with the Calvins and received a rebate of 33 1/3 percent on the $510 salvage bill.⁵

Cornwall: *The tow lines lie slack as the* Cornwall *and an associated vessel prepared to pull this stranded steamer off the bottom. Note that the steel girders, so prominent in the later pictures of* Cornwall *in this era, have not yet been erected.*

16–17 September 1912, steamer *Caspian,* Presqu'ile Point: Within a week of returning to Kingston, the *Cornwall* was dispatched to the rescue of the *Caspian* (her ex-running mate, the *Passport*). The Caspian spent less than a day aground at Presqu'ile (south of Brighton) before the *Cornwall* arrived and quickly pulled her off. Damage was so slight that the excursion steamer proceeded on her way to Rochester with six tons of the *Cornwall*'s coal. The bill (including $27 for the coal) was $651.15.⁶

Appendix D: Salvage Operations

22–23 September 1912, steamer *Rapids Prince,* Aultsville: Like the *Bartlett* and *Augustus,* fog led the Richelieu and Ontario Navigation Company steamer *Rapids Prince* astray. The *Cornwall* towed her off a shoal near Aultsville and then accompanied her back to the Kingston dry dock. The bill was $862.75.⁷

26–29 October 1912, steamer *Rock Ferry,* Charity Shoal: A break of nearly a month followed before the *Rock Ferry* was reported aground on Charity Shoal, a dangerous reef just off the head of Wolfe Island. One of the first generation of wooden-hulled, steam-engined bulk carriers on the Great Lakes, the *Rock Ferry* was at considerable risk as the seas picked up over Sunday. The following day the *Cornwall* drew her off and, in company with her running mate, the tug *Frontenac,* escorted the *Rock Ferry* to Ogdensburg for repairs. This bill was $1,986.00 and included fourteen meals to the crew of the *Rock Ferry* at thirty-five cents each.⁸

23–25 November 1912, Motorship *Toiler,* Wolfe Island: The final job of this highly successful first season involved the motorship *Toiler,* "a hoodoo" in some eyes because of the propensity of her machinery to break down. She was on a mud bank at the lower end of Wolfe Island. A crowd of vessels, including the *Cornwall,* had little trouble pulling her off. The tug *Frontenac* was also involved in this job.⁹

1–2 July 1913, barge *Winnipeg,* Bay State Shoal: Forty-two hours work in getting to, and lightering the barge. *Cornwall* also towed down the "whirlie" *Lydon,* presumably to assist in the lightering job.¹⁰

5–6 July 1913, steamer *Olcott,* 1000 Islands Park: The steamer *Olcott* called for help, but released herself before it could arrive. The call came at 5:30 p.m. *Cornwall* was dispatched by

8:00 p.m. and had returned by 3:30 a.m. Nevertheless Calvins submitted a bill for nine hours futile steaming at $135.00.[11]

8–9 July 1913, steamer *A.E. Ames,* Salmon Point: The work on the *Ames* must have seemed especially satisfying to the Calvins. The rival Donnelly outfit had been called up to Salmon Point on Saturday, 5 July. In the heavy weather over the weekend Donnelly's lighter, the barge *Grantham,* broke away and ran ashore herself. Monday night *Cornwall* and her lighter, the *Maize,* set off for Prince Edward county. Early Wednesday morning she released the *Ames* and brought her into the Montreal Transportation Company elevator in Kingston.[12]

1–2 August 1913, barge *Quebec,* Alexandria Bay: Again used as a lighter as well as towing off the barge. An unusually large crew of twenty wreckers were aboard on this occasion. The bill was $1,144.10. A precautionary letter to their insurance people in Montreal said that the *Cornwall* while alongside the *Quebec* and in tow of the tug *Thompson* was in a slight collision with a steamer at Prescott.[13]

15 August 1913, steamer *North King,* Point Anne: The *North King* went aground about 10:00 p.m. on the 14th. *Cornwall* was dispatched at 7:30 a.m. However, the tug *Frontenac* was already at Belleville and released the vessel before the *Cornwall* arrived. That the *Cornwall* was sent on a fool's errand didn't prevent the Calvins from billing $150.00 for fifteen hours of her time.[14]

31 October–3 November 1913, barge *Cornwall,* Cornwall Canal: One of the last of her wrecking ventures as a Calvin vessel has been the cause of some confusion over the years. The Montreal Transportation Company owned a barge that was also called the *Cornwall.* Like her steamboat namesake, this barge was

Appendix D: Salvage Operations

prone to mishaps. She had been sunk in the Soulanges canal by the *Dundurn* in 1906, at Smith's Island near Brockville in 1907, and stranded on Howe Island in 1911.[15] Late in October 1913 the barge *Cornwall* was running down to Montreal loaded with grain when she sank at Dickinson's Landing at the upper end of the Cornwall Canal. The steamer *Cornwall* was dispatched with her wrecking gear. Anyone who has cooked rice might imagine what was happening in the meantime. The wet grain swelled and burst the sunken barge. All the wreckers could do was strip the salvagable equipment from her deck and return home. Sandford Calvin sent a bill for $1,425.85.[16]

11–12 November 1913, steamer *A.E. McKinstry*, above Murray Canal: The steamer *McKinstry* of the Merchant's Mutual Line of Toronto, was bound for Fort William with a load of cement from Point Anne. Calvin's received the call at 4:30 p.m. and got the *Cornwall* away within two hours. She returned by 6:00 p.m. the next day having pulled the steamer off. The *McKinstry* was not damaged and continued on her way.[17]

18–20 November 1913, steamer *Hecla*, below Alexandria Bay: Owned by the George Hall Coal Company of Ogdensburg, the *Hecla* ran ashore before dawn on the 18th, while running up the river light (without cargo). *Cornwall*, the tug *Frontenac*, and the Montreal Transportation Co. tug, *Bartlett*, tried in vain to pull her off. They left behind the steam pumps. On the 25th Donnellys were awarded a contract for removing the stricken vessel. It finally took the *Donnelly* and the *Saginaw* until 5 December get her clear. Calvin's bill was for $3,701.50, and included none of the Donnelly work.[18]

25 April 1914, steamer *Georgia*, Carleton Island: With lighter *Harriet D.*, removed 300 tons of coal from *Georgia*, then towed the steamer down to Brockville.[19]

The River Palace

30 April 1914, schooner *Keewatin,* Adolphustown: *Cornwall* pulled off the *Keewatin* and took her to Collins Bay to discharge the coal.[20]

2 May 1914, tug *Umbria,* Carleton Island: Calvins had dispatched their tug *Frontenac* to this vessel at the same time as *Cornwall* had gone to the aid of the *Keewatin.* When *Cornwall* finished at Collins Bay she went to the assistance of the *Umbria,* which subsequently required repairs in Kingston.[21]

22–24 May 1914, steamer *Nicaragua,* Point Vivian: Another of the Hall Coal Co. vessels out of Ogdensburg, the *Nicaragua* on this occasion ran aground between Clayton and Alexandria Bay. The *Cornwall* and the lighter *Harriet D.* took off about 600 tons of coal. *Cornwall* brought the steamer back to the Kingston Dry Dock for repairs.[22]

11–16 July 1914, steamer *Sarnor,* Goose Neck Island: The steamer went aground on Goose Neck Island near Morrisburg. Like most of the Hall steamers, *Sarnor* was in the coal trade. After *Cornwall* had been on the scene a couple of days, *Saginaw* was called in to assist in getting the steamer off.[23]

22 July 1914, schooner *Maple Leaf,* Brothers Islands: This schooner had been chartered by young men of the St. Catharines YMCA (Young Mens' Christian Association) for a cruise of Lake Ontario and the St. Lawrence River. *Cornwall* got them off the same day.[24]

19–20 August 1914, steamer *Northmount,* Point Vivian: *Cornwall* took less than twenty-four hours to release the *Northmount* from the shore near Alexandria Bay.[25]

18–19 September 1914, steamer *J.H. Plummer,* Cataraqui Bay: The *Plummer* was a CSL package freighter that lost its way in the

Appendix D: Salvage Operations

fog. The *Harriet D.* was along to receive some 300–400 tons of iron from her forward hold. The balance of the cargo was shifted to the steamer *Tagona*.[26]

20 September 1914, steamer *Arabian,* Main Duck Island: *Arabian* got ashore in the fog. The newspaper accounts are incomplete as to the outcome of this particular story.[27]

23–26 September 1914, steamer *Samuel Marshall,* Sparrowhawk Point: The *Samuel Marshall* was an old American-built hull, then operated by the Central Coal Company of Brockville. She was downbound with grain from Port Colborne to Montreal when she went ashore on Sparrowhawk Point, just below Cardinal. *Cornwall* and *Harriet D.* removed about 12,000 bushels of grain. A Montreal Transportation Company tug finally pulled her up out of the swift current.[28]

1–3 May 1915, steambarge *Jeska,* Northport: Bound from Oswego to Trenton with a load of coal, the steam-barge *Jeska* ran on a shoal in the Bay of Quinte. To this site *Cornwall* carried pumps and diving gear. The divers had to patch the hull before it could be pumped out. About forty tons of coal was also removed.[29]

19–22 May 1915, steamer *Fred Mercur,* Cardinal: The *Mercur,* one of the Hall Coal Company fleet, ran aground at the Cardinal lock. *Cornwall* and *Harriet D.* lightered 350 tons of coal after which she refloated.[30]

5 June 1915, schooner *Horace Taber,* Snake Island: The *Taber* was one of the many schooners for whom the only paying cargo left was coal, shipped into the smaller way ports. She had shipped coal at Oswego for Gananoque, when she ran ashore near Snake Island at the entrance to Kingston harbour. *Cornwall* pulled her off.[31]

The River Palace

11 September 1915, tug *Emerson* with barge *Quebec,* Main Ducks: Again the tug and her consort were loaded with coal. Both were pulled off with little damage.[32]

26–29 September 1915, steamer *Arabian,* Wilson, NY: *Arabian* was bound for Washburn, Minnesota with a cargo of sodium nitrate valued at some $50,000. She blew ashore in a storm four miles (about six kilometres) east of Niagara and began pounding on the rocks. Two days later, after pumping her out and removing some 100 tons of lighterage, *Cornwall* drew the steamer off. *Arabian* was examined by divers at Port Dalhousie, and ordered taken to Toronto for repairs.[33]

18–25 October 1915, steamer *Byron Whitaker,* Cardinal: After breaking her rudder and wheel, the *Whittaker* ran aground near Cardinal. *Cornwall* and *Harriet D.* were dispatched to lighter some of the 42,000 bushels of wheat.[34]

Rock Ferry *ashore on shoal by Main Duck Island, May 17, 1916.*

Appendix D: Salvage Operations

Cornwall *assisting* Rock Ferry *aground on Main Duck Island, May 1916: The pumps are spewing water over the side of the* Rock Ferry *while the* Cornwall *stands by.*

Cornwall *towing the* Rock Ferry*: Smoke belching from its stacks, after five days of pumping out lake water and shifting part of* Rock Ferry's *cargo of coal,* Cornwall *is towing her off the shoal.*

16–21 May 1916, steamer *Rock Ferry,* Main Duck Islands: Among the many salvage jobs undertaken by the *Cornwall* was towing the 1,445 ton *Rock Ferry* (which she had already extracted from Charity Shoal in 1912) off the Main Ducks. Stranded by a storm on a Tuesday, she had to be lightered of 500 tons of coal before being released the following Sunday. The barge *Cobourg* was used as lighter.[35]

12–13 August 1916, steamer *Rapids King,* Coteau Landing: The *Rapids King* got ashore below Coteau Landing on a Saturday evening. She worked herself free over the course of the night. Consequently the *Cornwall* and *Frontenac* had little to do.[36]

23–26 August 1916, steamer *Hamiltonian,* Iroquois: The *Hamiltonian* went ashore about a mile (1.5 kilometres) below Iroquois in a combination of heavy fog and smoke. *Frontenac, Cornwall,* and the *Harriet D.* went to the rescue. Nearly 300 tons of pulpwood were on board.[37]

26 August 1916, steamer *Wyoming,* Cardinal: Immediately after releasing the *Hamiltonian,* the Donnelly crews released the *Wyoming,* making some temporary repairs on the site.[38]

14–17 November 1916, steamer *Gowan,* Farren's Point: The *Gowan* had been towing the schooner *Holmes* down the river. They were reported to have been headed out to sea for the Atlantic Coast/Cuba trade. Perhaps because she was not on very hard, only the *Cornwall* was sent to the scene. The next day the *Johnston* came to her assistance. The job eventually required a combination of lightering and tugging.[39]

27–30 April 1917, steamer *Hecla,* Jackass Shoal: Bound from Oswego to Montreal with coal, the *Hecla* ran aground on Jackass Shoal below Morrisburg. *Cornwall* and the *Harriet D.* were sent to remove some 700 tons of her cargo of 1,100 tons of

Appendix D: Salvage Operations

coal before she could be pulled off. They also deployed two 12-inch pumps.⁴⁰

4 May 1917, ferry *John Webster*, Morristown: One of the more unusual cases for the Kingston-based salvage outfit was the *John Webster*, which fell between her launching ways. Where the tug *Frontenac* failed to get her off, the *Cornwall* succeeded.⁴¹

4–5 May 1917, barge *Isabel Reid*, Farran's Point Canal: The *Reid* got onto the beach above the canal. She had to wait until the *Hecla* and the *John Webster* were taken care of.⁴²

15–16 May 1917, tug *Magnolia*, Johnson's Light: The *Magnolia* went ashore near pirate Bill Johnson's light with the barges *Winnipeg* and *Condor*. The new Kingston salvage outfit, Pyke Wrecking and Salvage, got the contract for the barges while *Cornwall* and *Frontenac* went to work on the tug. They pumped her out, pulled her off, and brought her back to Kingston for repairs.⁴³

21 May 1917, barge *Brighton*, Brockville Narrows: *Cornwall* and her lighter, *Harriet D.*, appear to have made fairly light work of the barge *Brighton*. They took off some 14,000 bushels of wheat.⁴⁴

22–28 August 1917, steamer *John S. Thom*, Devil's Neck: The *Thom* ran ashore 20 miles (32 kilometres) above Charlotte [Rochester]. *Cornwall* released her and towed her back to Kingston for repairs. At one stage a rumour circulated that *Cornwall* had been lost in the heavy seas on the Lakes, but this proved to be misconceived.⁴⁵

4–6 September 1917, steamer *Howard W.*, Rock Island Light: *Cornwall* and the tug *Johnston* were involved in raising this steamer. Rock Island Light was the other name for Johnston's Light.

14–20 September 1917, steamer *Avon*, above Lachine: Not often did the Donnelly company venture as far downriver as the Lachine Rapids. However, *Avon* was owned by the Ogdensburg Coal and Towing Company, with whom the Donnelly reputation was well established. She was running upriver fairly light. *Frontenac* and *Cornwall* went down to meet her, the *Cornwall* lightering some 200 tons of package freight and taking it on down to Montreal.[46]

26 September 1917, tug *Thompson*, Snake Island: Early morning fog shrouded the Snake Island shoal at the entrance to Kingston harbour from the Montreal Transportation Company tug. By 8:00 p.m. *Cornwall* had worked her safely off.[47]

12–19 October 1917, steamer *Richard W.*, Wolfe Island: The wooden-hulled *Richard W.*, owned by the Canada Import Company of Montreal, got ashore on the south side of Wolfe Island, opposite Cape Vincent. Donnelly sent *Cornwall*, *Frontenac* and the *William Johnston* to the scene. *Cornwall* was used to lighter the cargo of coal.[48]

25–26 October 1917, steamer *Viking*, Brockville Narrows: The *Viking* had on board some 58,000 bushels of grain owned by the British government. She was released by the *Cornwall* and the *Frontenac*.[49]

30 October–8 November 1917, barge *Hamilton*, Point Peninsula: The Montreal Transportation Company tug *Joyland* was towing the *Hamilton* from Port Colborne to Montreal. The barge was loaded with 65,000 bushels of wheat. She broke lose in the morning, and the *Joyland* was unable to recapture her. The crew put into Cape Vincent and telephoned for assistance. Despite fairly high seas, *Cornwall* was sent to track her down. As it turned out *Hamilton* did run ashore. The lighter *Harriet D.* was brought to the site. Nevertheless,

Appendix D: Salvage Operations

it took several days to get the barge off.⁵⁰

3 June 1918, barge *Melrose,* near Cornwall: The Montreal Transportation Company's barge *Melrose* went ashore near Cornwall with a load of grain. *Cornwall* and the *Harriet D.* went down to lighter her. She was later towed up to Kingston.

24–28 April 1919, schooner *Horace Taber,* Reid's Bay: Four years after the *Cornwall* rescued her from Snake Island, the *Taber* was still carrying coal from Oswego to Kingston. On this occasion she sprang a leak and was deliberately beached. *Cornwall* towed her into Portsmouth.⁵¹

24 August–18 September 1919, steamer *Cabotia,* Main Duck Islands: On Sunday, 24 August 1919, the thirty-nine-year-old wooden hulled *Cabotia,* went aground off the Main Duck Islands downbound from Ashtabula to Montreal with coal. The crew fetched up at Cape Vincent, 20 more miles (32 more kilometres) down the lake. A telephone call to Kingston set the crew of the *Cornwall* back in motion. With the *Cabotia*

Cornwall, Harriet D., *and* Cabotia *off Main Duck Island, August 1919.*

seriously exposed and the gale continuing to run, the *Cornwall* spent several days in Prince Edward county's South Bay. Five days after the accident, the *Cornwall* and her lighter, the *Harriet D.*, finally arrived at the Ducks. The *Cabotia*'s crew reported she had broken in two, a total loss, and claimed the wrecking crew were merely attempting to save as much of the 1,200 tons of coal as possible. Nevertheless, a week later, Donnellys bought the wreck and set about saving her. On Thursday, 18 September, with another serious storm threatening, they pulled her off with 500 tons of coal still aboard. She made Portsmouth harbour partially under her own steam.[52]

26 September–1 October 1919, barge *Hilda*, Stoney Point: The delay in the lightering and salvage of the *Hilda* stemmed from continuing bad weather. Aground on an exposed shore south of the Stoney Point lighthouse the *Hilda* had narrowly missed escaping into Sackets Harbor. There the Donnelly fleet, including *Cornwall* and the lighters *Harriet D.* and *Cobourg* took shelter. They lightered some 5,000 bushels of dry grain from *Hilda*'s cargo of 35,000 bushels.[53]

11 May 1920, schooner/steam barge *Robert McDonald*, Kingston harbour: The *McDonald* was abandoned by owner George Sudds in front of the city, virtually in front of city hall. The city hired Donnelly's to get the eyesore out of sight. It took but one tug to pull her free. There was some question of dumping her in Back Bay at Garden Island but when the Calvin's objected the *Cornwall* towed her further up the lake.[54]

1 July 1920, telephone cable, Clayton: *Cornwall* and *Harriet D.* spent Dominion Day on the American side fishing up a 17-ton roll of submarine telephone cable which had escaped into the river while being loaded into a scow. It was eventually installed between Alexandria Bay and Peacock Island.[55]

Appendix D: Salvage Operations

17–29 August, 1920, steamer *Phelan*, Iroquois Point: See text for extended description

17–21 September 1920, steamer *Vinmount*, Cascade Point: The steel *Vinmount*, running upbound light, sank at the foot of the Soulanges Canal. She was brought up to the Kingston Dry Dock for repairs.[56]

2 November 1920, steamer *Stormount*, Cornwall Canal: *Stormount* sprang a leak in the canal while downbound to Montreal with grain.[57]

29 April–1 May 1921, steamer *Mapleboro*, Windmill Point, Prescott: Running upriver empty, *Mapleboro* struck shore in a fog. *Cornwall*, *Frontenac*, and *William Johnston* released her. The soft mud bottom meant she could be pulled off with no damage.[58]

11–13 July 1921, steamer *Mapleboro*, below Prescott: For the second time in 1921 the Donnelly Salvage crews went to work on CSL's *Mapleboro*. This time she was loaded with package freight from Montreal and had broken her propeller. Again, *Cornwall*, *Frontenac*, and *William Johnston* were required.[59]

14 August 1921, steamer *Beaverton*, Sister Island Light: Loaded with grain from the elevators at Port Colborne, the *Beaverton* ran ashore in the early hours of a Sunday morning near Alexandria Bay. The *Harriet D.* brought the lightered grain to Kingston, while the rest of the cargo was unloaded at Prescott.[60]

29 September–4 October 1921, steamer *Bessemer No. 2*, Farran's Point: The ex-car ferry, owned by the Walkerville Navigation Company, was bound for Montreal with a load of coal. *Frontenac*, *Cornwall*, and the lighter *Harriet D.* were sent to the scene. Together they lightered some 350 tons of coal, leaving but 40

tons aboard. Thus lightened, the Donnelly vessels were able to pull her off. The *Bessemer* was undamaged, so the coal was reloaded into her holds before the salvagers left.[61]

17–23 November 1921, steamer *Aragon*, Salmon Point: Bound for the Edwardsburg Starch Company at Cardinal with a load of corn, the *Aragon* was out of Chicago. *Cornwall* and *Harriet D.* were dispatched to lighter the cargo. They were able to remove only about 4,000 bushels of corn because the heavy seas continued to rage for several days pushing the hull still further ashore. For periods of time *Cornwall* and the *Harriet D.* had to run for shelter themselves. She was abandoned. The Russell outfit of Toronto returned to the site in the early spring to find that her hull had caved in and she was almost a total loss.[62]

19–28 December 1921, steamer *Keybell*, Kingston: In a late season storm, the *Keybell* blew onto the Royal Military College shore near the causeway. Not only was she hard aground, but a few days later a second storm delayed proceedings. The rescue effort included cables stretched across the harbour manipulated with block and tackle. Once these were in place, the salvagers were hoping for a good westerly blow that would raise the water level at the eastern end of the lake in general and under the *Keybell* in particular. Finally at 2:30 p.m. on 28 December the *Frontenac*, *Johnston*, and *Cornwall* were able to finish the job.[63]

16–30 November 1922, steamer *Moulton*, Charity Shoal: Most of the work at rescuing the *Moulton* was undertaken by the *Frontenac*. The steamer had been running up light from Montreal to Port Colborne, when she ran well up on the shoal. After several attempts were made to pull her off, Donnelly went back in to Portsmouth for more help. A few days later they were driven off the site by heavy seas, and then were distracted by the rescue of the steamer *Andasta* from the

Appendix D: Salvage Operations

grip of Carleton Island, and the schooner *Daryaw* at Four Mile Point. Two weeks after the grounding, clear weather, 100-ton jacks, a large gang of men, and the *Frontenac* and *Cornwall* combined to get the *Moulton* clear.[64]

18–19 May 1923, steamer *Wahcondah*, Prescott: Bound from Port Colborne to Montreal with 60,000 bushels of grain, the *Wahcondah* struck an old wharf at Prescott and sprang a leak. *Cornwall* and *Harriet D.* were sent down to lighter her.[65]

16–17 May 1924, steamer *Elmbay*, Grenadier Island: In company with the steel lighter *Cobourg*, the *Cornwall* went to the assistance of the *Elmbay*. Seven thousand bushels of wheat were lightered before the steamer could be refloated.[66]

25–27 April 1925, steamer *Elmbay*, Fairhaven: Apparently on her final salvaging expedition, the *Cornwall* was once again sent with the lighter *Cobourg* to the rescue of the steamer *Elmbay*, this time at Fairhaven, NY. Crossing in fog, the two vessels were late in arriving. About 160 tons of coal were removed from the steamer, after which *Cornwall* was able to release her.[67]

Elmbay *at Toronto: The subject of* Cornwall's *last two salvage efforts,* Elmbay, *had been built in France, and was transferred to Brazilian registry after the Second World War.*

Notes

ABBREVIATIONS:

ANQ-M: Archives nationales du Québec — Montréal
CC: Calvin Company
CSL: Canada Steamship Lines
DCB: *Dictionary of Canadian Biography*
DBW: *Daily British Whig* (Kingston)
DN: *Daily News* (Kingston)
MMGL: Marine Museum of the Great Lakes
LAC: Library and Archives Canada
QUA: Queen's University Archives

INTRODUCTION

1. Robert Cellem, comp., *Visit of His Royal Highness the Prince of Wales to the British North American Provinces and the United States, in the Year 1860* (Toronto: Henry Rowsell, 1861), 153.

2. *Ibid.*

3. Gardner D. Englehart, *Journal of the Progress of H.R.H. the Prince of Wales* [London, 1860?], 38.

Notes

4. Basil Greenhill, *The Life and Death of the Merchant Sailing Ship, 1815-1965* (National Maritime Museum, The Ship, Vol. 7, London: Her Majesty's Stationery Office, 1980), 30.

5. James Cooke Mills, *Our Inland Seas: Their Shipping & Commerce for Three Centuries* (Chicago: A.C. McClurg & Co., 1910, rep. 1976), 179.

6. Mills, *Inland Seas*, 177-80. *History of the Great Lakes* (Chicago: J.H. Beers, 1899), Vol. 1, 428-30. H.A. Musham, "Early Great Lakes Steamboats: Warships and Iron Hulls, 1841-1846," *American Neptune*, 8 (April 1948), 132-49. Especially see note 3 for a review of early civilian experiments with iron ship construction in the United States.

7. Walter Lewis, "Steamboat Promotion and Changing Technology: the Careers of James Sutherland and the *Magnet*," *Ontario History*, 77 (September 1985), 207-30.

8. *Argus*, 4 August, 6 November 1846. *British Whig*, 15 June, 3 July 1847. Queen's University Archives [henceforth QUA], James Sutherland Papers, James to Margaret Sutherland, 2 June 1846. Library and Archives Canada [henceforth LAC], Record Group [henceforth RG] 12 Department of Transport, A1, Vol. 206, No. 94, 302-7.

Chapter 1: The Iron Steamboat

1. *Daily British Whig* (Kingston) [henceforth DBW], 12 November, 14 November 1853.

2. There are not many good biographies of John Hamilton. Start with the one by Peter Baskerville in the *Dictionary of Canadian Biography* [henceforth DCB], Vol. 11, 377-79. For his association with the Royal Mail Line see Walter Lewis, "Until Further Notice: The Royal Mail Line and the Passenger Steamboat Trade on Lake Ontario and the Upper St. Lawrence River, 1838-1875" (Queen's University, M.A. thesis, 1983). On the *Traveller* consult, Walter Lewis, "Steamboats in the Ice," *Beaver*, Vol. 70, No. 6 (December 1990-January 1991): 23-28.

3. DBW, 30 November 1853, ad.

4. Hamilton's assets were largely tied up in steamboat property. He did, however, have small investments in other craft, and a substantial amount of undeveloped real estate scattered across the province. His Commercial Wharf was on the best waterfront site in Kingston. Like many other mid-nineteenth century Canadian businessmen he had a few securities, which included a substantial number of shares in the Commercial Bank of Canada. Indeed he was also president of the Bank. See Lewis, "Until Further Notice."

5. Fred M. Walker, *Song of the Clyde: A History of Clyde Shipbuilding* (Cambridge: Patrick Stephens, 1984), Chapter 15. Michael S. Moss and John R. Hume, *Workshop of the British Empire: Engineering and Shipbuilding in the West of Scotland* (London: Heinemann, 1977), Chapter 6.

6. University of Glasgow Archives, Upper Clyde Shipbuilding [henceforth UCS], 1/34/3 and 1/35/1.

7. *Ibid.,* UCS, 1/34/3, f. 242. and UCS, 1/93/40, List of Ships.

8. *Montreal in 1856: A Sketch prepared for the Celebration of the Opening of the Grand Trunk Railway of Canada* (Montreal: John Lovell, 1856), 43–44.

9. *Montreal Business Sketches with a Description of the City of Montreal, Its Public Buildings and Places of Interest and the Grand Trunk Works at Point St. Charles, Victoria Bridge &c. &c.* (Montreal: Canada Railway Advertising Company, 1861), 133–36.

10. Archives nationales du Québec — Montreal [henceforth ANQ-M], John H. Isaacson, No. 2712, E. E. Gilbert and W.P. Bartley, 17 May 1853; *Ibid.,* No. 2757, same parties, 30 June 1853; *Ibid.,* No. 2850, William Patrick Bartley and James Dunbar, 29 September 1853. R.G. Dun ledgers cited by Kris E. Inwood, *The Canadian Charcoal Iron Industry, 1870–1914* (New York: Garland Publishing, Inc., 1986), 206. Quote from Gerald J.J. Tulchinsky, "John Frothingham" DCB Vol. 9, 288.

11. ANQ-M, J.H. Isaacson, No. 3853, Protest of Bartley & Dunbar to Hon. John Hamilton, 15 August 1855.

12. DN, 30 September 1854 quoting *Montreal Transcript*.

Notes

13. Ewan Corlett, *The Iron Ship: The Story of Brunel's SS Great Britain* (London: Conway Maritime Press, 2nd ed., 1990), 194.

14. *Montreal Gazette*, 18 November 1854. Quoted in DBW, 25 November 1854.

15. Province of Canada. Legislative Council. *Journals* (1854). Hamilton was notoriously poor in attendance. The session started on 6 September. He would not appear until 9 November, stayed to 13 November, was absent for the launch, returned till 9 December, and then left early. His attendance coincided with the introduction of legislation concerning the Commercial Bank (he was president) and the abolition of the Clergy Reserves (he was Chairman of the Board of Trustees of Presbyterian Queen's University). The following spring session ran from 23 February to 30 May 1855. Hamilton was present only on 19 March, when he introduced a petition from Queen's.

16. *Upper Canada Herald*, 22 May 1833. John Mills, *Canadian Steam Vessels*, Supp. 2, No. 1556.

17. ANQ-M, J.H. Isaacson, No. 3853, Protest of Bartley & Dunbar to Hon. John Hamilton, 15 August 1855.

18. DBW, 20 February 1855. The Royal Mail Line had evolved through a series of complicated arrangements that are unravelled in Lewis, "Until Further Notice."

19. ANQ-M, J.H. Isaacson, No. 3540, Protest of James Shearer to Hon. John Hamilton, 21 February 1855.

20. *Buffalo Daily Republic*, 20 January 1855. (Thanks to Bill McNeil for this reference.)

21. The calculations are based on evidence in QUA, CSL, Vol. 183, *The Richelieu and Ontario Navigation Company* (Montreal: Imprimerie Générale, 1885), 26, which includes the capital cost of the *Montreal* (1862) and *Quebec* (1866). The cost of *Montreal*'s furniture was low and would tend to bias the estimate of costs downward. Costs could have been as high as $90,000. Currency conversions are based on Table 43 in A.B. McCullough, *Money and Exchange in Canada to 1900*, 292.

22. *Daily News* (Kingston) [henceforth DN], 21 August 1855 quoting *Montreal Daily Advertiser*. See also DBW, 22 August 1855.

23. *Ibid.*

24. *Ibid.*

25. DN, 25 October 1856.

26. DN, 21 August 1855, quoting *Montreal Daily Advertiser*. Similarly, in the description of James Shearer's work on the interior of the *Champion*: "The capitals of the pilasters, which divide the sides into compartments, are surmounted by the national emblems of England, Ireland, Scotland, Canada, and the United States, carved and gilt. The light gilding of the scroll work, with that of the angels of the pilasters, while it affords relief to the uniformity of the white color of the walls, gives an air of chasteness to the saloon, which is wanting, when the profuse use of the gold raises the idea of a tawdry extravagance, as in the case on some boats, particularly in the United States." DBW, 1 September 1851, quoting *Montreal Gazette*.

27. DN, 29 September 1855 quoting *Montreal Pilot*.

28. DN, 21 August 1855.

29. DN, 29 September 1855 quoting *Montreal Pilot*.

30. This description is a composite of the early accounts of the *Kingston* cited with the specific quotes, the registration, and the description of her as *Bavarian* in 1873, and early photographs of the vessel. There is little evidence that the *Bavarian* differed much in her general arrangements from what had gone before. For the registry of the *Kingston* see LAC, RG 12, A1, Vol. 206, No. 93, 292–99.

    The rigging supporting the mast and smoke stacks was probably iron after its introduction to the area in the 1860s. One of the first vessels to do so was the Royal Mail Line's *Grecian* in 1863. DN, 7 March 1864.

    On the ship's boats see Province of Canada, *Statutes*, 16. Vict. (1853), cap. 167, sec. I; amending 14 & 15 Vict. (1851), c. 126, sec. IX.

Notes

Chapter 2: John Hamilton's *Kingston*

1. *Globe*, 28 August, 8 September, and 15 September 1855. *Montreal Gazette*, 25 August and 19 September 1855.

2. Edward Marion Chadwick, *Ontarian Families: Genealogies of United Empire Loyalist and other Pioneer Families of Upper Canada* (rep. Belleville: Mika Silk Screening, 1972), 148. Headstone in Cataraqui Cemetery, Kingston. DBW, 10 November 1915, 2.

3. DBW, 25 October 1855.

4. DBW, 20 November and 30 November 1855.

5. *Globe*, 21 November 1855.

6. DBW, 23 April 1856.

7. DN, 25 April 1856.

8. DBW, 13 August 1857.

9. DBW, 15 June 1857.

10. DBW, 13 July 1857.

11. DBW, 18 May 1857.

12. DN, 3 August 1857.

Chapter 3: The Floating Palace

1. Cellem, *Visit*, 155.

2. Cellem, *Visit*, 156. A British Canadian [Henry J. Morgan], *The Tour of H.R.H. the Prince of Wales through British America and the United States* (Montreal: John Lovell, 1860), 90.

3. Kinahan Cornwallis, *Royalty in the New World; or the Prince of Wales in*

America (New York: M. Doolady, 1860), 92.

4. Cornwallis, *Royalty*, 101.

5. DBW, 1 September 1860.

6. "Ship Wales used in 1860 now Wrecker at Kingston," *Kingston Whig-Standard*, 17 December 1927, 6.

7. Cellem, *Visit*, 197.

8. Donald Swainson, *Garden Island: A Shipping Empire* (Kingston: Marine Museum of the Great Lakes at Kingston, n.d.), quoting the unpublished reminiscences of Anthony Malone.

9. J.D. Livermore, "The Orange Order and the Election of 1861 in Kingston," in Gerald Tulchinsky, ed., *To Preserve and Defend: Essays on Kingston in the Nineteenth Century* (Montreal: McGill-Queen's University Press, 1976), 245–46. Anne MacDermaid, "The Visit of the Prince of Wales to Kingston in 1860," *Historic Kingston*, 21 (1973): 50–61.

10. DBW, 7 September 1860.

11. Edwin C. Guillet, *Cobourg, 1798–1948* (Oshawa: Goodfellow Printing Co., 1948), 41–45.

12. Cellem, *Visit*, 214.

13. *Weekly British Whig*, 21 June 1861. DBW, 24 June, 27 June 1861.

CHAPTER 4: THE *KINGSTON* AND THE CANADIAN NAVIGATION COMPANY

1. For a detailed discussion of the financial background of the Grand Trunk see A.W. Currie, *The Grand Trunk Railway of Canada* (Toronto: University of Toronto Press, 1957).

2. Lewis, "Until Further Notice," Chapter 4.

Notes

3. Province of Canada, Commission Appointed to Inquire into the Affairs of the Grand Trunk Railway, *Report* (1861) Appendix, 33–35. It was also known as the Langton Commission after its chairman.

4. Lewis, "Until Further Notice," 98, Note 36.

5. *Globe* (Toronto), 21 May 1860.

6. Langton Commission, *Report*, esp. 49, 76–77.

7. Thomas E. Appleton, *Ravenscrag: The Allan Royal Mail Line* (Toronto: McClelland & Stewart, 1974). Brian Young and Gerald J.J. Tulchinsky, "Sir Hugh Allan," DCB, Vol. 11, 5–15.

8. Province of Canada, *Statutes,* 20 Vic., c. 169; 22 Vic., c. 125. See also Walter Lewis, "The Canadian Navigation Company, 1861–1875" *FreshWater*(Spring 1986), Vol. 1, No. 1, 4–14.

9. LAC, RG 12, A1, Vol. 206, No. 93, 292–299; *Ibid.*, No. 94, 302–307.

10. Lewis, "Canadian Navigation Company," esp. 10.

11. Note that several of these names were also used for Allan's Atlantic liners: including *Bavarian* (1899), *Bohemian* (1859–64), *Corinthian* (1870), *Corsican* (1907), and *Grecian* (1880). See Appleton, *Ravenscrag,* 198–211.

12. See Lewis, "Canadian Navigation Company," 9–10.

13. For freight delivered at Niagara see Ontario Archives, Ms 193, Niagara Historical Society Papers, Niagara Dock & Harbour Co., Vol. 4, 25 July 1859 through 21 September 1860 for entries of *Kingston, Passport,* and *Champion.* Freight included fish, claret, ash kettles, horses, cod fish, sugar, butter, and miscellaneous boxes, parcels, and kegs.

14. *Montreal Gazette,* 14 May 1861.

15. *Montreal Gazette,* 13 May 1861.

16. DN, 5 July 1862, 13 June 1863, 8 June 1866, 27 June 1866. DBW, 23 May 1863.

17. DBW, 3 June 1870. For example of troop movements see also DN, 30 May 1864, 22 November, 23 November 1865, and 17 July 1866.

18. ANQ-M, Greffes de Joseph Mayer, No. 28, 5 June 1865, Protest of Andrew Dunlop. DN, 5 June, 6 June, and 9 June 1865.

19. DN, 6 June 1865. This kind of "damage control" for public relations purposes had been standard fare since the 1820s. Just about every newspaper that cared to continue to receive advertising contracts from the company printed them as offered.

20. ANQ-M, Greffes de J.S. Hunter, No. 11309, 12 July 1865, Supplementary Declaration by Andrew Dunlop, Master of Steamer *Kingston*.

21. DN, 6 July 1865 quoting *Montreal Telegraph*.

22. DN, 17 July 1865.

23. DBW, 21 August 1865.

24. DBW, 5 September 1866.

25. DBW, 9 November and 11 November 1867.

26. Marine Museum of the Great Lakes, Calvin Company Coll. [henceforth MMGL, CC Coll.], Character Book, Cornwall.

27. DN, 19 July 1871. DBW, 26 October 1871.

28. DBW, 21 June, 22 June 1870. A rather confused news account in the spring of 1870 suggested that much of the *Kingston*'s machinery had been replaced. What it failed to note was that the company had equipped their new iron steamboat *Corsican*, with the salvaged engines of the *Grecian*. DBW, 24 March 1870.

29. The first testimony came from the coroner's inquest at Brockville, reported in *Brockville Recorder*, 20 June 1872. In the published coroner's inquest testimony Carmichael indicated that the flames came from stateroom 19. His testimony, reported in *Lower Canada Jurist*, Vol. 19, 269–75, Canadian Navigation Company (app.) and Andrew Hayes (res.), implied that it might

have been in the rented cabin that the fire started. The evidence in this case is available from the ANQ-M. This was appealed from Hayes v. Canadian Navigation Company. See also, ANQ-M, J.S. Hunter No. 5759, Extension of Protest by Captain Charles D. Carmichael, Master of Kingston, 20 June 1872.

30. DBW, 12 June 1872. Quote from *Brockville Recorder,* 13 June 1872. See also Canada, *Sessional Papers,* 1873, No. 8, 46, 196.

31. Company president, Sir Hugh Allan, had had a tough string of luck with ships lost in the same era: *Canadian* (below Quebec City, 1856), *Indian* (off Nova Scotia, 1859), *Hungarian* (off Cape Sable Island, 1861), *Canadian* (near Belle Isle, 1861), *North Briton* (on Mingan Island, 1861), *Anglo-Saxon* (off Cape Race 1863), *Norwegian* (St. Paul's Island, 1863), *Bohemian* (off Cape Elizabeth, 1864), *Jura* (in Mersey, 1864), and *Saint George* (near Seal Island, 1869). Appleton, *Ravenscrag,* 83–102, 198–211.

32. DBW, 12 June, 15 June 1872. At the annual meeting of the Canadian Navigation Company in February 1873 it was reported that only $32,000 had been received in insurance, and that the cost of rebuilding the *Kingston* would be $60,000. These numbers do not include the full range of liabilities and expenses attendant on paying off the passengers and crew and salvaging the hull. Nor do they begin to account for loss of business. DN, 8 February 1873. See also *Brockville Recorder,* 20 June 1872 for the companies that had reinsured the liability of Citizens' Insurance Company.

33. DBW, 13 June 1872 quoting *Montreal Star.* Rumour of the fire in the canal was revealed in the correspondence of "Sir Herbert" after the *Bavarian* disaster. DN, 25 November 1873.

34. Labour dispute from DN, 12 June 1872.

35. DN, 15 January and 5 February 1873.

36. *Lower Canada Jurist,* Vol. 19, 269–75, Canadian Navigation Company (app.) and Andrew Hayes (res.). This case was appealed from Hayes v. Canadian Navigation Company. The company would appear to have had the last word on this case. In 1874 the federal government passed "An Act Respecting Carriers by Water (Canada, *Statutes* 37 Vic., chap. 25) that relieved carrier from liability for loss of any goods by reason of fire or the dangers of navigation. It capped the liability for personal baggage at $500.

37. DBW, 11 July 1872.

Chapter 5: The *Bavarian*

1. ANQ-M, J.S. Hunter, number 18127, Contract & Agreement for building Boilers for steamer *Kingston* between W.C. White Esq. and the Canadian Navigation Company, stipulated for by Sir Hugh Allan, 21 October 1872. The specifications and technical drawings were attached to the contract (see Appendix B).

2. Erik Heyl, "The Steamboat *Kingston*: Was She Rebuilt into the Steamboat *Bavarian*?" *Inland Seas*, Vol. 16 (1960), 309–12. See also letters from Anna G. Young and correction by the author, Vol. 17 (1960), 79 and 81. Also Erik Heyl, *Early American Steamers* (the author), Vol. 3: 208. This may, in part, have been the result of a confused article in DBW, 4 April 1873 that reported the *Bavarian* as well as a new vessel, *Egyptian* rebuilt from the "old *Kingston*." The later was clearly being confused with *Bohemian*, which also came out that season.

3. *Evening Star* (Montreal), 6 May 1873. See also DN, 7 May and 8 May 1873.

4. DN, 25 November 1873.

5. DBW, 4 July 1873, ad.

6. *Democrat and Chronicle* (Rochester), 26 August 1873. *Union & Advertiser* (Rochester), 26 August 1873.(Thanks to Gerry Girvin for these references.)

7. The safety legislation required only two boats on ships under 200 tons that had to be capable of seating twenty people. For larger vessels, like the *Bavarian*, a third boat was required. One was to be "made of metal, fire-proof,... capable of sustaining, inside and out-side, fifty person, with life-lines attached to the gunwale at suitable distances." Province of Canada, *Statutes,* 22 Vict. (1859), cap. 19 "An Act to consolidate and amend the several laws regulating the Navigation of the Waters of Canada, and providing for the security of person and property thereon."

8. *The Merchant* (Bowmanville), 7 November 1873.

Notes

9. The testimony from the inquest was published in the following papers: *Globe*, 11 November, 19 November, 20 November, 21 November, 22 November, and 28 November 1873; *Gazette*, 18 November, 19 November, 20 November, 21 November, 22 November 1873. DN, 26 November, and 27 November 1873.

10. DN, 25 November 1873. "Sir Herbert" may well have been Herbert C. Jones, the lawyer who represented the interests of the late Mrs. Sibbald of Brockville at the Inquiry. (*Gazette*, 19 November 1873)

11. Report of Investigation, 360, 362–3.

12. "Burning of the Steamer *Bavarian*," *Gazette*, 21 November 1873.

13. *Gazette*, 20 November 1873.

14. *Gazette*, 21 November 1873.

15. Canada, *Statutes*, 46 Vict. (1883), cap. 28, Masters and Mates of Inland Vessels Act.

16. DBW, 11 December 1873. *Globe*, 11 December 1873.

17. *Gazette*, 18 November 1873.

18. *Gazette*, 18 November 1873.

19. Canada, *Statutes*, 37 Vict. (1874), chap. 30.

20. Report of Investigation, 361.

21. *Ibid.*, 363.

22. Canada, *Statutes*, 37 Vic. (1874) cap. 25 (liability of carriers by water); 38 Vic. (1875) cap. 29 (Extension of Seaman's Act of 1873); 46 Vic. (1883) cap. 28 (Masters and Mates of Inland Vessels).

    The extension of the Seaman's Act required all vessels, including steam, over twenty tons to have an agreement between master and crew. None have survived for the *Kingston/Bavarian/Algerian/Cornwall*.

The River Palace

Chapter 6: The *Algerian*

1. DBW, 7 November 1873.

2. DBW, 19 November 1873.

3. DN, 5 April 1862. Chancery Sale in Alexander Campbell, Orton Hancox, Robert Smith, and James Harvey v. Kingston Marine Railway and Wm. George Hinds, George Davidson, Alexander Campbell, John Carruthers, Alexander Gunn, John McKay, Donald McKay, George Thurston, Joseph Bruce, Michael Doran, Alexander Begg, George Barnsted, and James Gardiner. Final order dated 8 December 1860. See also Province of Canada, *Statutes*, 27 Vict. (1863), cap. 65, An Act Respecting the Kingston Marine Railway.

4. DBW, 10 June 1873. DN, 3 February, 17 February, 8 April 1874. Power was born on Prince Edward Island, raised in Quebec City, and later trained there and in New York. He had practiced in Quebec before superintending the Montreal shipyard of the St. Lawrence Engine Works for Bartley & Gilbert. He then formed a partnership with the Tate brothers. See DBW, 13 September 1881, 29 August 1899 for summaries of Power's career.

5. ANQ-M, Hunter, No. 19180, 2 January 1874, Contract and Agreement for building an engine between Ebenezer E. Gilbert, Esq. and the Canadian Navigation Company, stipulated for by Sir Hugh Allan. Enclosed specifications. The document is reproduced in Appendix B.

6. See obituary in *Canadian Society of Civil Engineers*, Vol. 3 (1889) 364–65. Inwood, 206–7. He later patented a system for "submarine rock blasting and excavation," which was used in a series of government contracts to deepen the rapids of the St. Lawrence. It might also be noted that Gilbert was a brother-in-law of the Honourable L.H. Holton, sometime Minister of Finance in the pre-Confederation government of Macdonald and Dorion. Inwood, *Canadian Charcoal Iron Industry*, 207.

7. Canada. Department of Consumer Affairs, Patent Office, No. 2618, 14 July 1873, to E.E. Gilbert for a patent for Improvements on Valve Motions. This also received U.S. Patent No. 143,819, 21 October 1873.

8. DBW, 17 April, 26 May, and 6 July 1874. DN, 16 April, 17 April, 23 June, 30 June, 2 July, and 7 July 1874.

Notes

9. QUA, Canada Steamship Lines [henceforth CSL] Papers, Vol. 183, *Richelieu and Ontario Navigation Company* (1885), 28, 31, and 33.

10. DBW, 17 October 1891.

11. *Globe*, 1 July 1881, 8.

12. DBW, 16 August 1875.

13. DBW, 16 August 1875.

14. DBW, 17 August, 20 August 1875. The Department of Marine and Fisheries, Statement of Wreck & Casualty for 1875, suggests a partial loss of only $200.

15. DBW, 13 October 1880.

16. On *Spartan*, see W.R. Wightman, "The Canadian Steam Packet Service of the Upper Lakes," *Inland Seas*, 46 (Winter 1990): 255. The *Gazette*, 21 September 1892 account is quoted at length in Peter Charlebois, *Sternwheelers & Sidewheelers: The Romance of Steamdriven Paddleboats in Canada* (Toronto: NC Press Limited, 1978), 72–73.

17. Lewis, "Canadian Navigation Company."

18. *The ABC Railway and Steamboat Travellers' Guide, No. 5* (August 1880), 78.

19. DBW, 4 August 1890. Among those on board for this trip were two former captains: Captain Clarke Hamilton, then Collector of Customs at Kingston, and Captain Thomas Howard, who had retired as superintendent of the R & O to become harbour master at Montreal.

20. J. Ross Robertson, *Landmarks of Toronto: A Collection of Historical Sketches of the Old Town of York from 1792 Until 1833, and of Toronto from 1834 to 1914* (Toronto: J. Ross Robertson, 1894–1914, six volumes.) Vol. 2, 977.

21. Captain Mac, *Canada, from the Lakes to the Gulf: The Country, Its People, Religions, Politics, Rulers and Its Apparent Future: Being a Compendium of Travel Through the Upper and Lower Provinces ...* (Montreal: For the author, 1881), 50.

22. This was confirmed some years later by the Donnellys in a discussion of changes in marine salvage in "Marine Wrecking Record During the 1918 Season," DBW, 9 December 1918, 9.

23. QUA, CSL, Vol. 15, 14 October 1879, 252.

24. QUA, CSL, Vol. 15, 12 December and 19 December 1882, 344–45.

25. QUA, CSL, Vol. 182, 20 August 1890, 75; *Ibid.*, 5 November 1890, 82; *Ibid.*, 10 November 1891, 135–36.

26. Robert Taggart, "The Role of the Paddle-wheel in Maritime History," *A.S.N.E. Journal*, (August 1958), 443–61, esp. 447. "Paddle Steamer," in Peter Kemp, ed., *The Oxford Companion to Ships and the Sea* (Oxford: Oxford University Press, 1988), 625. G.W. Hilton, R. Plummer, J. Jobe, *The Illustrated History of Paddle Steamers* (New York: Two Continents Publishing Group, 1976), 39.

27. QUA, CSL, Vol. 182, 9 December 1891, 141; *Ibid.*, Vol. 23, 25 August 1894, 240; *Ibid.*, Vol. 24, 8 August 1900, 322; *Ibid.*, 26 September 1900, 332. *Picton Gazette*, 10 May 1901.

28. QUA, CSL, Vol. 23, 20 March 1895, 228.

29. QUA, CSL, Vol. 182, 8 February 1890, 50.

30. DN, 10 July 1882. Canada, Sessional Papers, Department of Marine and Fisheries, Board of Steamboat Inspection, *Report,* Steam Vessels Inspected Quebec Division. 1887–1906.

31. QUA, CSL, Vol. 182, 21 October, 27 October, and 18 November 1892, 213–17.

32. DBW, 28 May 1880, quoting *Hamilton Times*.

33. QUA, CSL Papers, Vol. 183, *The Richelieu and Ontario Navigation Company* (Montreal: Imprimerie Générale, 1885), 15–16.

34. QUA, CSL, Vol. 23, 20 March 1895, 238.

Notes

35. DBW, 29 March 1898. This practice was also discussed in the wake of the *Bavarian* disaster.

36. QUA, CSL, Vol. 15, 10 October 1882, 340.

37. QUA, CSL, Vol. 15, 22 March 1884, 385.

38. ANQ-M, J.S. Hunter, No. 14811, Lease of Bar Saloons by the Canadian Navigation Company to Martin Finn, 2 April 1869; No. 15555, Lease of Bar Saloons by Canadian Navigation Co. to Martin Finn, 10 January 1870; No. 16752, Lease of Bar Saloons, The Canadian Navigation Co. to Martin Finn, 24 April 1871; No. 17615 Lease of Bar Saloons, Canadian Navigation Co. to Martin Finn, 6 March 1872. In 1883 Victor Olivon had chartered the bars as well as the restaurant at $500 a vessel. QUA, CSL Papers, Vol. 15, 17 March 1883, 351. The following season Jos. Monnette chartered the bars, paying $400 for each of the bars of the western steamers, including the *Algerian*. (*Ibid.*, 382.) *The Richelieu and Ontario Navigation Company*, (1885), 38.

39. ANQ-M, J.S. Hunter, No. 14811, 2 April 1869, Lease of Bar Saloons by the Canadian Navigation Company to Martin Finn.

40. See, for example, *QUA, CSL Papers, Vol. 15*, 29 March 1884, 386. *The Richelieu and Ontario Navigation Company*, (1885), 37, cites the Dominion News Company, C.R. Chisholm, manager as having the contract for $2,500 to sell books, advertisements, frames, etc. The News Company also paid $200 for the board of its news sellers.

41. DBW, 25 September 1877.

42. QUA, CSL, Vol. 15, 1 June and 3 June 1881, 306–7.

43. QUA, CSL, Vol. 15, February 1880, 262. Note that the higher reductions were on salaries over $3,000, while the 5 percent reduction was on salaries over $500. It was not clear whether those making less than $500 (the majority of the crew) were affected by this resolution at all.

44. QUA, CSL, Vol. 15, 5 June 1883, 259.

45. QUA, CSL, Vol. 182, 15 March 1893, 256.

46. QUA, CSL, Vol. 15, 25 February to 6 June 1882, 321–333.

47. QUA, CSL, Vol. 182, 3 October 1891, 127.

48. One has to be careful with the term "new leadership." When Louis Senécal died, the presidency was passed to Thomas McGreevy and then to N.K. Connolly and his brother Michael. All three with Senécal had been implicated in a series of highly political railway deals surrounding the various incarnations of Quebec's North Shore Railway. McGreevy and N.K. Connolly would go to jail in 1893 for defrauding the public treasury of some $3,000,000. For McGreevy see his biography in the DCB, Vol. 12, 626–31.

49. QUA, CSL, Vol. 182, 129–30 and 137–41.

50. QUA, CSL, Vol. 23, 14 February 1894, 44; *Ibid.*, 13 March 1894, 63. See also Anna G. Young, *Great Lakes' Saga: The Influence of One Family on the Development of Canadian Shipping on the Great Lakes, 1816–1931* (Owen Sound: Richardson, Bond & Wright Limited, 1965), 85–88.

51. QUA, CSL, Vol. 23, 21 March 1894, 66. Canada, *Statutes* 57–58 Vict. (1894), Chap. 105.

52. QUA, CSL, Vol. 23, 29 January 1895, 208; *Ibid.*, 19 February 1895, 214.

53. *Ibid.*, 16 October 1894, 169.

54. QUA, CSL, Vol. 24, 20 July 1897, 104.

55. *Ibid.*, 17 November 1897, 127.

56. Normand Lafrenière, *Canal building on the St. Lawrence River: Two Centuries of Work, 1779–1959* (Coteau-du-Lac National Historic Park Series, Booklet No. 1, Parks Canada, 1983), 45. The Soulanges canal was completed in 1899, the Cornwall enlargements in 1900, the Lachine enlargements in 1901 and the Williamsburg canals by 1903. George Washington Stephens, *The St. Lawrence Waterway Project: The Story of the St. Lawrence River as an International Highway for Water-borne Commerce* (Montreal: Louis Carrier & Co., 1930), 263–68.

Notes

57. QUA, CSL, Vol. 24, 8 August 1900, 322; *Ibid.*, 26 September 1900, 332.

58. QUA, CSL, Vol. 24, 1 February 1899, 216, contains a resolution to fit up the *Algerian* for this service. The evidence from Toronto Harbour Commission, RG2/6, Arrivals of Vessels, Vol. 5, 1894–1901, is that this service began in 1900.

59. QUA, CSL, Vol. 24, 26 September 1900, 332.

60. Toronto Harbour Commission, RG2/6, Arrivals of Vessels, Vol. 6, 1902–10.

Chapter 7: The Cornwall

1. QUA, CSL, Vol. 183, untitled document. See also *Ibid.*, Vol. 25, 22 December 1904, 156. Other changes at the same time included *Canada* to *Ste. Irenée*, *Cultivateur* to *St. Helen*, *Carolina* to *Murray Bay*, *Saguenay* to *Chicoutimi*, and *Virginia* to *Tadousac*.

2. Heyl, *Early American Steamers*, 3: 208.

3. "*Algerian*: Ship of the Month No. 158" *Scanner*, Vol. 20, No. 2, (November 1987), 11.

4. QUA, CSL, Vol. 25, 212.

5. *Le Sorelois*, 14 October 1904.

6. QUA, CSL, Vol. 25A, 48. *Le Sorelois* (13 April 1906) noted that captains would be named for the *Cornwall*, *Chicoutimi*, and *Belleville* "plus tard." Later that month, the *Cornwall* was actually put into service.

7. *The Richelieu and Ontario Navigation Company* (1885), 4–6. P.-André Sévigny, *Trade and Navigation on the Chambly Canal: A Historical Overview* (Studies in Archaeology, Architecture and History, Parks Canada, 1983), esp. 58–59.

8. QUA, CSL, Vol. 25A, 18 September 1907, 177. For her service in 1906 see *Le Sorelois*, 26 April 1906, 2 and 3.

9. *Ibid.*, 21 November 1907, 209. *Le Sorelois,* 3 May, and 22 November 1907.

10. QUA, CSL, Vol. 25A, 265.

11. *Ibid.*, 30 July 1908, 304.

12. *Ibid.*, 12 August 1909, 402.

13. *Ibid.*, 410 and 438. John O. Greenwood, *Namesakes, 1920-1929* (Freshwater Press, 1984), 135, shows the *Hamilton* cut down to a barge.

14. *Ibid.*, 19 May 1910, 497.

15. For the origins of CSL see Edgar Andrew Collard, *Passage to the Sea: The Story of Canada Steamship Lines* (Toronto: Doubleday Canada, 1991), esp. Chapter 1.

Chapter 8: The *Cornwall* and the Calvin Company

1. QUA, CC Coll., Series 1B, Box 55, *Railway and Marine World* to the Calvin Company, 10 February 1912. *Railway and Marine World,* March 1912, 157.

2. MMGL, CC Coll., Daily Journal, 4 December and 7 December 1911; Letter Book 22, Calvin Co. to Capt. Gilbert Johnston, R. & O.N. Co., 8 December 1911, 142.

3. Donald Swainson, *Garden Island.*

4. DBW, 3 August and 4 August 1881.

5. DBW, 21 August, 22, August, 23 August, and 25 August 1911.

6. MMGL, CC Coll., Daily Journal, 25 March, 30 March, and 3 April 1912. QUA, CC Coll., series 1B, Box 55, Thos. Brian to [J.D. Calvin], 15 April 1912.

7. QUA, CC Coll., Richelieu & Ontario Navigation Company to Calvin Company, Invoices dated 8 March, 14 March, 15 April, 29 April, 20 May, 13 June, 17 July, 3 September, and 14 September 1912. Also Series 3, Vol. 55, Day Book, 1908-1923, 359, 362, and 372.

Notes

8. MMGL, CC Coll., (980–150–304g), file July 1912, Bill of Sale of the *Cornwall*, 23 July 1912. See also CSL, Vol. 183, "Release of the Steamer *Cornwall* by the Montreal Trust Co. in favor of the Richelieu & Ont. Navigation Co., 25 June 1912." This document suggests that the Montreal Trust still had a right to the vessel despite another document in the same box, which is an official Bill of Sale of *Cornwall* from Montreal Trust & Deposit Company to the Richelieu & Ontario Navigation Company for $1.00, dated 30 October 1907.

9. MMGL, CC Coll., Letterbook 22, Hiram A. Calvin to Capt. Gilbert Johnston, 10 May 1912, 465.

10. *Ibid.*, H. A. Calvin to Xavier Hamelin, 21 May 1912, 495.

11. MMGL, CC Coll., Character Book of the Calvin Company Fleet. See also MMGL, Port of Kingston Customs Collection, *Cornwall* file, "Certificate of Survey," Kingston, 13 May 1912. Note that other documents in the same file show a nominal horse power of eighty-eight (Transcript of Register for Transmission to Registrar-General of Shipping and Seamen, 7 August 1912) and 65 1/2 (Declaration of Ownership on behalf of a Body Corporate, 21 November 1912).

12. MMGL, CC Coll., Inland Marine Policy of Insurance, Dale & Co., No. 1843, 4 May 1912; Letterbook 22, Calvin Co. to Dale & Co., 21 March 1912, 371.

13. MMGL, CC Coll., Letterbook 22, Steam Pumps & Wrecking Plant, 31 December 1912, 899.

14. QUA, CC Coll., Series IV, Vol. 80, Minute Book, 27 July 1912, 119.

15. M. Stephen Salmon, "British Competition: 'Canadian' Great Lakes Vessels Built in United Kingdom Shipyards, 1854–1965," *FreshWater*, Vol. 5, No. 2. (1990), 20–26.

16. MMGL, CC Coll., Letterbook, Invoice, Underwriters and Owners Barge *Hiawatha* & Cargo to the Calvin Company Limited, 29 June 1912, 612.

17. MMGL, CC Coll., Letterbook 23, Hiram A. Calvin to J.W. Norcross, October 1913, 501; *Ibid.*, 29 October 1913, 501; Memorandum of Sale, Calvin Co. to Sandford C. Calvin, 29 October 1913; Daily Journal, 29 October 1913.

18. DBW, 8 December 1913. See also MMGL, Customs House Collection, *Cornwall* file.

19. DBW, 9 December 1913, 5.

CHAPTER 9: THE *CORNWALL* AND THE DONNELLY SALVAGE AND WRECKING COMPANY

1. James A. Cowan, "Salvaged! The Saga of the Donnellys who for sixty years have been snatching ships from Davy Jones," *MacLean's Magazine*, 13 June 1928, 36.

2. QUA, CC Coll., Series 4, Vol. 80, Minute Book, 4 October 1915, 148.

3. Captain John Donnelly "One of the Early Boats," *Kingston Whig-Standard*, 29 June 1927. Mills reports the *Raftsman* (No. 2383, Garden Island, 1840) as broken up in 1854 and the *William Johnston* (No. 3097, Garden Island, 1878) as two separate vessels. The first was 100 feet overall, the second initially seventy-three feet; the first a paddlewheeler, the second a screw propeller.

4. DBW, 2 November 1917.

5. DBW, 25 October 1919.

6. Quote from "T.P. Phelan revisited," *Scanner*, (October 1990), 14. See also Ronald F. Beaupre, "Rosamond Billett and *T.P. Phela*n," (Ship of the Month No. 182), *Scanner*, (April 1990), 4–14. DBW, 18 August, 20 August, 25 August, 30 August, and 31 August 1920.

7. On the regulatory environment of Canadian shipping in the 1920s see two papers by M. Stephen Salmon, "'Fool Propositions': Mackenzie King, the Dominion Marine Association and the Inland Water Freight Rates Act of 1923," *FreshWater*, Vol. 2, No. 1 (Summer 1987), 8–19;. and "'Rank Imitation and the Sincerest Flattery': The Dominion Marine Association and the Revision of the Canadian Coasting Regulations, 1922–1936," *The Northern Mariner/Le Marin du nord*, Vol. 1, No. 3 (July 1991), 1–24. On the fate of Canada's largest carrier in those years see Edgar Andrew Collard, *Passage to the Sea: The Story of Canada Steamship Lines* (Toronto: Doubleday Canada

Notes

Ltd., 1991), esp. Chapter 3. On the great storm of 1913 see Frank Barcus, *Freshwater Fury,* (Detroit: Wayne State University Press, 1960).

8. *Kingston Whig-Standard,* 30 September, 4 October, 17 November, and 19–29 December 1921.

9. *Kingston Whig-Standard,* 1 December 1922, 18 May 1923, 19 May 1924, and 27 April 1925. The article in the *Palladium* (Oswego), 29 April 1925, about the trouble at Fairhaven seems to have been lifted from the marine column of the *Kingston Whig-Standard.* (Our thanks to Gerry Girvin for the reference.)

CHAPTER 10: THE *CORNWALL* AND SIN-MAC LINES LIMITED

1. *Canadian Railway and Marine World,* 32 (January 1929), 52.

2. *Canadian Railway and Marine World,* 32 (February 1929), 115.

3. *Canadian Railway and Marine World,* 32 (May 1929), 330. *Kingston Whig-Standard,* 8 January, 2 February 1929. Donnelly was originally reported to have been against the merger, and in the announcement of his firm's inclusion, uncharacteristically had nothing to say to the local press.

4. *Canadian Railway and Marine World,* (February 1932), 106.

5. *Canadian Railway and Marine World,* 37 (November 1934) 503; *Ibid.,* 38 (May 1935), 236.

APPENDIX A: CAPTAINS

1. DN, 1 January 1853, 25 January 1858, 5 August 1858, 8 November 1859, 28 April 1856, 13 February 1862, 9 October 1861, 22 July 1862, and 9 May 1863. *Weekly British Whig,* 21 March 1861, 19 April, and 26 April 1861. DBW, 14 April 1866 and 10 November 1915. QUA, CSL Papers, Vol. 172, Canadian Inland Steam Navigation Company, Dividend Book. With 140 of the 1,680 outstanding shares on 3 February 1863, Clarke owned just under 10 percent of the company. See same volume: "List of Shareholders in the Canadian Navigation Co'y, February 4th, 1874." James Croil, *Steam Navigation:*

The River Palace

Its Relation to the Commerce of Canada and the United States, (Toronto: William Briggs, 1898), 327. Cataraqui Cemetery, Kingston. Edward Marion Chadwick, *Ontarian Families: Genealogies of United Empire Loyalist and other Pioneer Families of Upper Canada* (rep. Belleville: Mika Silk Screening, 1972), 148. *Railway and Marine World*, December 1915, 492.

2. DBW, 12 April 1855, 4 May 1849, 30 March 1850, 18 May 1857, 9 October 1861, 14 April 1864, 10 May 1867, 18 July, 31 October 1868, and 20 May 1869. DN, 9 December 1854, 16 July 1869, 8 October 1870, 26 April 1871, 6 September 1871, 7 September 1871, and 10 September 1875. QUA, CSL, Vol. 172.

3. *Montreal Gazette*, 11 April 1898, 3. *British Whig*, 30 November 1850, 3 April 1861, 15 March 1864, and 2 February 1874. LAC, RG 12, A1, Vol. 206, No. 82, 173–86; *Ibid.*, Vol. 179, 50. QUA, CSL Coll., Vol. 172.

4. Farrell was aged thirty-three in 1854 according to Harvard University, Baker Library, R.G. Dun & Co. papers, Canada, Vol. 15, 121, 239. DBW, 27 June 1849, 28 March 1850, 26 April 1851, 22 March and 14 April 1855, 10 April 1858, 13 January 1859, 15 March 1862, 5 April 1862, 14 April 1863, 22 July 1871, 20 February and 20 April 1872, and 28 June 1880. C.M. Johnston, "John Farrell," DCB, Vol. 10, 277–78. DN, 21 April 1855, 16 May 1856, 30 March 1858, (Kingston assizes), and 29 April 1858. *Canada Gazette*, 1857, 209. QUA, CSL, Vol. 172.

5. Thomas Flynn, *Directory of the City of Kingston for 1857*, (Kingston, ON: T.W. Robinson, 1857), 56. QUA, CSL Papers, Vol. 182, 21 January 1892, 151; *Ibid.*, 16 August 1892, 201; *Ibid.*, 22 February 1893, 240; QUA, CSL Papers, Vol. 23, 21 February 1894, 47; *Ibid.*, 7 April 1896, 389; QUA, CSL Papers, Vol. 24, 31 March 1897, 82; *Ibid.*, 1 March 1899, 227; *Ibid.*, 6 April 1900, 300; *Ibid.*, 6 March 1901, 356; QUA, CSL Papers, Vol. 25, 21 March 1902, 9; QUA, CSL Papers, Vol. 25A, 19 September 1907, 177. Toronto Harbour Commission, RG2/6 Arrivals of Vessels, Vol. 5, 1894–1901. *Railway and Marine World*, October 1907, 767–69. *Le Sorelois* (Sorel), 28 April 1905, 2. DBW, 13 May 1876, 6 March 1877, 19 December 1879, 31 March 1890, 21 February 1918, and 22 February 1918.

6. Marriage licences, York County, 1864, 2: 135. DN, 8 November 1873 (quoting *Toronto Mail*). *Toronto City Directory, 1868–9* (Toronto: W.C. Chewett & Co., 1868) 162. *Montreal Gazette*, 21 November 1873.

Notes

7. Census of Canada, 1861, Kingston, Rideau ward, 207. Frontenac County, Surrogate Court Register, 1871–1903, 61, No. 1564. Also will. DBW, 17 October 1891.*Trade & Shipping on the Great Lakes*, 77.

8. LAC, RG 12, Vol. 1450, Certificates of Masters & Mates, 7, No. 96. *Kingston Whig-Standard*, 29 June 1927, 14. QUA, CSL Papers, Vol. 183, *The Richelieu and Ontario Navigation Company* (Montreal: Imprimerie Générale, 1885); QUA, CSL Papers, Vol. 182, *Ibid.*, 22 February 1890, 53; *Ibid.*, 28 December 1891, 147; *Ibid.*, 12 October 1892, 209; *Ibid.*, 22 February 1893, 240; *Ibid.*, 6 June 1894, 95; QUA, CSL Papers, Vol. 24, 21 September 1897, 110. *Railway and Marine World*, (April 1908), 297. *Canadian Railway and Marine World*, August 1917, 500; *Ibid.*, September 1927, 557. DBW, 8 January 1898 and 28 May 1928.

9. LAC, RG 12, Vol. 1450, Certificates of Masters & Mates, No. 96, 7. DBW, 14 June 1892 and 7 June 1921, 7. QUA, CSL Papers, Vol. 183, *The Richelieu and Ontario Navigation Company* (Montreal: Imprimerie Générale, 1885);QUA, CSL Papers, Vol. 182, *Ibid.*, 16 August 1892, 201; *Ibid.*, 11 July 1893, 333; QUA, CSL Papers, Vol. 24, 1 March 1899, 227; *Ibid.*, 6 March 1901, 356; QUA, CSL Papers, Vol. 25, 21 March 1902, 9. *Railway and Marine World*, May 1907, 351.

10. QUA, CSL Papers, Vol. 183, *The Richelieu and Ontario Navigation Company* (Montreal: Imprimerie Generale, 1885); QUA, CSL Papers, Vol. 23, 21 February 1894, 47; QUA, CSL Papers, Vol. 24, 23 February 1898, 151; *Ibid.*, 1 March 1899, 227; *Ibid.*, 6 April 1900, 300; *Ibid.*, 6 March 1901, 356; QUA, CSL Papers, Vol. 25, 21 March 1902, 9. DBW, 16 May 1892 and 24 March 1899.

APPENDIX C: ACCIDENTS

1. DN, 4 September 1866.

2. DBW, 9 October 1867.

3. DN, 8 November, 15 November, and 20 November 1867.

4. DBW, 26 October 1871.

5. *Democrat & Chronicle*, (Rochester), 26 August 1873. *Union & Advertiser*, (Rochester), 26 August 1873.

6. DBW, 15 September 1875.

7. DBW, 2 September, 7 September, 8 September, 9 September, 19 September, 20 September, 25 September, 2 October 1876, and 13 February 1877.

8. QUA, CSL, Vol. 15, 31 October 1882, 341.

9. DBW, 28 June 1884.

10. DBW, 27 July 1885.

11. DBW, 8 September 1885 quoting *Marine Record*.

12. DBW, 13 August 1887.

13. *Brockville Recorder*, 1 August, 2 August, 3 August, 5 August, 6 August, and 7 August 1889. *Montreal Gazette*, 2 August 1889. The Dept. of Marine & Fisheries, Statement of Wreck and Casualty for 1889 suggests a loss of about $300.

14. *Brockville Recorder*, 7 September 1889, quoting *Rochester Herald*, 4 September 1889.

15. DBW, 17 June 1890.

16. DBW, 19 August, 22 August, and 25 August 1890.

17. DBW, 12 September 1890.

18. DBW, 9 July 1891.

19. QUA, CSL, Vol. 182, 25 May 1892, 186.

20. DN, 10 June 1892.

21. DBW, 14 June 1892.

Notes

22. *Ibid.*

23. CSL, Vol. 182, 22 June 1892, 194; *Ibid.*, 16 August 1892, 201; *Ibid.*, 28 December 1892, 222.

24. QUA, Canada Steamship Engineering Ltd., Coll. 2246, Vol. 2, Dry Dock Entry Book 1891–1922.

25. QUA, CSL, Vol. 182, 24 October 1893, 380.

26. *Gazette,* 9 August and 10 August 1894. QUA, CSL, Vol. 23, 8 August 1894, 128.

27. DBW, 24 August 1894.

28. DBW, 2 July 1896.

29. DBW, 10 September and 11 September 1896.

30. DBW, 5 August and 7 August 1897.

31. DBW, 19 July and 21 July 1898.

32. DBW, 5 August 1898.

33. DBW, 16 August 1898.

34. Canada. *Sessional Papers,* 1900, No. 11, Department of Marine and Fisheries, Steamboat Inspection Report, Casualty Report for 1898/99. DBW, 1 March 1900 reporting Langlois v. Canadian Forwarding and Export Company.

35. DBW, 30 June 1900.

36. DBW, 4 June 1902.

Appendix D: Salvage Work

1. MMGL, CC Coll., Letterbook 22, Underwriters & Owners Barge *Winnipeg* & Cargo to Calvin Company Limited, 29 June 1912, 593, corrected 612.

2. *Ibid.*

3. DBW, 22 June, and 24 June 1912. MMGL, CC Coll., Letterbook 22, Underwriters & Owners Str. *Alexandria* to Calvin Company, 26 June 1912, 583. Daily Journal, 1912, 22 June 1912 [ordered 6:45 a.m., left 8 a.m., back 11:00 a.m.].

4. DBW, 26 August, 27 August, 29 August, 30 August, 3 September, and 9 September 1912. They finally retrieved the *Britannic* from Weaver's Point, but at a cost of $9,367.60. MMGL, CC Coll., Letterbook 22, Underwriters and Owners Steamer *Britannic* to the Calvin Company Limited, 31 October 1912, 824.

5. DBW, 9 September, 10 September 1912. QUA, CC Coll., ser. III, Vol. 55, Day Book, 1908–23, 376, 431.

6. DBW, 16 September, 17 September 1912. QUA, CC Coll., Vol. 55, 402. MMGL, CC Coll., Letterbook 22, Underwriters & Owners Str. *Caspian* to the Calvin Company Limited, 25 September 1912, 744.

7. DBW, 23 September, 24 September 1912. QUA, CC Coll., Vol. 55, 402.

8. DBW, 26 October, 29 October 1912. QUA, CC Coll., Vol. 55, 408. MMGL, CC Coll, Letterbook 22, Underwriters and Owners Str. *Rock Ferry* to the Calvin Company Limited, 30 October 1912, 819.

9. DBW, 25 November 1912. QUA, CC Coll., Vol. 55, 415. MMGL, CC Coll., 23–27 November 1912; Letterbook 22, Invoice, Motor Ship *Toiler* to the Calvin Company Limited, 28 November 1912, 869; *Ibid.*, Letterbook 23, Invoice, Underwriters & Owners Motor Ship *Toiler* & Cargo To the Calvin Company Limited, 28 November 1912, 28 ($1,308).

10. MMGL, CC Coll., Letterbook 23, Underwriters and Owners Barge *Winnipeg* and Cargo to the Calvin Company Limited, 2 July 1913, 385 (for $697.90).

11. MMGL, CC Coll., Letterbook 23 Underwriters & Owners Str. *Olcott* to the Calvin Company, 10 July 1913, 335. Daily Journal, 1913, 5–6 July 1913.

12. MMGL, CC Coll., Daily Journal 1913, 8–9 July 1913. DBW, 5 July, 8 July, and 9 July 1913.

Notes

13. MMGL, CC Coll., Letterbook 23, Underwriters & Owners Barge *Quebec* and Cargo to the Calvin Company Limited 2 August 1913, 388; also *Ibid.*, Calvin Company to Dale & Co., Montreal, 373. See also, DBW 2 August 1913.

14. MMGL, CC Coll., Letterbook 23, Underwriters & Owners Str. *North King* To the Calvin Company Limited, 16 August 1913, 400, ($289.09); Daily Journal, 15 August 1913; DBW, 15 August 1913.

15. DBW, 15 September and 21 September 1906; 10–20 June 1907; and 13–21 November 1911.

16. DBW, 1 November and 3 November 1913. MMGL, CC Coll., Letterbook 23, Underwriters & Owners Barge *Cornwall* & Cargo to Sandford C. Calvin, 10 November 1913, 530.

17. MMGL, CC Coll., Daily Journal, 11–12 November 1913; *Ibid.*, Letterbook 23, Underwriters & Owners Str. *McKinstry* & Cargo to Sandford C. Calvin, 19 November 1913, 535. DBW, 12 November, and 13 November 1913.

18. MMGL, CC Coll., Letterbook 23, Underwriters and Owners Steamer *Hecla* to Sandford C. Calvin, 6 December 1913, 553; Daily Journal, 18 November and 21 November 1913. DBW, 18 November, 21 November, 22 November, 25 November, 1 December, 2 December, and 5 December 1913.

19. DBW, 27 April 1914, 6.

20. DBW, 30 April 1914, 1 and 5.

21. DBW, 30 April 1914, 5; *Ibid.*, 4 May 1914, 4.

22. DBW, 22 May 1914, 2 [mistakenly the *Niagara*]; *Ibid.*, 26 May 1914, 2; *Ibid.*, 28 May 1914, 2.

23. DBW, 11 July 1914, 8; *Ibid.*, 14 July 1914, 3; *Ibid.*, 18 July 1914, 8.

24. DBW, 22 July 1914, 2; *Ibid.*, 23 July 1914, 5.

25. DBW, 19 August 1914, 2; *Ibid.*, 20 August 1914, 6.

26. DBW, 18 September 1914, 5; *Ibid.*, 21 September 1914, 4.

27. DBW, 22 September 1914, 5.

28. DBW, 24 September 1914, 5; *Ibid.*, 26 September 1914, 2; *Ibid.*, 28 September 1914, 5.

29. DBW, 1 May 1915, 5; *Ibid.*, 4 May 1915, 5.

30. DBW, 20 May 1915, 2; *Ibid.*, 22 May 1915, 8.

31. DBW, 7 June 1915, 8.

32. DBW, 13 September 1915, 3.

33. DBW, 27 September 1915, 1; *Ibid.*, 30 September 1915, 2.

34. DBW, 19 October 1915, 5; *Ibid.*, 20 October 1915, 8; *Ibid.*, 25 October 1915, 5.

35. DBW, 18 May 1916, 2; *Ibid.*, 19 May 1916, 2; *Ibid.*, 22 May 1916, 2; *Ibid.*, 23 May 1916, 2.

36. DBW, 14 August 1916, 5.

37. DBW, 23 August 1916, 2; *Ibid.*, 24 August 1916, 2; *Ibid.*, 28 August 1916, 2.

38. DBW, 28 August 1916, 2.

39. DBW, 15 November 1916, 5; *Ibid.*, 16 November 1916, 2; *Ibid.*, 18 November 1916, 6.

40. DBW, 27 April 1917, 2; *Ibid.*, 1 May 1917, 5; *Ibid.*, 4 May 1917, 5; *Ibid.*, 8 May 1917, 6.

41. DBW, 8 May 1917, 6.

42. DBW, 8 May 1917, 6.

43. DBW, 15 May 1917, 5; *Ibid.*, 16 May 1917, 2 and 6.

44. DBW, 22 May 1917, 2.

45. DBW, 22 August 1917, 2; *Ibid.*, 28 August 1917, 2 and 6.

46. DBW, 17 September 1917, 5; *Ibid.*, 20 September 1917, 2.

47. DBW, 27 September 1917, 5.

48. DBW, 15 October 1917, 3; *Ibid.*, 19 October 1917, 2.

49. DBW, 25 October 1917, 2; *Ibid.*, 26 October 1917, 16.

50. DBW, 30 October 1917, 2; *Ibid.*, 1 November 1917, 5; *Ibid.*, 3 November 1917, 10; *Ibid.*, 6 November 1917, 5 and 8.

51. DBW, 28 April 1919, 3.

52. Almost daily reports appeared in the DBW from 26 August to 19 September 1919.

53. DBW, 27 September 1919, 2; *Ibid.*, 29 September 1919, 2; *Ibid.*, 30 September 1919, 7; *Ibid.*, 1 October 1919, 7; *Ibid.*, 3 October 1919, 2.

54. DBW, 11 May 1920, 2; *Ibid.*, 12 May 1920, 2.

55. DBW, 2 July 1920, 2.

56. DBW, 17 September 1920, 14; *Ibid.*, 22 September 1920, 13.

57. DBW, 3 November 1920, 2.

58. DBW, 30 April 1921, 20; *Ibid.*, 2 May 1921, 3.

59. DBW, 11 July 1921, 2; *Ibid.*, 12 July 1921, 2; *Ibid.*, 13 July 1921, 2.

60. DBW, 15 August 1921, 11; *Ibid.*, 17 August 1921, 2; *Ibid.*, 18 August 1921, 2.

61. DBW, 29 September 1921, 4; *Ibid.*, 30 September 1921, 5; *Ibid.*, 3 October 1921, 2; *Ibid.*, 4 October 1921, 2.

62. DBW, 17 November 1921, 15; *Ibid.*, 19 November 1921, 7; *Ibid.*, 21 November 1921, 2; *Ibid.*, 23 November 1921, 3; *Ibid.*, 27 March 1922, 1; *Ibid.*, 10 May 1922, 1; *Ibid.*, 11 May 1922, 15.

63. DBW, practically daily from 19 December to 29 December 1921. See especially 28 December 1921, 1 and 11.

64. DBW, 16 November 1922, 2; *Ibid.*, 17 November 1922, 18; *Ibid.*, 18 November 1922, 2; *Ibid.*, 20 November 1922, 15; *Ibid.*, 21 November 1922, 14; *Ibid.*, 22 November 1922, 2; *Ibid.*, 23 November 1922, 7; *Ibid.*, 25 November 1922, 18; *Ibid.*, 27 November 1922, 2; *Ibid.*, 28 November 1922, 2; *Ibid.*, 30 November 1922, 15; *Ibid.*, 1 December 1922, 14; *Ibid.*, 2 December 1922, 5.

65. DBW, 18 November 1923, 2; *Ibid.*, 19 November 1923, 20.

66. DBW, 19 May 1924, 2.

67. DBW, 27 April 1925, 11. *Palladium* (Oswego), 29 April 1925, 2. (Thanks to Gerry Girvin for this last reference.)

Bibliography

PRIMARY SOURCES:

Manuscript Collections

Archives nationales du Québec — Montréal
    Court of Queen's Bench

Canada, Department of Consumer Affairs
    Patent Office Records

Harvard University, Baker Library
    R.G. Dun & Co. papers

Library and Archives Canada
    RG12, Department of Transport

Marine Museum of the Great Lakes
    Calvin Company Collection
    Customs House Collection, *Cornwall* file

Ontario Archives
    Niagara Historical Society Papers
    Marriage licences, York County

Queen's University Archives
    Calvin Company
    Canada Steamship Engineering Ltd., Coll. 2246
    Canada Steamship Lines
    James Sutherland Papers

Toronto Harbour Commission
    RG2/6, Arrivals of Vessels

University of Glasgow Archives
    Upper Clyde Shipbuilding

Newspapers

Argus (Kingston)
Buffalo Daily Republic
British Whig (Kingston) also *Daily British Whig* and *Weekly British Whig*
Brockville Recorder
Daily News (Kingston)
Democrat and Chronicle (Rochester)
Evening Star (Montreal)
Globe (Toronto)
Kingston Whig-Standard
The Merchant (Bowmanville)
Montreal Gazette
Palladium (Oswego)
Picton Gazette
Le Sorelois (Sorel)
Union & Advertiser (Rochester)
Upper Canada Herald (Kingston)

Journals

Canadian Illustrated News
Canadian Society of Civil Engineers
Frank Leslie's Illustrated Newspaper
Illustrated London News
Lower Canada Jurist

Bibliography

New York Illustrated News
Railway and Marine World (later *Canadian Railway and Marine World*)

Government Publications

Province of Canada, Commission Appointed to Inquire into the Affairs of the Grand Trunk Railway, *Report* (1861)
Province of Canada. Legislative Council. *Journals*
Province of Canada, *Statutes*
Canada, *Sessional Papers*

Books

The ABC Railway and Steamboat Travellers' Guide.

A British Canadian [Henry J. Morgan], *The Tour of H.R.H. the Prince of Wales through British America and the United States.* Montreal: John Lovell, 1860.

Captain Mac, *Canada, from the Lakes to the Gulf: The Country, Its People, Religions, Politics, Rulers and Its Apparent Future: Being a Compendium of Travel Through the Upper and Lower Provinces, …* Montreal: for the author, 1881.

Cellem, Robert, comp., *Visit of His Royal Highness the Prince of Wales to the British North American Provinces and the United States, in the Year 1860.* Toronto: Henry Rowsell, 1861.

Chadwick, Edward Marion, *Ontarian Families: Genealogies of United Empire Loyalist and Other Pioneer Families of Upper Canada.* Rep. Belleville: Mika Silk Screening, 1972.

Cornwallis, Kinahan, *Royalty in the New World; or the Prince of Wales in America.* New York: M. Doolady, 1860.

Croil, James, *Steam Navigation: Its Relation to the Commerce of Canada and the United States.* Toronto: William Briggs, 1898.

Englehart, Gardner D., *Journal of the Progress of H.R.H. the Prince of Wales.* [London, 1860?]

Flynn, Thomas, *Directory of the City of Kingston for 1857.* Kingston: T.W. Robinson, 1857.

Grant, George M., ed., *Picturesque Canada.* Toronto: Art Publishing Co., 1881–82.

Green's Marine Directory of the Great Lakes. Cleveland: Fred W. Green, 1916.

Lovell, John, *The Canada Directory for 1857-58: Containing Names of Professional and Business Men, and of the Principal Inhabitants, in the Cities, Towns and Villages Throughout the Province : Alphabetical Directories of Banks, Benevolent and Religious Societies.* Montreal: John Lovell, 1857.

Memoirs and Portraits of One Hundred Glasgow Men Who Have Died During the Last Thirty Years, and in Their Lives Did Much to Make the City What It Now Is. Glasgow: J. Maclehose, 1886.

Montreal Business Sketches with a Description of the City of Montreal, Its Public Buildings and Places of Interest and the Grand Trunk Works at Point St. Charles, Victoria Bridge &c. &c. Montreal: Canada Railway Advertising Company, 1861.

Montreal in 1856: A Sketch Prepared for the Celebration of the Opening of the Grand Trunk Railway of Canada. Montreal: John Lovell, 1856.

Richelieu & Ontario Navigation Co., *From Niagara to the Sea.* Printed by The Matthews-Northrup Co., Buffalo, NY, 1901.

Toronto City Directory, 1868-9. Toronto: W.C. Chewett & Co., 1868.

Secondary Sources

Books

Appleton, Thomas E., *Ravenscrag: The Allan Royal Mail Line.* Toronto: McClelland & Stewart, 1974.

Bibliography

Barcus, Frank, *Freshwater Fury*. Detroit: Wayne State University Press, 1960.

Charlebois, Peter, *Sternwheelers & Sidewheelers: The Romance of Steamdriven Paddleboats in Canada*. Toronto: NC Press Limited, 1978.

Collard, Edgar Andrew, *Passage to the Sea: The Story of Canada Steamship Lines*. Toronto: Doubleday Canada, 1991.

Corlett, Ewan, *The Iron Ship: The Story of Brunel's SS Great Britain*. London: Conway Maritime Press, 2nd ed., 1990.

Currie, A.W., *The Grand Trunk Railway of Canada*. Toronto: University of Toronto Press, 1957.

Dictionary of Canadian Biography. Toronto: University of Toronto Press, 1966-2005, 15 vols.

Greenhill, Basi, *The Life and Death of the Merchant Sailing Ship, 1815-1965*. National Maritime Museum, The Ship, Vol. 7, London: Her Majesty's Stationery Office, 1980.

Greenwood, John O., *Namesakes, 1920-1929*. Freshwater Press, 1984.

Guillet, Edwin C., *Cobourg, 1798-1948*. Oshawa: Goodfellow Printing Co., 1948.

Heyl, Erik, *Early American Steamers*. Published by the author, 1953-69.

Hilton, G.W., Plummer, R. and Jobe, J., *The Illustrated History of Paddle Steamers*. New York: Two Continents Publishing Group, 1976.

History of the Great Lakes. Chicago: J.H. Beers, 1899.

Hume, John R., *Workshop of the British Empire: Engineering and Shipbuilding in the West of Scotland*. London: Heinemann, 1977.

Inwood, Kris E., *The Canadian Charcoal Iron Industry, 1870-1914*. New York: Garland Publishing Inc., 1986.

Kemp, Peter, ed., *The Oxford Companion to Ships and the Sea*. Oxford: Oxford

University Press, 1988.

Lafrenière, Normand, *Canal Building on the St. Lawrence River: Two Centuries of Work, 1779-1959.* (Coteau-du-Lac National Historic Park Series, Booklet No. 1: Parks Canada, 1983.)

McCullough, A.B., *Money and Exchange in Canada to 1900.* Toronto, ON : Published by Dundurn Press in cooperation with Parks Canada and the Canadian Govt. Pub. Centre, Supply and Services Canada, 1984.

Mills, James Cooke, *Our Inland Seas: Their Shipping & Commerce for Three Centuries.* Chicago: A.C. McClurg & Co., 1910, rep. 1976.

Robertson, J. Ross, *Landmarks of Toronto: A Collection of Historical Sketches of the Old Town of York from 1792 Until 1833, and of Toronto from 1834 to 1914.* Toronto: J. Ross Robertson, 1894-1914, six volumes.

Sévigny, P.-André, *Trade and Navigation on the Chambly Canal: A Historical Overview.* Studies in Archaeology, Architecture and History, Parks Canada, 1983.

Stephens, George Washington, *The St. Lawrence Waterway Project: The Story of the St. Lawrence River as an International Highway for Water-borne Commerce.* Montreal: Louis Carrier & Co., 1930.

Swainson, Donald, *Garden Island: A Shipping Empire.* Kingston: Marine Museum of the Great Lakes at Kingston, n.d.

Tulchinsky, Gerald, ed., *To Preserve and Defend: Essays on Kingston in the Nineteenth Century.* Montreal: McGill-Queen's University Press, 1976.

Walker, Fred M., *Song of the Clyde: A History of Clyde Shipbuilding.* Cambridge: Patrick Stephens, 1984.

Young, Anna G., *Great Lakes' Saga: The Influence of One Family on the Development of Canadian Shipping on the Great Lakes, 1816-1931.* Owen Sound, ON: Richardson, Bond & Wright Limited, 1965.

Bibliography

Articles

[Bascom, Jay] "*Algerian:* Ship of the Month No. 158" in *Scanner,* Vol. 20, No. 2, (November 1987).

———, "T.P. Phelan revisited," in *Scanner,* (October 1990).

Beaupre, Ronald F., "*Rosamond Billett* and *T.P. Phelan,*" (Ship of the Month No. 182), in *Scanner,* Vol. 22, No. 7 (April 1990).

Cowan, James A., "Salvaged! The Saga of the Donnellys Who for Sixty Years Have Been Snatching Ships from Davy Jones," in *MacLean's Magazine,* 13 June 1928.

Heyl, Erik, "The Steamboat *Kingston:* Was She Rebuilt into the Steamboat *Bavarian?*" in *Inland Seas,* Vol. 16 (1960).

Lewis, Walter, "The Canadian Navigation Company, 1861-1875" in *FreshWater,* Vol. 1, No. 1 (Spring 1986).

———, "Steamboat Promotion and Changing Technology: the Careers of James Sutherland and the *Magnet,*" in *Ontario History,* 77 (September 1985).

———, "Steamboats in the Ice," *Beaver,* Vol. 70, No. 6 (December 1990-January 1991).

MacDermaid, Anne, "The Visit of the Prince of Wales to Kingston in 1860," in *Historic Kingston,* 21 (1973).

Musham, H.A. "Early Great Lakes Steamboats: Warships and Iron Hulls, 1841-1846," in *American Neptune,* Vol. 8 (April 1948).

———, "'Fool Propositions': Mackenzie King, the Dominion Marine Association and the Inland Water Freight Rates Act of 1923," in *FreshWater,* Vol. 2, No. 1 (Summer 1987).

———, "'Rank Imitation and the sincerest flattery:' The Dominion Marine Association and the Revision of the Canadian Coasting Regulations, 1922-1936," in *The Northern Mariner/Le Marin du nord,* Vol. 1, No. 3 (July 1991).

Salmon, M. Stephen, "British Competition: 'Canadian' Great Lakes Vessels built in United Kingdom Shipyards, 1854–1965," in *FreshWater*, Vol. 5, No. 2. (1990).

Taggart, Robert, "The Role of the Paddle-wheel in Maritime History," *A.S.N.E. Journal*, (August 1958).

Wightman, W.R., "The Canadian Steam Packet Service of the Upper Lakes," *Inland Seas* 46 (Winter 1990).

Theses

Lewis, Walter, "Until Further Notice: The Royal Mail Line and the Passenger Steamboat Trade on Lake Ontario and the upper St. Lawrence River, 1838–1875," Queen's University, unpublished M.A. Thesis, 1983.

Index

A. E. Ames (steamboat), 188
A. E. McKinstry (steamboat), 131, 189
Abyssinian (steamboat) *See Ontario*
Adolphustown, ON, 190
L'Aigle (steamboat), 47
Alexandria (steamboat), 183
Alexandria Bay, NY, 104-105, 188-190, 198-199
Alford, Steve, 12
Alfred, Prince, 57
Allan, Andrew, 62
Allan, Hugh, Sir, 62, 83, 87, 100, 104, 114, 161, 164
Allen and Wells, 29
America (steamboat), 181
American Express Line *See* Lake Ontario Express Line
Ames, A. E. (steamboat) *See A. E. Ames*
Amherst Island, 144, 183
Andasta (steamboat), 200
Arabian (steamboat, 1851), 42, 44, 63
Arabian (steamboat, 1892), 191-192
Aragon (steamboat), 138, 200
Arcand, Elezcar, 110
L'Assomption (steamboat), 47
Athenian (steamboat) *See Bay State*
Augustus (barge), 143, 185
Aultsville, ON, 187
Avon (propeller), 153
Avon (steamboat), 196

Banshee (propeller), 153, 156
Banshee (steamboat), 63-64, 69, 75, 149

Baptiste, 50, 72, 110
Barriefield, ON, 157
Bartlett (tug), 186, 189
Bartley, William P., 29, 93
Bartley and Dunbar, 15, 27-33
Batten, William George, 110, 156-157
Bavarian (steamboat) *See Kingston*
Bay of Quinte, ON, 54, 101, 157, 191
Bay of Quinte (steamboat), 52-53
Bay State (later *Athenian*, steamboat), 68-69, 82, 157
Bay State Shoal, NY, 187
Beauharnois, QC, 69, 181
Beauharnois Canal, 41, 72
Beaupré (steamboat), 122
Beaver Foundry, Montreal, 93
Beaverton (steamboat), 199
Bedford, F., 110
Belleville, ON, 54, 101, 188
Belleville (steamboat) *See Spartan*
Beloeil, QC, 120-121
Bertram Engine Works Company, Toronto, 116
Bessemer No. 2 (steamboat), 138, 199-200
Bismarck (barge), 181
Board of Steamboat Inspection *See* Canada. Board of Steamboat Inspection
Bohemian (later *Prescott* steamboat), 67, 69, 82, 101, 119, 153, 158-159
Bonaventure (steamboat), 47
Bonsecours Market, Montreal 49, 104
Boston (steamboat), 152-153
Bowen, William, 65, 149

The River Palace

Bowmanville, ON, 44, 99, 101
Bowmanville (steamboat), 47
Bradley, Charles, 85-87
Brian, Thomas, 125-126, 129, 131
Brighton (barge), 195
Bristol (propeller), 156, 158
Britannic (steamboat), 184-185
Brockville, ON, 42, 51, 70, 76, 79, 82, 101, 177, 181, 189, 191
Brockville (steamboat) *See Columbian*
Brockville Narrows, 195-196
Brothers Islands, ON, 190
Brown, George, 61
Browne, Edward, 153
Bruno (propeller), 158
Bruce (steamboat), 77
Brush, George, 106
Buffalo, NY, 32
Burlington Bay, ON, 44, 95
Byron Whitaker (steamboat), 192

Cabotia (steamboat), 197-198
Cacouna, QC, 65
Caledonia (steamboat), 47
Calvin & Breck (later Calvin Company), 74-75, 124-133, 169
Calvin, Dileno D., 53-54, 133
Calvin, Hiram A., 124, 128, 130-131
Calvin, Jack D., 124-125, 130
Calvin, Sandford C., 130-131, 189
Canada (later *St. Irénée*, steamboat), 120
Canada Import Company, 196
Canada Marine Works, Montreal, 81-82, 163
Canada Steamship Lines (CSL), 123, 131, 135, 190
Canada. Commission of Inquiry into the Grand Trunk Railway (Langton Commission), 61
Canada. Department of Marine and Fisheries, Board of Steamboat Inspection, 90, 96, 163
Canada. Department of Public Works, 29
Canada. Dominion Wreck Commission,158
Canadian Inland Steam Navigation Company (later Canadian Navigation Company), 62-100, 112-113, 147-152, 164
Canadian Marine Association (later Dominion Marine Association), 156
Canadian National Railways (CNR), 21
Canadian Pacific Railway (CPR), 114
Canadian Railway News Company, 113
Cantin, Augustin, 81-82, 163
Cape Vincent, NY, 196-197

Captain Mac, 104-105
Cardiff, Wales, 155
Cardinal Canal, 137
Cardinal, ON (Edwardsburgh), 173, 191-192, 194, 200
Carleton Island, NY, 189-190, 201
Carmichael, Charles, 76, 86, 89, 154-155, 159
Cartier, George Étienne, 19, 59
Cascade Point, QC, 199
Cascades Rapids (*See also* Split Rock Rapids), 49, 72
Caspian (steamboat) *See Passport*
Cataract (steamboat), 56, 68-69
Cataraqui Yacht Club, Kingston, 146
Caughnawaga (now Kahnawake), QC, 20, 51
Cedars Rapids, 49, 67, 72, 100
Central Coal Company, Brockville, 191
Chabot, Julian, 115
Chambers, Captain, 151
Chambly, QC, 120-122
Chambly (steamboat), 120, 122
Champion (steamboat), 63-65, 69, 153-155
Charity Shoal, ON, 139, 187, 200
Charlotte, NY, 82, 174, 195
Chatham (steamboat), 156
Chicago, IL, 21, 200
Chicoutimi (steamboat), 122
Chieftain III (steamboat), 125
Chippewa (steamboat), 118
Citizens' Insurance Company, Montreal, 79
City of Montreal (steamboat), 156
City of Toronto (steamboat), 100
Clayton, NY, 104, 176, 198
Clyde (propeller), 157
Clyde (schooner), 156
Clyde Bank Foundry (later Clydebank Shipyard), Govan, Scotland, 25-26
Clyde, River *See* River Clyde
Cobourg, ON, 44, 54-56, 70, 101, 182
Cobourg (barge), 138-139, 143, 194, 198, 201
Cole, Mrs., 11
Collins Bay, ON, 183, 190
Colstack (brig), 155
Columbian (steamboat, 1847) *See Cataract*
Columbian (later *Brockville*, *Rapids Queen*, steamboat, 1892), 114-117, 119, 157-158, 181
Columbus (brig), 96, 155
Comet (later *Mayflower*, steamboat), 11, 47, 53
Commercial Bank of Upper Canada (later Commercial Bank of Canada), 24, 59
Condor (barge), 195

242

Index

Conley, Paul, 12
Connor, G. W., 110
Corinthian (steamboat), 60, 67, 69, 100-101, 152-154, 157-158, 163
Corliss Steam Engine Company, Providence, RI, 29
Cornwall, ON, 48, 69, 72, 84, 101, 181, 197
Cornwall (barge), 188-189
Cornwall (steamboat) *See Kingston*
Cornwall Canal, 72, 108, 110, 175-177, 181, 199
Corsican (later *Picton*, steamboat), 66, 68-69, 101, 119, 157-158, 182
Coteau Landing, QC (or Coteau-du-Lac, QC), 69, 72, 194
Coteau Rapids, 49, 72
Cunard Line, Liverpool, 25-26

Daryaw (schooner), 201
Davidson (barge), 153
Detroit, MI, 21, 57
Devil's Neck, NY, 195
Dick, D. J., Mrs., 154
Dickenson's Landing, ON, 48, 71-72, 189
Dixon, Obadiah, 83
Dominion (steamboat), 79
Dominion Towing and Salvage Company, Port Arthur, 140
Dominion Marine Association *See* Canadian Marine Association
Dominion Wreck Commission *See* Canada. Dominion Wreck Commission
Donnelly (steamboat), 134
Donnelly (tug) *See Mary Frances Whelan*
Donnelly Family, 11
Donnelly Salvage and Wrecking Company, Portsmouth, 15, 126, 131-140
Donnelly, John Jr., 131, 133
Donnelly, John Sr., 74, 124, 133, 176
Donnelly, Thomas, 131
Dorval, L'Île, QC, 51
Dufour, Napolèon, 84-85, 96
Dunbar, James, 29, 93, 154
Dundurn (steamboat), 189
Dunlop, Andrew, 73, 110, 152-154, 158, 180
Dunlop, Herbert, 154
Dunlop, James, 152
Dunlop, Robert, 152
Dunlop, Wallace, 154

Eagle Foundry, Montreal, 106
Eastern Townships, QC, 21
Ebenezer (ship), 155

Edward VII *See* Prince of Wales
Edwardsburg Starch Company (later Canada Starch Company), 200
Elgin (schooner), 156
Elgin, Lord (steamboat) *See Lord Elgin*
Elmbay (steamboat), 139, 201
Emblem (schooner), 156
Emerson (tug), 192
Empire Refining Company, Walkerville, ON, 122
Erin-go-bragh (ship), 155
Esford, Henry, 157

Fairhaven, NY, 139, 201
Fanny (schooner), 155
Farmers' Delight (schooner), 155
Farran's Point, ON, 71, 176, 194-195, 199
Farrell, John, Bishop, 151
Farrell, Peter, 151-152
Fenian Crisis, 65
Fenwick's Hotel, Kingston, 91
Finn, Martin, 113
Finucan, James, 83, 87
Finucan, William, 87, 159
Fire-fly (steamboat), 56, 151
Folger Family, 116
Forget, L. J., 119
Fort Henry, Kingston, 53
Fort William, ON, 140, 189
Fournier, Mr., 175
Fowler and Hood, Kingston, 64
Fred Mercur (steamboat), 191
Frontenac (steamboat), 23
Frontenac (tug), 131, 135-139, 185, 187, 189-190, 194-201
Frothingham and Workman, Montreal, 29

Galops Rapids, 71, 75, 104, 173-174
Gananoque, ON, 70
Garden Island, ON, 17, 53, 124, 127, 129, 131, 133, 171, 198
Geddes, W. A., Mrs., 156
Geddes Wharf, Toronto, 117
General Wolfe (schooner), 156
George Hall Coal Company, 189-191
George Marsh (schooner), 11
Georgia (steamboat), 189
Gilbert, Ebenezer E., 93-94, 128, 164, 170
Gildersleeve, Charles F., 67, 69, 115, 117, 153, 158
Gildersleeve, Henry (steamboat) *See Henry Gildersleeve*
Gildersleeve, James P., 52

243

Gildersleeve, Overton S., 52, 67, 149
Girouard, Mr., 88
Glasgow, Scotland, 25
Goodall, Jane, 154
Goose Neck Island, NY, 190
Govan, Scotland, 25
Gowan (steamboat), 194
Grand Trunk Railway (GTR), 21, 25, 33, 42, 45, 48, 54-55, 59-63, 69, 114, 120
Grantham (barge), 188
Great Britain (steamboat), 23
Grecian (steamboat), 66, 69, 147-148
Grenadier Island, ON, 76, 81, 139, 174, 201
Guelph, ON, 21

Ha Ha Bay, QC, 67
Hall Coal Company *See* George Hall Coal Company
Hall, Mary P. (tug) *See Mary P. Hall* (tug)
Hamilton, ON, 20, 42, 69-70, 83, 101, 175
Hamilton (barge), 196
Hamilton (steamboat) *See Magnet*
Hamilton, Clarke, 41, 62, 146-150
Hamilton, George, 22
Hamilton, John, Hon., 20-26, 29-31, 41, 46, 59, 61-62, 91, 146-150
Hamilton, Robert Jr., 23
Hamilton, Robert Sr., 22
Hamiltonian (steamboat), 194
Hannaford, Maitland, Mrs. 147
Harriet D. (barge), 135-136, 139, 143, 189-197
Harbottle, Thomas, 63
Hatch, Mr., 147
Havana (steamboat), 153
Hayes, Andrew, 80
Head, Edmund, Sir, 19
Hecla (steamboat), 131, 189, 194
Henderson, John, 83, 85, 110
Henrietta (schooner), 156
Henry Gildersleeve (steamboat), 151
Hercules (steamboat), 53
Hero (steamboat), 150
Hersee and Timmerman, Buffalo, NY, 32
Heyl, Erik, 119-120
Hiawatha (barge), 131, 183
Hilda (barge), 198
Hochelaga (steamboat), 47
Holmes (schooner), 194
Holmes, Mary Jane, 155
Hope (tug), 74-75
Horace Taber (schooner), 191,197
Howard, Thomas, 63, 80, 113, 149-150

Howard W. (steamboat), 195
Howe Island, ON, 189
Hudson Bay Company, 148
Huell & Laird, Montreal, 33
Hulburt W. Smith (steamboat), 133, 135

Ida (tug), 181
Ireland, Miss, 87
Iroquois Point, ON, 71
Iroquois, ON, 135, 194
Isabel Reid (barge), 195
Islander (steamboat)143, 181

J. F. Maynard (steamboat), 176
J. H. Plummer (steamboat), 190
Jackass Shoal, ON, 194
James McKenzie (steamboat), 47
Jeska (steambarge), 191
John Redpath (steamboat), 47
John S. Thom (steamboat), 195
John Watkins (schooner), 155
John Webster (ferry), 195
Johnson's Light, NY *See* Rock Island Light, NY
Johnston, Captain, 124
Johnston, William (tug) See *William Johnston*
Jones, Walter, Mrs. Dr., 79
Josephine (schooner), 151
Joyland (steamboat), 196
Jura (steamship), 26

Kate (tug), 153
Kathleen (steamboat), 153
Keewatin (schooner), 190
Kelley, John Ramage, 63, 146-148, 152
Kenny, Edward, 176
Keybell (steamboat), 139, 200
Kingston, ON, 22-24, 42, 44, 51-54, 70, 74, 91-92, 101, 124, 175
Kingston (schooner), 155
Kingston (later *Bavarian, Algerian, Cornwall*, steamboat, 1855): *Kingston*: construction, 20-21, 25-33; description, 33-40; operations, 41-45, 70-72; Royal Tour, 18-19, 46-58; accidents, 72-80; *Bavarian*: construction, 81-82; accidents, 82-90; *Algerian*: construction, 91-95; crew, 96, 108-114; operations, 100-105; accidents, 96-100; upgrades, 105-108; *Cornwall*: operations,119-120; Richelieu River, 120-123; rebuilding,124-130; salvage operations, 130-139; layup, 140-144; discovery, 11-12; diving, 13-18

Index

Kingston (steamboat, 1901), 116-117, 157
Kingston Curling Club, 146
Kingston Dry Dock, 93, 180, 187, 190, 199
Kingston Marine Railway, 24, 64, 91-92
Kinlock, Samuel, 41

L'Aigle (steamboat), 47
L'Assomption (steamboat), 47
Lachine, QC, 49, 72, 181, 196
Lachine Canal, 27, 29-31, 72, 75, 109, 153, 175, 182
Lachine Rapids, 20, 50, 71-72, 104, 107, 148, 176
Lake Ontario, 18, 21, 23, 25, 42, 45, 82, 84, 88, 100, 155, 190
Lake Ontario Express Line, 60-63, 82
Lake St. Francis, 72
Lake St. Louis, 72, 181
Langell, Simon (steamboat) See *Simon Langell*
Lanoraie, QC, 121
Lavaltrie, QC, 121
Levebre, J., 110
Lemoyne (steamboat), 137
Lévis, QC, 21
Lewiston, NY, 33, 68
London, ON, 74
Long Sault Rapids, 23, 48-49, 72, 102-104, 180
Lord Elgin (steamboat), 152
Lydon ("whirlie"), 187
Lyons, Lord, 19

Macassa (steamboat), 101
McAuslan, William, 30
Macdonald, John A., Sir, 53-54, 59, 83, 87
McDonald, Robert (steambarge) See *Robert McDonald*
McGrath, John, 110, 153, 157-158, 179-180
McKenzie, James (steamboat) See *James McKenzie*
McKinstry, A. E. (steamboat) See *A. E. McKinstry*
McLean, D., 114
McMahon, Mr., 94
MacNab, Allan, Sir, 19
Macpherson, Mr. [Purser], 88
Macpherson, Crane & Company, Montreal and Kingston, 22-23, 65
Macpherson, David Lewis, Sir, 23, 25
Macpherson, Frances Pasia, 23, 146
Macpherson, John, 23
Madden, John, 79
Magnet (propeller), 158

Magnet (later *Hamilton*, steamboat), 20, 25, 42, 44, 63, 65, 70, 75, 96, 115, 118-119, 122, 149, 157-158, 163, 166
Magnolia (tug), 195
Mail Line See Royal Mail Line
Main Duck Island, ON, 177, 191-192, 194, 197
Maize (barge), 188
Malton (steamboat), 139
Mamie (barge), 143
Maple Leaf (schooner), 190
Mapleboro (steamboat), 199
Mapleglen (steamboat), 137
Maria and Elisa (schooner), 155
Marine Museum of the Great Lakes at Kingston, 93
Marsh, George (schooner) See *George Marsh*
Mary Frances Whelan (later *Donnelley*, tug), 137-138
Mary P. Hall (tug), 137, 139
Marshall, Samuel (steamboat) See *Samuel Marshall*
Maynard, J. F. (steamboat) See *J. F. Maynard*
Masters and Mates Act, 89-90, 110, 156
Matilda (schooner), 155
Maxwell, Thomas, 63, 151
Mayflower (steamboat) See *Comet*
Meagher, John, 151
Melrose (barge), 197
Merchant's Mutual Line, 189
Mercur, Fred (steamboat) See *Fred Mercur*
Michigan (gunboat), 20
Milford, Wales, 96, 155
Milloy Family, 100
Milloy, Alexander, 62, 88-89, 149, 164
Mills, Daniel F., 110, 158, 179
Minnes, James, Mrs., 156
Mitchell, William, 114
Modjeska (steamboat), 101
Mohawk (gunboat), 20
Montgomery, John, 73
Montreal, QC, 15, 21-23, 27, 41-42, 48-49, 51, 67, 69-70, 72, 74-75, 95, 104, 113, 115, 120, 139, 150, 173, 176, 182
Montreal (steamboat), 37-38
Montreal and Southern Counties Railway, 121
Montreal Ocean Steamship Company (later Allan Line), 62
Montreal Safe Deposit Company, 115
Montreal Transportation Company, 185, 188-189, 191, 196-197
Montreal Trust Company, 141
Morgan Iron Works, New York, NY, 114

Morrisburg, ON, 71, 185, 190, 194
Morristown, NY, 195
Moulton (steamboat), 200
Mulgrave, Lord, 19
Mullen, John, 124, 131
Murray Bay, QC, 25, 65
Murray Canal, 101, 189

Napoléon (steamboat), 47
Neilson, Rick, 11-12
New Era (later *Empress*, steamboat), 56-57, 64, 69, 152-153
New York, NY, 93
New York Central Railroad, 116
Newcastle, Duke of, 53-54
Niagara Falls, ON, 100
Niagara Harbour & Dock Company, 65
Niagara Navigation Company, 117-118
Niagara-on-the-Lake, ON, 25, 192
Nicaragua (steamboat), 190
Nish, Robert, 178-179
Nixon, Sara Doremus, 146
Norcross, J. W., 131
Norseman (later *North King*, steamboat), 153, 158, 188
Northmount (steamboat), 190
Northport, ON, 191
Nottingham, William (steamboat) See *William Nottingham*

O'Donell, John, 73
Ocean (propeller), 182
Oddfellow (schooner), 173
Ogdensburg, NY, 68, 187, 189
Ogdensburg Coal and Towing Company, 196
Oka, QC, 72
Olcott (steamboat), 187
Olivon, Victor, 112
Ontario (steamboat, 1839), 23
Ontario (later *Abyssinian*, steamboat, 1847), 29, 68-69
Ontario Foundry, Kingston, 91
Orange Order, 53-55
Oshawa, ON, 87
Osprey (steamboat), 157
Oswego, NY, 74, 134, 191, 194, 197
Ottawa, ON, 50-51, 96, 114
Ottawa (schooner), 156
Ottawa (steamboat), 148
Ottawa River, 23, 51, 72
Owen Sound Transportation Company, 65, 100

Palm Bay (steamboat) See *Richard W.*
Palmer, William P., 135
Parisian (steamship), 182
Parker, Ben, 108
Parmenter, Jonas J., 84
Parrott, John, Mrs., 156
Parthia (tug), 125 128, 131, 136, 183
Passport (later *Caspian*, steamboat), 20, 24, 30, 41-44, 47, 63-64, 96, 101, 106, 115, 119, 148-149, 154-155, 157-158, 175, 181, 186
Peacock (schooner), 155-156
Peerless (steamboat), 56-57
Pense, Edward J. B., 147
Perth, ON, 74
Peterborough, ON, 56
Phelan, T. P. (steamboat) See *T. P. Phelan*
Phelix, James W., 127
Phoenix (steamboat), 51
Picton, ON, 101
Picton (steamboat) See *Corsican*
Pigeon Island, ON, 148
Pierrepont (steamboat), 53, 74
Playfair, James, 140
Plummer, J. H. (steamboat) See *J. H. Plummer* (steamboat)
Point Anne, ON, 188-189
Point de Bisser, QC, 74
Point Peninsula, NY, 196
Point Vivian, NY, 190
Poirier, F. X., 89
Pont de Beloeil, QC, 121
Port Arthur, ON, 140
Port Dalhousie, ON, 192
Port Darlington, ON, 44, 70, 76, 87, 99, 101
Port Hope, ON, 44, 56, 70, 75, 99, 101
Port Robinson, ON, 155
Port Stanley, ON, 156
Portland, ME, 21
Portsmouth, ON, 128, 135, 138, 142-143, 150, 185, 197-198
Power, William, 91-92, 164
Prescott, ON, 70, 82, 101, 104, 115, 131, 139, 148, 183, 188, 199, 201
Prescott (steamboat) See *Bohemian*
Presqu'ile Point, ON, 186
Prevost, D., 110
Prince of Wales, 17, 46-57, 61, 108
Protection (steamboat), 152
Putnam, Lester N., 148
Pyke Wrecking and Salvage Company, Kingston, 195

Index

Quebec, QC, 17, 23, 46, 60, 65, 74, 93, 96, 115, 124, 149
Quebec (barge), 188, 192
Quebec (steamboat), 46
Queen Elizabeth (steamship), 25
Queen Elizabeth 2 (steamship), 25
Queen Mary (steamship), 25
Queen's University, Kingston, 24
Queenston, ON, 22, 146
Queenston (steamboat), 23, 100

R. W. Stanley (steamboat), 156
Rapide Plat, 71
Rapids King (steamboat), 116, 157, 194
Rapids Prince (steamboat), 116, 187
Rapids Queen (steamboat) *See Columbian*
Rawley, Mr. [diver], 131, 183
Red Rover (schooner), 155
Redpath, John (steamboat) *See John Redpath*
Reid, Isabel (barge) See *Isabel Reid*
Reid Towing and Wrecking Company, Sarnia, 140
Restless (boat), 11
Richard W. (later *Palmbay*, steamboat), 143, 196
Richardson, T., Mrs., 156
Richelieu & Ontario Navigation Company (R & O), 17, 100, 104-127, 150
Richelieu Company, 63, 100, 121
Richelieu River, 120-121
Rideau Canal, 23, 55, 151
Rideau King (steamboat), 136
Risley, Samuel, 90
River Clyde, 14-15, 25, 130
Rivet (yacht), 54
Rivier, John, 83
Robert McDonald (steambarge), 198
Rochester, NY, 82, 134, 174, 186, 195
Rock Ferry (steamboat), 187, 192-194
Rock Island Light, NY, 195
Rollo, Colonel, 19
Rose, John, 19
Rothesay (steamboat), 114
Round Island, NY, 104
Royal Canadian Insurance Company, Toronto, 153
Royal Canadian Yacht Club, Toronto, 57
Royal Mail Line, 20-24, 31, 41-44, 59, 69, 72, 75, 82, 100, 106, 109-115, 149, 151
Royal Military College, Kingston, 139, 200
Russell, J. E., 138, 140, 200
Ruttle, Vic, 11, 143

Sackett's Harbor, NY, 198
Saginaw (tug), 133, 135-136, 185, 189-190
Saguenay River, 63-65, 115, 149
St. Antoine, QC, 121, 125
St. Basile-le-Grand, QC, 120
St. Catharines YMCA, 190
St. Charles, QC, 121
St. Clair River, 21
St. Denis, QC, 121
St. Helen's Island, QC, 48
Ste. Hélène (steamboat), 47
St. Hilaire, QC, 121
Ste. Irénée (steamboat) see *Canada* (steamboat)
St. Lawrence (propeller), 151, 156, 158
St. Lawrence (steamboat), 46, 53, 149, 152
St. Lawrence Engine Works, Montreal, 15, 27-29, 93
St. Lawrence Navigation Company, 114
St. Lawrence Seaway, 71
St. Lawrence River, (*See also* individual rapids and canals), 21, 23, 70-72, 89
St. Marc, QC, 121
Ste. Marie (steamboat), 47
St. Mathias, QC, 120
St. Ours, QC, 121
St. Patrick's Society, Portsmouth, 150
St. Roch, QC, 121, 123
St. Sulpice, QC, 121
Salaberry (steamboat), 47
Salmon Island, ON, 183
Salmon Point, ON, 138, 185, 188, 200
Samuel Marshall (steamboat), 191
Sanderson, Mr., 19
Sarnia, ON, 21, 140
Sarnor (steamboat), 190
Scotland, 21-22, 30
Shanly, Walter, 61
Shanly, Walter (steamboat) See *Walter Shanly*
Shaw, A. & D., 151
Shearer, James, 31-33, 112
Sherbrooke, QC, 51
Shinroan, Ireland, 149
Sibbald, Mrs., 87
Simard, Joseph, 141
Simla (steamboat), 137, 143
Simon Langell (steamboat), 143
Simpson, George, Sir, 148
Sin-Mac Lines, 16, 140-141
Sincennes-McNaughton Line, 122, 140
Sincennes-McNaughton Tugs Limited, 141
Sinclair, Capt., 63

247

Sister Island Light, NY, 199
Smith, Hulburt W. (steamboat) *See Hulburt W. Smith*
Snake Island, ON, 191, 196
Sorel, QC, 17, 111, 120-121, 124-125, 129, 171
Soulanges Canal, 189, 199
South Bay, ON, 98, 198
Sovereign (steamboat), 176
Sparrowhawk Point, NY, 191
Spartan (later *Belleville*, steamboat), 65-66, 69-70, 75, 98, 119, 122, 148, 150, 152-153, 158, 163, 169
Spence, John C., 32-33
Split Rock Rapids, 49, 66, 72-73, 75, 96, 175, 180
Stanley, R. W. (steamboat) *See R. W. Stanley*
Stoney Point, NY, 198
Stormount (steamboat), 137, 199
Stratford, ON, 21
Sudds, George, 198
Swansea, Wales, 55
Swift's Wharf, Kingston, 64, 100, 107, 169, 181

T. P. Phelan (steamboat), 135, 137
Taber, Horace (schooner) *See Horace Taber*
Taché, Étienne-Paschal, 19
Tacoussac, QC, 65, 101
Tagona (steamboat), 191
Tecumseh (steamboat), 153, 158, 178-179
Terrebonne (steamboat), 47, 121
Thames (schooner), 156
Thom, John S. (steamboat) *See John S. Thom*
Thompson (tug), 188, 196
Thomson, George, 25-26
Thomson, James, 25
Thomson, Robert, 26
Thousand Islands (*See also* individual islands and shoals), 76, 84, 92, 101, 116
Thousand Islands Park, NY, 104, 181, 187
Thunder Bay, ON, 21
Toiler (motorship), 187
Topsey (steamboat), 47
Toronto, ON, 42, 45, 56, 68-70, 74, 97, 101, 115, 118, 154, 173, 177, 192, 201
Toronto (schooner), 156
Toronto (steamboat), 116, 157
Toronto Ferry Company, 117
Traveller (steamboat), 23, 53
Trenton, ON, 191
Trois Rivières, QC, 46
Trowell, Belle, 156
Trowell, John, 96, 98, 110, 113, 155-156, 158

Trowell, John Valentine, 156
Twohy, Captain, 63

Umbria (tug), 190
Union Navigation Company, 68

Valois, L., 112
Van Horne, Cornelius, 114
Vandalia (propeller/steamboat), 96, 156
Vaughan Township, ON, 154
Verchères, QC, 46
Victoria (steamboat) 47
Victoria Bridge, Montreal, 21, 48-49, 72, 104, 128, 181
Viking (steamboat), 196
Vinmount (steamboat), 199

Wahcondah (steamboat), 139, 201
Wainwright, William, 114
Walker & Little, Montreal, 33
Walkerville Navigation Company, 199
Walter Shanly (steamboat), 53
Washburn, MN, 192
Watertown, ND, 156
Watkins, John (schooner) *See John Watkins*
Weaver's Point, ON, 184-185
Webster, John (ferry) *See John Webster*
West (propeller), 153
Whelan, Mary Frances (tug) *See Mary Frances Whelan*
Whitaker, Byron (steamboat) *See Byron Whitaker*
Whitby, ON, 56, 83, 91, 174
White, William C., 81, 105, 161, 169
William Johnston (tug), 131, 133, 135, 136, 138, 185, 194-196, 199-200
William Nottingham (steamboat), 133, 135
Williams, F., Sir, 19
Williamsburg Canals, 72
Williamsburgh, ON, 70
Wilson, Jane, 155
Wilson, NY, 192
Windmill Point, ON, 199
Windsor, ON, 57, 74
Winnipeg (barge), 131, 183, 187, 195
Wolfe Island, ON, 187, 196
Wonga Wonga (steamship), 26
Wreck Hunter (boat), 12
Wyoming (steamboat), 194

Zebra mussels, 14
Zimmerman (steamboat), 56

www.ingramcontent.com/pod-product-compliance
Lightning Source LLC
Chambersburg PA
CBHW020835160426
43192CB00007B/662